Exotic and Irrational

Exotic and Irrational

Opera in Denver — 1879-2006

by

Allen Young

> *For Barbara*
> *A lasting inspiration*

EXOTIC AND IRRATIONAL: Opera in Denver—1879-2006 by Allen Young

Text copyright © 2006, Allen Young

Book design copyright © 2006, Pilgrims Process, Inc.

www.pilgrimsprocess.com

All Rights Reserved

Front cover photos courtesy of Opera Colorado

Other photo credits page 218

ISBN: 978-0-9749597-8-8

Library of Congress Control Number: 2006904302

Printed in the United States of America

0 9 8 7 6 5 4 3 2 1

Set in Adobe Caslon Pro 11 pt over 14 pt

Forward

I first became acquainted with Allen Young about two years ago when I was developing a website for Opera in Old Colorado and a colleague referred me to him as the most informed Colorado opera historian. To my delight, I learned that Allen was then writing a history of opera in Denver. When I saw the finished manuscript, I recognized that here was a scholarly and absorbing work of great importance to our cultural history by a gifted writer uniquely qualified to create such an intimate record.

Allen Young was born in Washington, D.C. July 4, 1918. He moved to Denver in 1947 where he joined The Denver Post and in September 1948 became music critic, reviewing theater and film events and records. He did a record review program on classical radio station KFML from 1953 to 1957. He left the Post in 1957, and later that year created The Lively Arts, which he published and edited for two years before going to Cervi's Journal where he edited the arts pages from 1959 to 1963. From 1963 until 1970 he served as executive Director of Young Audiences, Inc. From 1972 until 1980 he was Associate Editor of the Rocky Mountain Medical

Journal for the Colorado Medical Society. Allen has done free lance work for Time magazine, Life magazine, The Los Angeles Times, Opera News and Musical America. A weekly columnist in The Daily Journal from 1967 to 1972, he wrote on environmental matters. From 1984 until 1987 he was music reviewer for the Rocky Mountain News and did occasional reviews for that paper until 1996. From 1963 until October 2004 he was Denver correspondent for Variety magazine. In 1993 Allen published a history of opera in Central City. (Young, Allen. *Opera in Central City*. Denver: Spectrographics, 1993.)

In the course of exchanges with Allen about early opera history in Denver, he invited me to add some biographical details about Denverites who figured prominently in the development of opera and to make editorial refinements to his manuscript. My wife, Reta, inevitably became involved with the work, serving invaluably by proofreading successive drafts and suggesting astute improvements. As we worked our way through the manuscript, we became ever more aware that it is a marvelous account of the 150 years of successes and failures by a great many remarkable people and diverse organizations, striving to create appreciative audiences for opera. We trust that many will eagerly read this book and agree that it is, indeed, a grand history of how this "exotic and irrational" enterprise, with which we are so enamored, finally flourished in Denver.

> Charles L. Ralph
> Professor Emeritus, Colorado
> State University and webmaster for
> www.operapronto.home.comcast.
> net/
> Fort Collins, CO
> 11 February 2006

Contents

Prelude ix

I   A Stop on Tour 1

II   The Grand Tradition 00

III   The Tradition Refreshed 00

IV   A Little Chamber Opera 00

V   The Dutch Tornado

VI   The Conductor and The Soprano 00

VII   Symphonic Overtures 00

VIII   Opera Goes to College 00

XI   A Little Yearning 00

X   Opera In-the-Round 00

XI   Merrill Innovations 00

XII   Opera Colorado Begins a Second Decade 00

XIII   Seifert Takes the Helm 00

XIV   Russell Arrives Cautiously Adventurous 00

XV   Always A New Beginning 00

Notes 00

Index 00

Prelude

In 1859 seekers and searchers, promoters and planters, miners and merchants, doctors and teachers came together on the banks of Cherry Creek at the Platte River to make a new life for themselves. This fertile soil was the stuff that would make Denver the "Queen City of the Plains." They came to build a community based on the kind of independence produced by business enterprise. With income, their vision widened. It was said that the first thing a rich man did was to build a safe in his home for his mining records and then build a theater. Grand mansions went up and the middle class had far finer homes than they had left behind. Mining and farming interests required lumber, hoists, wagon wheels, dynamite, plows, and other rudimentary equipment. The people of a growing town demanded amusement to distract them from the struggling and sweating that would lead the way to a better life.

Even before Denver became enough of a community to claim cityhood, the people saw the beginnings of theater, educational facilities, and church life. In 1859, its founding year, the Charles Thorne Theater Company arrived, and from then on there was a steady stream of plays; a favored recreation. Because actors could ride into town on a wagon, with a blanket for a curtain, and a kitchen chair as a prop, Denver quickly became known as a theater town.

William N. Byers, founder and editor of the Rocky Mountain News, was an eager publicist for theater and opera in Denver. From his first issue on April 23, 1859, he stressed the importance of all kinds of theater for Denver. As early as October 1859 he was reviewing the productions of the Charles Thorne company. He proclaimed Denver's thirst for culture the following year by writing "We want something rich and respectable in the amusement line." Not everyone thought amusements were respectable. Dean Martyn Hart, who had come to St. John's Cathedral in the Wilderness in 1878, led a successful effort to ban Sunday night entertainments. The opposition gathered, 500 strong, to attack the Dean's residence, destroying windows and doors, but the ban held.

From the outset, Denver's growth was rapid, drawing from New York, Boston, and Chicago and the farmlands of Missouri and Wisconsin. Denver was poised to become a cosmopolitan city as its potential for creating wealth became known in the East. Here was the escape desired by émigrés from the burgeoning eastern cities. They left an increasingly oppressive life for the opportunity to follow the Thoreauean concept that "Westward I go Free," later expanded into Horace Greeley's "Go west, Young Man. Go west."

Among those who set a tone of musical substance in early Denver was Frank Damrosch, older brother of the famed Walter, who came to Denver around 1870 to seek independence from his overpowering father, the distinguished Dr. Leopold Damrosch, and distance himself from Walter, his talented younger brother. He arrived in Denver with $25 he had earned plus $100 from his father.

Denver was not ready for an personable young man who had no talent except music. He was invited by a fellow boarder to come and work on his Wyoming ranch. Instead he took a job as a hatter's clerk, and next worked for a wholesale liquor establishment, loading 300-pound barrels of whisky on wagons for the mining camps. He played chamber music on Sunday mornings, and met musically interested members of Temple Emmanuel. He joined the Colorado

National Guard, for he enjoyed drills as well as the balls. Later he opened a music store on 16th Street between Curtis and Champa Streets.

Damrosch formed the Denver Choral Union with 80 singers in 1879 and in that year they performed Gilbert and Sullivan's *H.M.S. Pinafore* at Forrester's Opera House, first in May and again in September. He found his métier as music educator when he became the first superintendent of music in Denver public schools.

After his father's death in 1885, Damrosch returned to New York where his brother Walter wrangled Frank a position as chorus master at the Metropolitan Opera during what was known as the "German period." In time he replayed his Denver experience by becoming superintendent of music for New York. To this day, his Denver stay has not been sufficiently recognized; he brought much spirit to its musical life, leaving behind a grand tradition of choral work.

Denver lacked a good hall for theater and opera, and indeed was surpassed by Central City, Leadville, and Golden. Until the Tabor Grand Opera was built in Denver, at 16th and Curtis Street, there was a frustrating lack of proper performance sites. The Tabor Grand Opera House opening was on September 5, 1881, with the Emma Abbott Grand English Opera Company performing Wallace's *Maritana*. Abbott and her company continued through the next two weeks with a total of 13 performances, including *Lucia, Trovatore, Bohemian Girl*, and *Faust*. Grand opera had been introduced to Denver in 1877 and 1878 by the Richings-Bernard Grand English Opera Company, but it had performed in the dismal Forrester Opera House, formerly a drill hall for a military group. In the Tabor Grand, Denver now had a magnificent venue for grand opera.

In addition to demand for a proper place for performances, there now also was a concomitant surging of enthusiasm for participation in the performing arts. Local operatic energies were directed to clubs, such as the Denver Opera Club, organized by A. Kauffman and E. J. Passmore. It performed *The Pirates of Penzance* in May and again in October 1881. In that same year, the Denver Vocal Society gave a performance of Gilbert and Sullivan's *Trial by Jury*. The next year, at the request of former Governor Tabor, the Denver Opera Club offered *H.M.S. Pinafore* at the Tabor Grand Opera House, with Tabor bearing all costs of production. The Colorado Opera Club of Denver in 1882 produced a new work, *Brittle Silver*, by W. F. Hunt and Stanley Wood, both of Colorado Springs, the first bona fide opera written and produced in Colorado.

Choral singing was elevated in Denver when Dean H. Martyn Hart of St. John's in the Wilderness recruited a splendid succession of English organists and choir masters, including John H. Gower, Arthur Marchant, and Henry Housely, who brought a strong sense of English musical traditions to Denver. Gower had been organist and choir director at Royal Chapel of All Saints, Windsor, Great Park, by the time he was fourteen and later was organist for Queen Victoria's Princess Royal Chapel. He left St. John's to enter the mining field.

Upon Gower's departure, Dean Hart named Henry Houseley organist and choir director. Houseley also was organist for Temple Emmanuel where St. John's moved after a devastating fire in 1894. English born, he came to Denver in 1882 where he lived until his death in 1925. In 1890 Houseley directed a production of *The Sourcerer* by Gilbert and Sullivan, performed by a local group. In 1892 his own opera, *Native Silver*, the first opera composed by a Denver resident, was performed at the Broadway by a local ensemble. His second opera, *The Juggler*, was performed there in 1895 and again in 1898. His one-act opera, *Pygmalion*, premiered in 1900. Houseley directed a production of Wagner's *Parsifal* in 1906, performed by the Apollo Club and Sixty Ladies. Three one-act operas by Houseley, *Pygmalion and Galatea*, *Narcissus and Echo*, and *Love and Whist*, were performed in 1912. From 1900 until 1903, Houseley conducted Denver's initial symphony concerts at the Broadway Theater. At the time of his death, the Rocky Mountain News editorialized, "He was a musician of the first rank, and more than that, high-class music was a religion to him." In 1927 he was selected by

The Echo, a local music publication, as "the individual who had contributed the most to the development of music in Colorado."

The Emma Juch Grand English Opera Company presented seven operas in six days at the Metropolitan Theater in early 1890, and returned for the August 18, 1890 opening of the sophisticated Broadway Theater. Juch's company gave twelve performances of ten operas, opening with *Carmen*. In Denver, opera clearly had its foot in the door.

While Denver was busy building opera houses, hosting touring opera companies, and creating home-grown operas, some of its locally-trained singers attained international recognition. The first among them was Jeanne Lane Brooks, born in Denver in 1871, the daughter of Brig. Gen. and Mrs. Edward J. Brooks. She studied under her sister, Madeline Vance Brooks, and then under the French voice teacher Juliani, and studied opera acting under Jean de Rezke. Jeanne, as prima donna, toured the United States with the Henry W. Savage's Castle Square Opera Company, debuting in *Cavalleria Rusticana* in 1903. She went to Europe for further study, and when she made her European debut, singing in *Aida* in Paris, she took the name of Jeanne Brola. In 1909 she made her debut at La Scala in Italy in Samaras' *Rhea*, the first American diva to perform there. She received acclaim for her interpretation of various Wagnerian roles, including Eva in *Die Meistersinger*, Elsa in *Lohengrin*, and Elizabeth in *Tannhäuser*. Jeanne also was lauded for her Verdi roles, and later was known for her interpretation of Puccini heroines. In 1911, Puccini chose Jeanne for the role of Minnie in the English premiere at Covent Garden of *The Girl of the Golden West*. Later she sang with the Beecham Opera Company under the direction of Sir Thomas Beecham, who classed her among the six greatest interpreters of Tosca of all times. Jeanne was Tosca at the Shaftsbury Theatre in 1915, the first time the opera had been sung in English in London. In 1919 she starred in *La Bohème* at the Royal Opera House in London. Jeanne sang 39 lead roles in Europe, including Marguerite in *Faust*, Gilda in *Rigoletto*, and Suleika in *L'Africaine*. She sang to acclaim at Paris Opera and the Grand Opera of Nice and went to Cairo where she sang *Aida*. She returned to Denver in

1922 with her husband, John Harrison, who had been Professor of Voice at London's Royal Academy and one of the great voice teachers of Europe. They established the Brola-Harrison Voice Studios. She died in 1956 in Denver after suffering from cancer. She had never sung opera in Denver.

Born in 1874, in Ottumwa, IA, Rose McGrew, as a young girl, moved to Denver. When a senior in East Denver High School she took a position as soloist in a church choir. Mme. Biana Bianci, a noted prima donna, heard Rose sing and told her mother she should go to Germany to study voice. She first went to Dresden where she studied with Natalie Haenisch and Von Kotzebue, and then to Berlin for study with Zimmerman. In less than three years she had learned 12 operas. She was the prima donna in the Duke of Mecklenburg's Royal Theater in Schwerin for three years and in the Royal Theater in Hanover for three years. Rose returned to Denver for a visit in March, 1900, and gave a concert. When she returned to Germany it was to go to Breslau, where she was under contract for six years. In 1901 Rose married Alexander Schoenberg in Dresden. The New York Times for May 17, 1908, reported that in Breslau her repertoire was 52 operas. William, King of Prussia (the Kaiser), presented Rose with a certificate, giving her the Order of the Silver Laurel. In 1913 she was called home to Denver by her mother's illness. Her mother died soon after and she stayed to help her father reconstruct his home. By then, World War I had begun and it was dangerous to cross the Atlantic, so she began to sing on the concert stage in New York and Denver. From 1920 until 1947 she was a member of the voice faculty, teaching opera singing at the University of Oregon. Madam Rose's husband died in Germany in 1950. She died in 1956 in Eugene, Oregon. Again, Denver never heard her in opera.

Frances Rose Rosenzweig, born in Elmira, New York in 1874, moved with her family in 1888 to Denver where she attended the public school of Denver, graduating from East High. She then studied in Cleveland and Vienna, where she received the offer of prima donna of the Breslau Opera in Germany. There she began using the professional name Frances Rose. Frances sang leading roles in major European opera houses including Vienna, Berlin, Paris, and London. She was engaged by the Berlin Royal Opera from about 1908 to 1912. She made a recording singing Santuzza in *Cavalleria Rusticana* for the Odeon label in Berlin in 1909 and she sang Clytemnestra in the Berlin premiere of Richard Strauss' *Elektra* at the Royal Opera on February 15, 1909. Frances became noted for her roles in the operas of Richard Strauss and gave a series of concerts at Breslau and Magdeburg with the composer. Her program included the finale of *Salome* under the composer's baton and a group of his songs with Strauss at the piano. In 1909 she sang the title role in *Carmen* with Enrico Caruso as her Don José when the Kaiser, the Kaiserin and Crown Prince were present at the Kaiser's Royal Opera in Berlin. She married Theodore Konrad, a German from Cologne, in 1910 in London, where she was singing in *Elektra* at Covent Garden, after which the newlyweds returned to Berlin. She was recruited by the Metropolitan Opera for the 1909-10 and the 1912-13 seasons, but she refused the offers because she wished to be with her husband in Europe. She was in the United States at the outbreak of World War I and could not return to Germany. When in 1915 she sang in the Chicago Grand Opera Company's production of *Tannhäuser*, it was her American premiere. Frances' husband, a tenor with the Swedish Royal Opera Company, died in London in 1921. She returned to the family home around 1936, after retirement, where she remained until her death in 1956 in Denver. Hers was an international career that excluded Denver.

With the opening in 1908 of the city-owned Municipal Auditorium, that could be configured as a theater with a capacity of 3,300, Denver had another and larger venue for attending operatic events. The city had signed an agreement with the Shubert management, which brought major entertainment to Denver. However, visits by touring opera companies were becoming fewer and fewer.

As opera performances diminished, there was a concomitant increase in recitals by favorite operatic singers of the time: Enrico Caruso, Feodor Chaliapin, Rosa Ponselle, Amalita Galli-Curci, Lawrence Tibbetts, Lily Pons, and Kirsten Flagstad. The Denver management firms of Robert Slack and, later, Arthur M. Oberfelder brought in all the great singers and instrumentalists of the period.

Locally-produced opera began to fill the void resulting from fewer professional companies coming to Denver. In 1915, 1916, and 1917 Monsignor Joseph Bosetti staged operas for his Cathedral Opera Company with a cast largely drawn from his Denver Cathedral choir. In 1933 he founded the Denver Grand Opera. Thomas' *Mignon* was its first production. For the next 18 years Bosetti's company, every spring, gave Denver an opera production. Through the Denver Grand Opera's sponsorship by the Catholic diocese's Catholic Charities, its performances were invariably sold out. When guest artists appeared, they generally made a single appearance, giving their roles in subsequent performances to local singers. The final production of the Denver Grand Opera Company was *La Traviata* in 1951. The legendary company folded when Bosetti's health failed. He died at age 68 in 1954.

One of the most influential persons in the development of opera in Denver was Florence Lamont Hinman. Florence Lamont was born in 1884 in Michigan to Canadian parents but spent her early years in Canada, where she attended the London Conservatory of Music. When she was 17 she contracted tuberculosis of the hip and came to Denver for her health. During 1904-16, she regained her health, continued her studies, and engaged in professional singing and accompanying in Denver, New York, and other U.S. cities. With Leroy Hinman, whom she married in 1924, she founded the Lamont School of Music in that year, which became a part of the University of Denver in 1941. During her career, Florence lectured and taught music abroad and in many parts of the United States. Florence sang a principal role in Msgr. Bosetti's production, *Mignon*, in 1933. She wrote articles for music journals and, in 1934, published a book, *Slogans for Singers*. In 1934, she co-founded the Denver Post Summer Opera and she conducted the operas during the first two years. Florence was a former choral director of Central City Opera and a board member of the Metropolitan Opera Auditions for the Rocky Mountain region. Also, she was involved with the Lamont Singers, the Denver Symphony, the Treble and Bass Clubs, and the

Opera Club. She was awarded an honorary doctorate in music from the Denver Conservatory of Music. She retired from the Lamont School administration in 1953 but continued teaching singing there as a Professor Emerita. Among her successful students were Agnes Davis, Ina Rains (later Ina Souez), Frank Dinhaupt (later Francesco Valentino), and Jean Dickenson. She did have a major impact.

Agnes Davis, born in 1902 in Colorado Springs, attended grammar and high school in Colorado Springs and then studied at Colorado State Teachers College in Greeley. Coming to Denver, she taught physical culture in the public schools and never thought of a singing career until she won a singing prize of $500. It was then that she started to study music in earnest with Florence Lamont Hinman, and sang locally in hotel dining rooms, theaters, and churches. She won first place in the 1927 Colorado Atwater Kent singing competition, a gold medal, $5,000, and two years of free tuition. Agnes went to the Curtis Institute in Philadelphia and studied there for five years, graduating in 1934. She toured with Columbia Concerts from 1934-49 and taught at the Philadelphia Conservatory of Music from 1949-50. In June 1935, she sang before the Queen and King of England at the Coronation Silver Jubilee in London. She made her debut with the Metropolitan Opera in 1937 as Elsa in Wagner's *Lohengrin*. In the course of her career she sang several roles in operas such as Strauss' *Rosenkavalier*, Verdi's *Falstaff*, and Wagner's *Parsifal*, and sang under the direction of Fritz Reiner, Leopold Stokowski, Eugene Ormandy, and Otto Klemperer. When Walter Damrosch presented his revised opera *Cyrano* with the Philharmonic Symphony Society of New York at Carnegie Hall in 1941, he chose Agnes Davis as Roxanne. In 1938 Agnes returned home to sing in a concert at the Auditorium with the Denver Symphony Orchestra, under the direction of Horace E. Tureman. She also sang with the Denver Symphony Orchestra, directed by Saul Caston, at a Red Rocks Music Festival concert in 1949. Agnes enjoyed a notable career teaching voice at the Indiana University School of Music from 1950 until her death in 1967.

Ina Souez was born Ina Rains in 1903 in Windsor, Colorado, to a family of Cherokee descent. She graduated from the Lamont

School of Music in Denver where she was a pupil of Florence Lamont Hinman. Ina greatly impressed Denver audiences with her singing abilities, and in 1926, The Denver Post sponsored a Farewell Gala Concert at the Auditorium to raise funds for her travel to Milan, Italy, for further study. The advice of the several opera impresarios there was that she needed no additional study of vocal technique. Their opinion was that hers was a naturally placed voice backed by a prodigious technique and that she should concentrate on the coaching of operatic roles. Ina proceeded to coach with Ernesto Cadore (La Scala, Milan) and Alberto Conti (San Carlos, Naples). Her talent for learning a new opera role every month soon brought her to the attention of many of the smaller Italian opera houses. In two years, she had sung and mastered the roles of Mimi, Cio-Cio San, Marguerite, Leonora, and the leading soprano roles in *Mefistofele, Pagliacci,* and *Andrea Chenier.* She was then engaged at the Teatro Massimo (Palermo, Sicily) for six months. Upon completion of her contract there, Ina went to Paris to study the French repertoire. While in Paris, she was engaged to sing at the London Promenade Concerts under Sir Henry Wood's baton. These concerts brought her to the attention of the English music world and were the beginning of her singing career in that country. Her quick study talent stood her in good stead and she learned the role of Liu (*Turandot*) on thirty-six hours notice. Her performance of that role, during the Gala Coronation season, made her name a household word. With Sir John Barbarolli, Sir Thomas Beecham, and Sir Malcolm Sargeant Ina sang concerts all over the British Isles for the next two years. When she returned to Covent Garden, it was to sing Micaela in the history-making Conchita Supervia-Thomas Beecham performances of *Carmen*. These performances brought the young soprano to the attention of Dr. Fritz Busch, who was just then creating and establishing the Glyndebourne festival. He saw and heard Ina as the perfect Donna Anna (*Don Giovanni*) and Fiordiligi (*Cosi fan tutte*) for his productions. From its inception, that conductor, his company, and Ina Souez became a part of music history. The soprano was the leading Prima Donna of the Festival for six years and recorded both *Don Giovanni* and *Cosi fan tutte*. These superlative recordings of the Mozart operas are recognized as definitive.

Ina Souez came back to Denver in 1938 to sing in a Homecoming Concert at the Auditorium. A reception followed the next day in Windsor where she was fondly greeted by family and friends. The Souez performances of the Verdi *Requiem* with Jussi Bjoerling, Kirsten Thorborg, and Dr. Busch conducting, were performed all over Scandinavia and became one of the most sought after musical events of the season. World War II cut off projected plans for a recording of the work with this stellar cast and forced Miss Souez to return to the United States. She served in the U.S. Army WACS and when duty permitted, sang many concerts and orchestral engagements for Special Services. In 1946 she sang excerpts from Berg's *Wozzeck* with the Janssen Symphony of Los Angeles. When her voice began to lose its luster and she was trying to decide how to support herself, Spike Jones asked her to join his City Slickers. Her second career blossomed through the 1950s. When Jones waned in popularity, Souez moved to San Francisco to teach, and then to Los Angeles. She also helped judge regional auditions for the Metropolitan Opera. She specialized in Mozart and the Italian opera repertoire. She died at age 89 at a Santa Monica nursing home where she lived her last eight years. Ina was another great artist who never sang opera in Denver.

Josephine Louise Antoine was born in 1908 in Denver and adopted by Mr. and Mrs. Arthur H. Antoine. By 1914 her family had moved to Boulder. In 1921 she began studying voice with Alexander Grant, a faculty member at the University of Colorado. He remained her teacher until she graduated from the University of Colorado in 1929. That same year she won the Colorado Atwater Kent Audition Contest which provided her with scholarship money and the opportunity to study at an East Coast conservatory. In 1930-31 she was at Curtis, and from 1931-34 studied at Juilliard under the direction of Marcella Sembrich. In 1935 Josephine signed with the Metropolitan Opera Company and on January 4, 1936 made her premier lead role performance as Philine in *Mignon*. Her career with the Met lasted through 1947. During this period she also sang for other opera companies including the Chicago Opera, the San Francisco Opera, the Cincinnati Opera, and the

Chautauqua Opera. She sang concerts at the Denver Auditorium in 1936 and 1945. She also starred in *The Bartered Bride* in Central City in 1940 and in *The Red Mill* for the Denver Post Opera at Cheesman Park in 1949. After a successful opera career she taught at Indiana University (1947-48), University of Colorado (1948-49), Los Angeles Conservatory (1950-53), University of Texas (1953-57), Arizona State University (1959-66), and at Eastman School of Music (1957-59, and 1966-71). At the time of her death in 1971 she was a professor of voice at the Eastman School of Music.

Operatic expectations in Denver soared in 1954 when Dr. Antonia Brico led a performance of the doublebilled *I Pagliacci* and *Gianni Schicchi* with local singers who acquired their experience in Father Bosetti's productions. When German-schooled Walter Herbert arrived in Denver hopes again were lifted. There was a return to the Tabor with such admirable productions as *Madama Butterfly*, *Salome* and *Rigoletto*, all expertly staged by Edwin Levy of the University of Denver. Other productions were by John Newfield, who staged *The Marriage of Figaro* with the outstanding Norman Treigle, *La Traviata* with the stellar Licia Albanese, and *The Barber of Seville* among others. These attractive productions enticed a core of enthusiastic supporters, but the backers were unable to involve the elite of the city for their financial support. They were more interested in the Central City Opera scene. As a result, this effort collapsed in 1957 in financial disarray. Newfield then staged chamber opera at International House for two years, again to a highly enthusiastic audience unfortunately too small to count.

In the 1975, Central City had looked hopefully to Denver and for a time believed it could do opera there. Lacking Denver resources, it went to the Seattle Opera. There was a promise of a superior *Aida* but what arrived was a third-rate production. In 1976 a fine *La Bohème* was produced by Central City Opera at the Denver Auditorium with the wonderful Benita Valente, the up-and-coming Ashley Putnam, and George Shirley, who broke the race barrier in Denver opera with his fervently sung Rodolfo. Central City was having financial problems of its own, and decided against the Denver season that had been urged by some board members.

The travails of opera in Denver have been long and exhausting for those who worked to gather support. Opera is inherently costly, and is an entertainment which Denver would buy only with stars of international renown. Many had recollections of pleasurable times at the opera but their affections seemed more affixed to memories of Dorothy Kirsten, Licia Albanese, and Benita Valente than to the aura of the entire production.

Opera Colorado was founded in 1981 by Nathaniel Merrill and Louise Sherman, who came to Denver from long careers at the Metropolitan Opera in New York City. Their first performances were in 1983. Opera Colorado succeeded in finding deep pockets even though there were very tough years. Initially Opera Colorado depended on big-name singers but gradually Merrill's regard for fresh quality led him to the potential of less experienced singers like Stephen West, Hao-Jiang Tian, Steven Taylor, and Marcia Ragonetti, who made strong contributions to the total effort. Later, Colorado singers who had become known internationally, such as Cynthia Lawrence and Donald Kaasch, made impressive appearances.

There is no doubt that Opera Colorado permanently sealed a future for opera in Denver. The cosmopolitan life in Denver had produced an opera company that reflected the nature of the city with its international casts and repertory of German, French, and Italian opera. It had been necessary to build a foundation. The rough stones were now in place for a larger and more complex structure.

Frank Damrosch

Horace Tabor

Tabor Grand Opera House

Exotic and Irrational xxiii

Broadway Theater in its heyday, and as it was being demolished.

Jean Lane Brooks (Jeanne Brola)

Rose McGrew

Agnus Davis

Ina Souez

Frank Dinhaupt (Francesco Valentino)

Josephine Louise Antoine

A Stop on Tour

Denver from its beginning was a strong theater town, and audiences gathered whenever actors rode in on their wagons to deliver their crude melodramas. A whiff of opera arrived in December 1864. The Rocky Mountain News reported a planned presentation of Rossini's *A Daughter of the Regiment* by Mr. and Mrs. Gruenwald who had stopped over in Denver, traveling by stage coach on their way East from San Francisco, where they had appeared in Maguire's Opera House. The Rocky Mountain News spoke of disappointment in the event. For one thing, it was no more than a duet from the Rossini opera, among a potpourri of operatic song. Shortly thereafter the singers found their way to Central City where they were given a warmer reception by the musically inclined Welsh and Cornish miners.

The Howson Opera Troupe, a comic opera company, arrived in 1869 to deliver some Offenbach, farces, and burlesques at the Denver theatre. They performed at the Montana Theatre in Central City as well.

Though theater first came to Denver by stage coach or wagon, it was the extension of the Denver Pacific Railroad to Denver in 1870 that made it feasible to bring in opera with its superabundant cargo of singers, orchestra, costumes, and scenery. Audiences who once had known opera in the larger Eastern cities and Chicago were thrilled to welcome any kind of touring company. Denver's isolation had kept it in thrall to more accessible towns.

Comic opera was a national rage beginning in the late 1870s and it was visited on Denver by Marie Amiee's French Opera Company, Ware's Opera Bouffe Company, Alice Oates' Comic Opera Company and others.

The first authentic opera company to visit Denver was the Richings-Bernard Grand English Opera Company, which arrived in 1877 for a one-week stand. The troupe consisted of some thirty-odd people of which the principals were Mrs. Caroline Richings-Bernard, Miss Hattie Moore, Mrs. Henry Drayton, Miss Amy Phillips, Messrs. Harry Gates, W. A. Morgan, Will Kinross, Joe Dauphin, and Frank Howard. The remainder were chorus people and orchestra performers. Pierre Bernard was the conductor.

A company member described this tour in the Grand Army Magazine for April 1883 thus, "Denver was finally reached and we remained an entire week. The city had then about 20,000 to 22,000 inhabitants but opera was an entirely new feature in amusements, and the week's business was a very large one. We played at Guard's Hall under the management of Mr. Nick Forrester. The repertoire consisted of *Martha*, *The Bohemian Girl*, and *Maritana*. Also there were *Figaro's Wedding* and *Il Trovatore*. We closed the week's performances with a very largely attended concert in West Denver Turner Hall."

The Gilbert and Sullivan craze, fueled from London and spreading within weeks to the European continent and to New York, flowed a few months later into Denver. From 1876, when the Oates Comic Opera Company introduced *Trial by Jury*, until the 1929 appearance of the D'Oyly Carte Opera Company at the Broadway with its set of six operas, there were G & S productions galore. It was *H.M.S. Pinafore* that caught the attention of Denver, and the rest of the world, like nothing else before. In the 1879-1880 season there was a total of 15 Pinafore performances—by the Denver Choral Union, Mrs. Nate Forrester's Juvenile H.M.S. Pinafore Company, the touring New York 5th Avenue Pinafore Combination and Haverly's Church Choir Opera Company.

William Byers wrote in the Rocky Mountain News that "The Pinafore season has proved a success both in a financial and artistic sense. The audiences have from the first been large and appreciative and the performance has improved with each successive repetition." He also opined in May 1879 that "The man who comes in late and clambers over the back of his chair was at the 'Pinafore' performance last night, and those who sat near him uttered a silent prayer that the ship's crew would take him up and throw him overboard. He is a good deal more of a nuisance than the party who pretends to know all the music and hums it through the performance." Critically speaking, Byers wrote that "The slight blemishes in the performance noticeable to the audience were those which arose from the timidity of the ladies and gentlemen taking part, and while not marring the opera made many of the utterances on stage unintelligible to those in the rear of the hall."

Through the 1880s and 90s, many of the opera companies passing through Denver included a *Pinafore, Penzance, Mikado, Gondoliers* or other G & S fare in their repertoire. Among these were the Melville Opera Company in 1881, the Comley-Barton Company in 1882, Charles E. Ford's English Comic Opera Company, the C. Hess Acme Opera Company, the Chicago Church Choir Opera Company, and the Boston Ideal Opera Company in 1883, the Bijou Opera Bouffe Company in 1884, the Demorest English Opera Company, the Grau English Opera Company, and the Carleton Opera Company in 1885, the Chicago Opera Company, and J. C. Duff's Comic Opera Company in 1886, the Emma Abbott New Grand Opera Company and the Adelaide Randall Comic Opera Company in 1887, the California Opera Company in 1890 and so on, unabated year after year, until finally tapering off in the 1920s.

In December 1879 The Denver Daily Times observed plaintively that "Denver feels the want of a first class opera house more keenly than ever before. Why don't some Leadville millionaires take hold of the matter? It is a glowing opportunity to rid oneself of superfluous luck. Amateur and 'local' entertainments are about all the Denver public has an opportunity of encouraging."

Such productions as there were took place mostly in Governor's Guard Hall, Walhalla Hall, and the Turner Hall. Guard Hall was a combination armory and opera house, which had superseded plans for the Denver Opera House that Byers had been pushing. It had been erected at what is now 15th and Curtis. Its planning was unfortunate. Dressing rooms were at the front of the house, accessible to the stage only through the audience. The stage was only 20 feet deep, and the building was called "a masterpiece of incompetent planning." Company managers who came to look left despondently.

Walhalla Hall sat at 11th and Curtis streets and was considered the best of what there was. The Turner Hall was larger but considered to be inconveniently placed on what was then Holladay Street, near the red light district, now known as Market Street. Denver still had no proper theater.

The response to the Times editorial was not immediate but in March 1880 the Rocky Mountain News reported that H. A. W. Tabor had acquired seven lots at 16th and Curtis. In that summer he began construction of the Tabor Grand Opera House, working from lavish designs by W. J. Edbrooke. Horace Tabor saw to it that it was a marvel of extravagance. The cherrywood paneling, Persian carpets and pseudo-Moorish temple minarets over boxes and proscenium put all other theaters to shame. It cost about $850,000—a phenomenal sum for the time. The Tabor was such a showplace, all the competition was at a disadvantage.

For the 1956 *The Ballad of Baby Doe* author John Latouche has Tabor sing "I dreamed up this place myself. Imported them cherrywood pillars from Japan and mahogany from Honduras, carpets from Brussels and tapestries from Paris, France. It's a bang-up job, if I say it as shouldn't, smart as any opry house you're likely to see."

The Tabor Grand Opera House opened September 5, 1881, with the Emma Abbott Opera Company performing *Maritana*. Ms. Abbott also performed the "mad Scene" from *Lucia de Lammermoor*. The company continued the grand opening to present operas over the following two weeks. Abbott had formed her company in 1878 and with an ensemble of up to sixty members, toured the country during the 1880s, bringing opera to cities and towns that otherwise would never have experienced it. Welcome everywhere west of the Hudson River as "the people's prima donna," Abbott was called upon to inaugurate thirty-five new opera houses between 1879 and 1890, from Waterloo, Iowa, to Ogden, Utah.

It was not the whim of the audiences that brought opera to them. It was a green-visored clerk in New York or Chicago, with a timetable in one hand and an atlas in the other who determined where opera companies might travel. Denver always seemed to be the last desperate hope of the Eastern booking agents, for the railroad main line, the Union Pacific, ran through Cheyenne across southern Wyoming. Denver was an out-of-the-way stop. Therefore there was a need to assure the Tabor Grand could be a worthwhile stop financially.

Horace Tabor ordered William Bush, his long-term assistant and business associate from their Leadville days, who managed the Tabor Grand, to arrange the cooperation of other theater managers. By March 1884, Bush had a "Colorado Circuit" of five theaters: the Tabor Grand, Tabor Leadville, Colorado Springs, Central City, and Georgetown. Shortly thereafter, Bush was fired due to his being sympathetic to Tabor's divested wife, Augusta, and opposed to his marriage to Baby Doe McCourt. Thereupon, Peter McCourt, elder brother of Baby Doe, took over the management. McCourt proved to be an able and successful impresario, a position he held until 1921. By November 1884 he had added houses in Fort Collins, Canon City, Salida, and Pueblo. In July 1885, the Cheyenne Opera House joined the circuit, providing a critical link with the Union Pacific

Railroad. By 1886, McCourt had recruited opera houses in Greeley and Idaho Springs, and by 1888 the "Silver Circuit" included 13 houses: seven in Colorado, four in Utah, and two in Wyoming. The circuit eventually included as many as 20 theaters at a given time, as new ones were added and others dropped (or were lost to fires).

The Academy of Music was opened in April 1883 by P. T. Hughes, across the street from the Tabor. It was leased to Parker and Killen, with W. C. Hilker as business manager. It seated 1,000, with a stage 45 feet deep and 50 feet wide. The Academy of Music hosted the C. D. Hess Acme Opera Company, the Carleton English Opera Company, the Demorest English Opera Company, The Grau English Opera Company, and Her Majesty's Opera Company, featuring Minnie Hauck in Denver's first *Carmen*. When the inadequate Academy of Music burned in 1886 it was hastily rebuilt on a grander scale, reopening the following year as the Denver Music Hall with Adelina Patti in a grand operatic concert. In the summer of 1887 the Adelaide Randall Comic Opera Company offered *The Princess of Trebizonde*, *The Mikado*, and Audran's *The Mascot*. Later the company moved to the larger Mammoth Rink for two more weeks of performances, including the ever-popular *Pinafore*.

The Metropolitan Theater at Fifteenth Street and Cleveland Place, with a capacity of 2,384, aimed to draw on the uptown audience centered around the Brown Palace Hotel which was under construction at 16th and Broadway in 1888. It opened in September 1889. Because of inadequate income, a new ownership headed by J. Jay Joslin took over. Joslin installed L. G. Hanna as manager. After a $7,000 improvement it re-opened in January 1890. The Grand Italian Opera Company, the first resident company of the Metropolitan Opera of New York to visit Denver, arrived in early 1890 and presented four operas. Adelina Patti's aria "The Last Rose of Summer" during her performance of *Martha* was a sensation. Lillian Nordica was Leonora in *Trovatore* and Francesco Tamagno appeared in his famed role as Otello. Among the opera companies that performed there were the California Opera Company and Emma Juch Grand English Opera Company. It was named 15th Street Theatre for a while in 1890. Eventually coming under the ownership of Horace Tabor, the name was changed to People's Theatre and was managed by Philip McCourt, whose brother was Peter McCourt, manager of the Tabor Grand Opera House, and sister was Baby Doe Tabor. Only three years old, the theatre burned to the ground June 10, 1892.

Touring companies began to crest. With completion of the Brown Palace Hotel, the new theaters deserted the brilliantly lit marquees of Curtis Street for the areas adjacent to the new hotel. When the Broadway Theater opened across from the Brown in 1892 the Emma Juch Opera Company offered 12 performances. These drew on a repertory of ten operas, leading off with *Carmen* and including *Lohengrin*, the first Wagner opera performed in Denver. Its company numbered 150 in all, arriving on a special train.

Colorado's financial picture was grim in the early nineties after the devaluation of silver in 1893. The Broadway Theater suffered, and was closed for one-third of the 1895-96 season. There was a spectacular close to this season when the Damrosch Opera Company came with a trainload of Wagner—*Lohengrin, Die Walküre, Tannhäuser, Die Meistersinger,* and *Siegfried*. The Denver German community was thrilled. The 23-year old Johanna Gadski was a sensation as Elsa in *Lohengrin*. In December 1897 the Boston Lyric Stock Company arrived and remained through February, offering *Faust, Trovatore,* and a set of light opera favorites, including the mandatory *Bohemian Girl*. Going to a 10-20-25 cent admission heightened competition for a while. When Peter McCourt and W. H. Bush leased the Tabor from the Northwestern Mutual insurance Company and set a $1 fee at the Tabor and $1.50 at the Broadway, presentations were more frequent and of higher quality.

Although theater companies toured steadily from the 1870s through the present, operatic costs cut into the ability of managements to send out first-class companies. Denver had a reputation as a strong theater town, despite its local managers perennially being on the brink of financial disaster. The large eastern theater trusts began to take over the presentation of theater and opera. Tabor allied himself with the Hayman, Klaw, and Erlanger interests, and in March 1897 his theater interests were assumed by Northwestern Mutual Life Insurance Company. In June 1899 the Tabor was sold by Northwestern Mutual to the Bimetallic Investment Company for $425,000. John Campion, who owned the Little Johnny Mine in Leadville, was a leader in this group. Among subsequent alterations to the theater was the changing of the date on its cornerstone from 1881, its actual opening, to 1899.

The Broadway became the leading theater in the 1898-1899 and 1899-1900 seasons. Shortly thereafter, Nellie Melba with the Damrosch-Ellis Grand Opera Company took its stage for standing room only performance. The Charles A. Ellis Opera Company gave three opera performances in 1899. The Lambardi Italian Opera Company opened August 28 with a repertory of 14 operas, including *Norma, Aida* and *La Gioconda*. In 1900 the second Metropolitan company, the Maurice Grau Grand Opera Company, came to the Broadway for five performances with the splendors of the reigning sopranos, Melba in *La Bohème,* Gadski in *Les Hugenots,* and Nordica in *Lohengrin*. $160 was bid for a box seating eight, and over 6,000 persons attended these performances with resultant receipts of $24,000. In 1901, when the Boston Lyric Opera Company performed *Carmen* at the Broadway, the three Italians in the cast sang in Italian and the others sang in English. No one sang in French.

By the end of this season Peter McCourt was the dominant theater manager in the city, as well as in Colorado, Wyoming, and Utah, managing both Broadway and Tabor theaters, although he was controlled in turn by the big national theater chains.

There were always new opera companies being formed. In April 1904 the Rose Cecelia Shay English Grand Opera Company arrived at the Broadway. Juvenile opera companies from New Zealand came to Colorado, Pollard's Australian Juvenile Opera Company in 1902 and Pollard's Lilliputian Opera Company in 1905, performing in Peter McCourt's Silver Circuit houses. Named for the founding family that came from Tasmania, their adult and juvenile companies toured mostly in New Zealand and Australia during the 1880-1910 decades. The Lambardi Opera Company came to the Broadway in

1909 and 1910 and in between was the International Grand Opera Company of 100 members. Denver took opera when it was available, not being in a position to wheedle for a better balance.

In 1908 the Municipal Auditorium was opened, affording a theater with a large capacity of 3,300 and a flying proscenium which when raised could permit seating for 10,000 for recitals, orchestra, and band concerts. By arrangement with the Shubert organization, this city-owned facility set its tickets at a range from 25 cents to $1. Mayor Speer arranged for free Sunday afternoon programs. Unexpectedly, the Municipal Auditorium became the principal opera house of Denver.

The first of many operatic performances there was a concert by the Conreid Opera Company on October 21, 1908. Emma Calvé, Olive Fremstad, and Marcella Sembrich gave recitals there within the first year. In 1912 the Chicago Grand Opera Company gave its first performance in Denver, at the Auditorium. It was Wolf-Ferrarri's *The Secret of Suzanne*. In 1913 it again hosted the Chicago company, with a retinue of 150 and Mary Garden in *Thais* and Luisa Tetrazzini in *Lucia di Lammermoor*. Its repertory also offered a matinee program of *Hansel and Gretel* and Act II of *The Tales of Hoffman*. In April 1914, Chicago offered *Aida*, *Tosca*, and *Cavalleria Rusticana/I Pagliacci*. Denver was on Chicago's tour in 1921, 1922, 1924, and its final one, in 1928. Chicago Grand Opera touring companies performed 21 times in Denver between 1912 and 1928. The 1928 tour starred Rosa Raisa in *Aida* and Mary Garden in *Resurrection*.

Mary Garden was the company's great star in those days. When in Denver, she was the guest of John Charles Shaffer, owner of the Rocky Mountain News and the Denver Times and developer of the Ken-Caryl Ranch near Morrison. He was a patron of the arts and spearheaded the fund drive for building Chicago's opera house. Shaffer would engage opera companies to perform at the Denver Auditorium and house the cast in the Manor House at his ranch.

The National Grand Opera Company of Canada was scheduled to perform four operas in the Auditorium in February 1914.

They delivered the first, *Samson and Delilah*, but when the star tenor demanded his fee and left for New York and the local manager revoked part of the guarantee funds, the other members refused to appear. The company's baggage was seized to indemnify the audience which had assembled for the second performance. (The tenor had succeeded in getting two of his 235 trunks before departure.) A few days later, the company gave two benefit performances and a concert, and with help from the business community were able to get back to New York. The departing tenor was the famous Leo Slezak, father of the movie character actor, Walter Slezak.

Fortune Gallo's San Carlo Grand Opera Company, 100 strong including 30 instrumentalists, made the first of many visits in December 1917 and returned often until it disbanded in the 1950s. In 1918 came a quartet from the Metropolitan Opera with Frances Alda, Giovanni Martinelli, Carolina Lazzari, and Giuseppi DeLuca. Local ambitions were high with the Municipal Music Commission presentation, at the Municipal Auditorium, in June 1920 by 300 Denver singers of *Aida*.

Denver and its Auditorium garnered a unique distinction by broadcasting in 1921 the first opera to be presented in its entirety over radio. The opera *Martha*, performed by a local group as part of Denver Music Week, aired twice, May 19 and 20, from 9ZAF, a station founded by Dr. William (Doc) Reynolds, a dentist, at his 1124 S. University home in Denver in 1919. The studio was on the front porch and the transmitter in the back yard. Florence Lamont-Abramowitz was Betsy Anne in the May 19 performance. Also in the cast was Leroy R. Hinman, whom she would marry in 1924. Florence and Leroy would later create the Lamont School of Music.

During the twenties Denver had the opportunity to hear the greats of opera in recital at the Auditorium. Among these were Enrico Caruso, Renato Zanelli, Amelita Galli-Curci, Geraldine Ferrar, Rosa Ponselle, Alma Gluck, Lucrezia Bori, Feodor Chaliapin, Frieda Hempel, Ernestine Schuman-Heink, Louise Homer, Titto

Schipa, Paul Althouse, and John McCormack. These were glorious operatic presences but they were never heard in complete operas.

The opera companies that came during the twenties offered clumsy affairs, scenically threadbare, dramatically primitive, and instrumentally pedestrian, except for the Metropolitan Opera. It was costly to send out a company like the Metropolitan when the proceeds of a Denver engagement were not large. Operatic costs steadily cut into the ability of managements to send out first class companies.

The full Wagner "Ring" cycle was done by the German Grand Opera Company in 1930, returning the following year with d'Albert's *Tiefland, Tristan and Isolde*, and *The Flying Dutchman*, but few opera troupes visited Denver as the Great Depression dragged on. In the thirties and forties the San Carlo Opera Company was the most reliable, and not on a very high plane. When Hizi Koyke sang her charming Cio-Cio-San in authentic costumes and, when Coe Glade sang her spirited Carmen, audiences were satisfied.

Two citizens galvanized local enthusiasts to fill the operatic void. A Catholic priest, Joseph J. Bosetti, an opera advocate for two decades, founded the Denver Grand Opera Company and produced its first opera, *Mignon*, in 1933. Thereafter, for the next 21 years Bosetti mounted one or more operas on the Auditorium stage.

Additionally, Helen Bonfils rallied interest in Denver Post sponsored productions staged in Cheesman Park, starting in 1934. This series began as sets of grand opera selections but in 1936, with the performance of *Vagabond King*, it became an operetta and musical series that continued annually until 1972, with the exception of the war years, 1944 and 1945, when there were no productions. Jean Dickenson had starring roles in the first two Post productions.

All through the thirties and most of the forties the yearly operatic cycle traditionally consisted of a visit by the San Carlo Opera, a Denver Grand Opera production, the Post's Cheesman Park performance, a college production or two, and a few recitals by leading singers. Oberfelder and Slack, who had now combined their booking businesses, saw to it that Denver heard the finest operatic voices through recitals—Kirsten Flagstad, Lotte Lehman, Gladys Swarthout, Elizabeth Rethberg, Ezio Pinza, Bidu Sayao, Lauritz Melchoir, James Melton, Risë Stevens, Jan Peerce, Jussi Bjoerling, Ferruccio Tagliavini, Jennie Tourel, and Lily Pons, as well as the stars that now were achieving fame in the movies, including Grace Moore, Nelson Eddy, and Jeanette MacDonald. Dorothy Kirsten and Leonard Warren performed with the Denver Symphony. These talented singers kept interest in opera alive.

It had been decades since opera had been done at the Tabor. After a long, lusty life, it had become a movie theater, acoustically wrecked when its walls were altered for talking pictures. Already many in Denver had forgotten the glorious days of opera. Then, early in 1948, came the announcement by Denver's leading impresario of the thirties and forties, Arthur M. Oberfelder, that he would present the Metropolitan Opera in April at the Auditorium Theater in three productions, *Aida, La Bohème,* and *Carmen,* three operas unsurpassed in popularity. This was a major operatic event, for it brought the Met to Denver for the first time since 1900. Casting was typically that of the Met on the road, ranging from Risë Stevens' admirable Carmen to Licia Albanese's classic Mimi. Leonard Warren's commanding Amonasro was the standout voice in *Aida* which featured the uneven singing of Stella Roman and Kurt Baum.

In The Denver Post Richard A. Moore described opening night, "The silver fingers of a searchlight swept the sky. Flash bulbs popped. Limousines, family cars, and convertibles unloaded their passengers at City Auditorium Monday night, and one chair collapsed in a box." Cecil Effinger, before becoming nationally known as a composer and inventor, was the Post music critic from 1946 to 1948. He wrote of "An important page for the history of music in Denver—the long-awaited tour by the Metropolitan added to its success as a packed house drawn from all the Rocky Mountain area heard... a superb performance of *Aida*." Later Effinger wrote of the Met's visit that "There is no question that the opera audience in this area will welcome another such visit. Perhaps new opera could be included along with the best of some lesser known standard works."

Sure enough, Oberfelder was able to announce a second Met visit in May 1949. With a somewhat less orthodox lineup than in the previous year's visit, the Met brought Verdi's *Otello*, Thomas's *Mignon*, and Donizetti's popular *Lucia di Lammermoor*. The casting had brilliance. In December 1947 when Toscanini performed *Otello* for NBC Radio, Ramon Vinay was the Otello and Giuseppe Valdengo the Iago (as they were in Denver). Both had prepared and sung under Toscanini's demanding direction a score he had mastered in many performances. Licia Albanese was the luminous Desdemona. Fritz Busch conducted a towering performance which benefited from Herbert Graf's potent stage direction as well as Donald Oenslager's handsome settings.

The Met's resident leader of French opera, Wilfred Pelletier, led the *Mignon* cast, which had the splendid Risë Stevens in its lead, with Jerome Hines, already a local favorite for his 1946 triumph in Central City's *The Abduction from the Seraglio*, and Giuseppe di Stefano who misgauged the Auditorium's acoustics and shouted. The final act did find him in fine, controlled voice. Patrice Munsel's Lucia was not what it should have been for she had not yet found herself as a dramatic coloratura. A very young Frank Guarrera made a strong impression as the villainous Enrico, years before his presence became an annual event at Central City.

The three performances were sold out, and it seemed the Met would always have a welcome in Denver, however within the year it was concluded that Denver would not henceforth figure in Met touring plans. That pleasure was saved for Dallas and Houston.

The welcome mat was out for the Boston Grand Opera Company when it arrived in November 1949. The name reminded some old-timers of the good, old touring company of that name, but the company that arrived in Denver was not only creaky, it had a company manager anxious to purchase a critic's good word under the counter. He found no takers.

Its sure-fire repertory consisted of one performance each of *Carmen, Rigoletto,* and *La Traviata.* The *Carmen* was born in Dallas as Leonora Cohron, and changed her name to Leonora Corona when she went to the Met in 1927, where she stayed until 1935. At the Met she achieved a certain notoriety through Lawrence Gilman's review of the 1929 revival of *Don Giovanni* in its first performance at the Met since 1908. He wrote, "Of Miss Leonora Corona who substituted for the ailing Rosa Ponselle (as Donna Anna) it will perhaps be sufficient to say that she made Miss Ponselle's indisposition seem a costly thing indeed for the Metropolitan."

A performance such as Madame Corona gave as Carmen in Denver might have set opera back many years but, fortunately, the audience was slender. Those who were there chortled at the memorable operantics, happenings matched only by those in the Marx Brothers *A Night at the Opera* or in Rene Clair's *Le Million.* Madame Corona flounced across the stage, flashing her teeth, flirting with the teen-agers drafted to play the soldiers, entangling her mantilla on the epaulets of one soldier, and her shawl on another's. In the final act she was distracted by a falling comb and even more by the displacement of her artificial bosom. This appeared to concern her more than the possibility of death at the hands of Don Jose. No one tried to subdue the laughter, and certainly no vocal effort could have saved the evening.

The Don Jose, Rene Casteler by name, was, I wrote in The Denver Post, "sung from somewhere near the top brass button of his red tunic. His singing was uneven in tone, possessed quavers and breaks, and the music seemed well out of his range." The supers had been gathered from local high schools and colleges, and some of the soldiers would more suitably have filled the roles of the children playing at soldiering than of supposedly virile men.

The next evening's *Traviata* promised more of the same but there was a surprise in the personable competence of soprano Elvira Helal. Improved orchestral support was helpful, but one looked in vain for comparable competence in the balance of the cast.

In February 1950 the Oberfelder management brought the San Carlo Opera Company for four performances. *Madama Butterfly, La Traviata, Il Trovatore,* and *Aida* comprised a heady listing. Hizi Koyke was the predictable Cio-Cio-San with her small, carefully used soprano and her charmingly animated characterization. Conductor Carlo Moresca struggled with unrehearsed instrumentalists.

Belle Udell was Aida, arriving on stage like one who believed she really was a serving girl to Amneris. This new production was gaudy but inept. Several singers drew positive reaction. Stefan Ballinari was an unusually stalwart Count di Luna for *Il Trovatore* and David Poleri was a fresh-voiced young tenor as Manrico, showing the promise that would carry him to a national career. Poleri achieved notoriety at the New York City opera when, in the final act of *Carmen,* he gave into impulse and left the stage, leaving the Carmen, Gloria Lane, to stab herself in order to die.

Denver audiences turned out for these performances, popularly priced as they were. People knew better than to expect first-class singing, thus the law of low expectations ran its course.

Among the organizers of operatic tours the name of Charles L. Wagner deserves a high rank. He actually listened to his singers' auditions. He had been connected with the original Boston Opera Company and that company had utilized such great singers as Nordica and Destinn. In building his company he managed to hear some of the best available. Some of these, like Jon Crain, Margaret Roggero, and Richard Torrigi, became known nationally. Conductor Paul Breisach had conducted at the Metropolitan and in San Francisco, and Desiree Defrere had been a stage director at the Met.

In March 1950 on the tiny Phipps Auditorium stage, the Wagner company did its best for a good crowd with the popular double bill of *Il Pagliacci* and *Cavalleria Rusticana.* Subsequently Wagner wrote to me of his efforts to provide the best in touring opera, boasting of thorough rehearsals and good voices. He had lost $1,600 in Denver on this single performance.

It was November 1955 before Wagner sent another company into Denver. This time he took over the Denver Theater, a large motion picture house which had a pit and a decent stage. There were two performances of *La Bohème,* an English language matinee and an evening one in its original Italian. A promising Josephine Asaro was an affecting Italian language Mimi. Because of acoustical treatment as a film theater, the Denver Theater did not work as a live theater venue. Thomas Martin, who with his wife Ruth, translated many standard operatic works into English, was the conductor.

The ghost of the Boston Opera Company stood in the wings of the rebuilt Auditorium Theater when the New York Opera Festival brought *Carmen* into town. Francesco Foti, who had come to Denver with Leonora Corona, came again for another disaster but not so many laughs this time.

La Bohème and *La Traviata* were brought in yet again by the New York Opera Festival. The sensitive Mimi was the lovely Maria di Gerlando, while the strutting Rudolph Petrak, all teeth and shrill voice, was the Rodolfo. The colorless Violetta was Josephine Guido but there was something of a surprise in the Irish baritone James Buckley who sang the elder Germont.

Another inevitable *Butterfly* and a perhaps slightly less obvious *Rigoletto* came in October 1959 with the bland Josephine Guido back as Cio-Cio-San and Eddy Ruhl as a Pinkerton of some promise. Under correct supervision, Ruhl's hefty tenor might have been made more palatable. He would figure in Central City opera lore when he replaced an ailing William Olvis as Rhadames in *Aida* opposite Beverly Sills in 1960. Both Ruhl and Olvis soon vanished from national view.

It was again *Rigoletto* when in 1963 Community Concerts of Denver brought in the Goldowsky Grand Opera Theater in its tradition of touring the best young singers and giving them operatic experience. Exactly what they were to provide audiences was uncertainly stated.

Boris Goldowsky is best recalled for his rich Russian accent, familiar to all who listened to the Saturday afternoon broadcasts from the Metropolitan in the forties and fifties. As producer of opera at the Tanglewood Music School in the Berkshire summer home of the Boston Symphony, he had done such notable performances as that of the first American *Idomeneo* and the first Britten *Peter Grimes*.

Goldowsky had developed a bizarre notion that stage acting was simple, so easy that young, inexperienced singers could realize characters if there were something for them to do which related to the role they were playing. His idea was to prevent them from being distracted from important musical matters. The result: a busy stage. A mess might be closer to the mark.

It is good to recall the performance of Sherrill Milnes as Rigoletto. In 1963 he was a very young version of the great singer he would become, while his stiff acting would in time bend. Many in the audience were excited to be hearing a young Denver tenor, Eric Davis, who was singing the Duke. He had been a tenor of promise in many local productions. Despite illness, he insisted on singing because of the support he had received from Denver in the past. This unwise move meant he was unequal to the demands of the role.

Other company singers went on to achieve distinction, among them Thomas Paul, Gwenlynne Little, Ara Barberian, Marcia Baldwin, Nancy Williams, and Louise DeSett. It was a fine group of singers in a terrible production. In March 1965 Milnes again toured for Goldowsky as Masetto in *Don Giovanni*, notable for this being the opera's premiere in Denver.

It would be more than a decade before another touring company came to Denver. There was imposing lineage in the sponsors: the Central City Opera House Association would present a widely hailed regional opera company, the Seattle Opera Company in *Aida* at the Auditorium. Seattle committed itself to offering a first-rate production in 1975, a good cast and with lavish settings to be supervised by its general manager, Glynn Ross, directed by Lincoln

Clark, its principal stage director, and conducted by Henry Holt, its principal conductor.

The cast came together for the first time in Denver, which went against promises made for a first-rate production. The inadequate leads were Rolf Bjoerling, son of the great Jussi Bjoerling, as Rhadames, Betty Jones as Aida and Marguerite Yauger as Amneris. The only exceptions to poor casting were Robert Mosely as Amonasro, Archie Drake as Ramfis and as the King, Stephen West of Denver, the only singer who could be readily understood.

Because of Duain Wolfe's attentive leadership of a large local chorus and the miracle achieved by choreographers Mattlyn Gavers, who had worked at Central City, and Maria Ferrera of Denver, who provided good dancers with lively dance, the triumphal entry scene worked its excitement. Conductor Holt was negative in his work with the Denver Symphony Orchestra, and this was reflected in lackluster playing. The shallow pit of the Auditorium Theater had always been a problem, and the balance of singers and orchestra was poor.

This major effort to present a prime opera company fizzled. A strong sales pitch had sold out the two performances. So large-scaled a disappointment killed the relationship with Seattle, which was to have led to further collaboration. With a loud thud, touring opera had come to an end. It did, however, have the effect of kindling Denver's growing interest in having its own opera company.

Exotic and Irrational 19

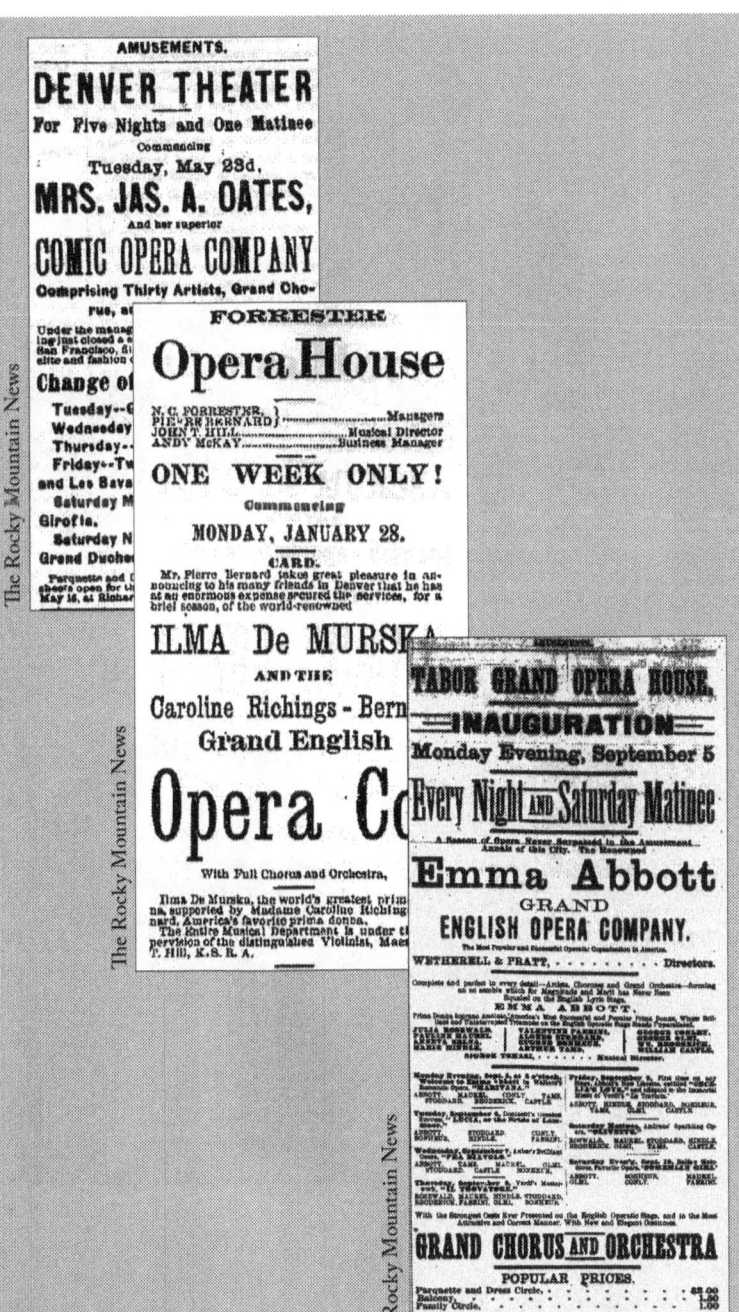

Governor's Guard Hall

Feodor Chaliapin

*Florence Lamont
(Abramowitz) Hinman*

Denver Municipal Auditorium

Monsignor Joseph Bosetti

Frances Rose Rosenzweig
(Frances Rose)

Rosa Ponselle

Enrico Caruso

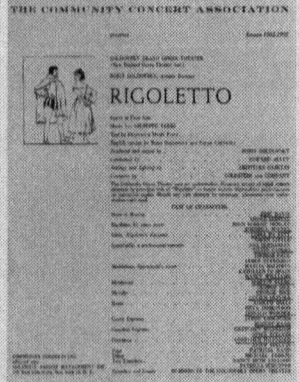

Mary Garden

Sherrill Milnes

The Grand Tradition

The life of Joseph J. Bosetti, a Catholic priest, whose death in January 1954 ended nearly 45 years of intense, untiring effort, showed Denver what it meant to have a musician dedicated to Italian opera in its midst. Bosetti had seen Verdi when he came to dedicate a home for retired musicians across the street from his childhood home in Milan. Verdi provided funds for this residence and took a great interest in its talented occupants, so he was an occasional visitor, often glimpsed by the young Bosetti. For all his life Bosetti was to seek activities that would bring him close to the heart of music, though he made his way as a churchman. It was not the world of music alone that engrossed him. He was intrigued by all the major matters of the mind.

Welby, the small Italian coal-mining town north of Denver, where Father Bosetti arrived as a missionary in 1909, offered sparse outlet for his interests. He found little there to glorify the spirit, but he filled the position of assistant to the parish priest dutifully and, in addition, was linguist for an Italian coal company.

In Denver, the Cathedral of the Immaculate Conception was completed in 1912 as the grandest church in the state. Soon after, Father Bosetti was appointed assistant pastor of the Cathedral. There he organized a large, male choir which he trained in classical music. With a strong background in harmony, counterpoint, and theory, and a constantly expanding ability to play the organ, he exactly suited the needs of the Cathedral.

He taught French at the Cathedral school, along with philosophy and psychology. His success in this latter field was such that he was invited to teach a course in psychology at the University of Colorado in Denver. Also, while in Switzerland for his first teaching duties, he had learned to ski, and was able to give ski instruction from this experience. Bosetti soon became Vicar General, then Chancellor, and later Dean of the Denver Deanery. With such firmly rooted connections to Colorado, it is not surprising that he refused to return to Italy in 1914 to fight in World War I against his new home, as an Italian government draft measure called on him to do.

From the outset he struggled to build up the Cathedral choir, extending the quality of musical literature, reaching out into the community for the best singers, no matter what the denomination. Thursday evenings he would gather members of the chorus and other musical friends as he played through the scores of his favorite operas, commenting on the action and creating interest in this secular music he loved so much. The annual concert by Father Bosetti and the Cathedral choir became an anticipated event. Programming was original, for the Mozart Requiem might occupy the first half, with light opera to follow. Prominent Denver singers participated in these concerts. From society there was Mrs. Charles McAllister Wilcox. Many promising young singers were introduced in these concerts, including young Frank Dinhaupt.

There was special praise for *Bethlehem*, a Christmas cantata written by Bosetti and performed at the Broadway in 1922. It and other works were done when the choir traveled to Greeley, Colorado Springs, and other communities, with expenses covered by these towns. When the singers went to Colorado Springs to sing for patients at the Penrose Hospital, Mrs. Spencer Penrose saw to it that the singers were put up at The Broadmoor, the lavish pleasure dome her husband owned. As choir members persuaded singing friends to join, the choir enlarged. This meant more attendance for concerts. A concert to raise money for Cathedral school football uniforms brought in parents and friends of parents.

Father Bosetti relished the out-of-doors when there was opportunity. The Denver Diocese considered the value of having a summer camp for boys, and negotiated with co-owners of 165 acres prime acreage near Estes Park. The deal fell through but Bosetti was able to purchase the property which has long operated as Camp St. Malo, with the assistance of several wealthy parishioners.

In 1915 Father Bosetti thought it time to do an opera. Naming his ensemble the Cathedral Opera Company, he presented *Cavalleria Rusticana* at the Auditorium. Buoyed by a good response, the following year he leased the Broadway Theater and presented a full-scale production of Thomas' *Mignon* with Florence Lamont-Abramowitz, later to be Hinman, in the lead. During rehearsals she slipped out of a cart and broke an ankle. Despite this, she went on for the opening night.

In 1917, Gounod's *Romeo and Juliet* had its Denver premiere under the auspices of Catholic Charities, the pre-eminent organization of the Diocese's charitable giving, which earned proceeds out of ticket sales. This performance was again at the Auditorium Theater, with Elizabeth Young as Juliet, Stiles Richards as Romeo, and the reliable bass, George Kerwin, as Friar Lawrence. One young dancer in the production was Martha Wilcox, whose father, John W. Wilcox, was music critic for The Denver Post. Later Martha became a prominent advocate of modern dance, a teacher of renown, first at Colorado College, then at the University of Denver.

Not until 1933 would Bosetti organize another opera production. In that year, in May, he formed the Denver Grand Opera Company and produced *Mignon* at the Auditorium. From then on, every spring for the next 18 years, the Denver Grand Opera

Company, in the Auditorium, performed an opera (two operas were produced in 1935, one in the spring and one in December), with a mix of stars from major opera houses and local talent. The productions were double cast, each performing on alternate dates. The Metropolitan Opera's General Manager, Edward Johnson, once attended a performance and was astonished by the size of the 200-strong chorus.

For a 1934 revival of *Romeo and Juliet*, Josephine Neri and Arch Cannon, both prominent teachers, and also wife and husband, led the cast. Alternates were Anne O'Neill and Karl Jorn. In 1935 the opera was *La Traviata* with Jean Dickenson, alternating with Anne O'Neill, and tenor Joseph Clifford with Frank Dinhaupt.

Frank Valentine Dinhaupt was born in New York, but came to Denver with his parents when he was 11. He was a choir boy at the Cathedral of the Immaculate Conception, under the direction of Bosetti, and graduated from Regis High School. He studied voice with Florence Lamont Hinman. In 1926, sponsored by a prominent Denver woman, he went to Milan, Italy and, a year later, made his operatic debut in Parma under the name Francesco Valentino, in the role of Germont in *La Traviata*. Throughout the 1930s he sang in major European opera houses, including La Scala and Glyndebourne (notably as Macbeth, 1938-39). Loyal to his mentor, Bosetti, Valentino returned in 1935 to sing with the Denver Grand Opera Company in *La Traviata* in the spring and *La Somnambula* in December; in 1937 his lone Wagner effort, *Lohengrin* with Denver favorites Anne O'Neill, Joseph Clifford, and Karl Jorn; 1946, *Il Trovatore*; and 1948, *The Barber of Seville*. He was at Central City for six seasons—1946, *La Traviata*; 1950, *Madama Butterfly*; 1951, *Romeo and Juliet*; 1951, *Amelia Goes to the Ball*; 1952, *The Marriage of Figaro*; and 1954, *Faust*. Valentino began singing with the Metropolitan Opera in 1940, making his debut on December 7, 1940, as Enrico in *Lucia* with Lily Pons. Later he sang such Verdi roles as Rigoletto and Amonasro in *Aida*. He appeared in 26 different roles during the next 21 seasons, never missing a scheduled performance. He also sang with the San Francisco Opera and in concerts with orchestras, among them Toscanini's. After his retirement from singing in 1962, Valentino joined the faculty of the Peabody Conservatory of Music in Baltimore, where he taught for 15 years. He died in Fairfax, Virginia, in 1991.

Jean Dickenson was born in Montreal in 1914, to American parents. Her mother, May F. Dickenson, was a noted writer, and her father, an engineer, was a faculty member at the University of Pennsylvania and Columbia. As her father traveled abroad extensively in his profession, she lived in India and South Africa, as well as Canada and the USA. Jean became a student at the Lamont School of Music of Florence Lamont Hinman. In 1932 Jean won the Colorado Atwater Kent Radio Auditions, sponsored by the Rocky Mountain News. She got her professional start singing on KOA radio in Denver, and then was employed as the soprano on CBS radio's weekly Hollywood Hotel, which featured host Dick Powell, singer Frances Langford, and guest celebrity stars. With the Denver Grand Opera Company, she sang Juliet in *Romeo and Juliet* in 1934, Violetta in *La Traviata* in 1935 and the title role in *Lucia di Lammermoor* in 1939. With the Denver Post Opera Company she was Gilda in selections from *Rigoletto* in 1934 and Lucia in selections from *Lucia di Lammermoor* in 1935. Jean appeared with the San Carlo Opera Company in 1937 at the Denver Auditorium in the role of Gilda in *Rigoletto*. She became a regular performer 1937-51 on the NBC radio program, American Album of Familiar Music. A favorite of radio audiences, she was known as the "Nightingale of the Airwaves." She appeared in concert with the Denver and Milwaukee symphony orchestras, the Promenade Symphony Concerts, and the Little Symphony of Montreal. Jean sang numerous concerts throughout the United States and Canada under the management of the National Concert and Artists Corporation of New York. At age 26, coloratura soprano Dickenson made her Metropolitan debut January 26, 1940, as Philine in *Mignon*, with Risë Stevens in the title role. She subsequently became a protégé of the celebrated opera star, Lily Pons. Jean married Daniel Edward Marcy Jr. in Cincinnati in 1942. The Marcys currently reside in Briarcliff Manor, New York.

In the late forties the dances in the Denver Grand Opera productions were choreographed by Lillian Covillo and Friedann Parker, founders of the Colorado Ballet. The orchestra for these productions was basically the Denver Civic Symphony, founded in 1912. Bosetti would not tolerate any levity or foolishness in the pit or on the stage. He tolerated dance episodes but did not enjoy them, as he resented their distracting him from the work of instructing singers in the essentials of operatic singing.

The sets were done by Walter Keeley, who designed out of his love for opera and familiarity with the grand traditions of 19th century opera. A Western Union technician who learned scenic design at the Elitch's Garden Theater, in 1934 he asked Bosetti for permission to design his productions. Keeley always believed, as did his contemporaries, that more was always better. Sets had to be large because there were always so many chorus members. He was always very conscientious about the need for good painting, and his settings rarely offended, even if they reflected the Golden Age of Opera, the time warp of his musical tastes. In outdoor scenes, there were always "the hanging gardens of Babylon," those mossy-looking swoops of green-painted canvas which hid the wrinkled skies from view. Aside from his delight in designing these productions, he loved to listen to recordings from his large library of 63 operas which he would delightedly play for friends.

John Carbone, a Denver businessman, loved opera about as much as Bosetti, and he would order tickets for The Metropolitan Opera and Bosetti and Carbone would go to The Met to listen to and engage singers for the following year's production. In addition to Carbone, the Weckbaugh and Minnisale families supported these productions.

The intermixture of international singers and talented local singers was sometimes alarming and sometimes quite palatable. Prior to the arrival of the imports, local singers would rehearse roles they might never sing on stage. There were occurrences during these productions which would today be laughable. When Francesco Valentino performed as the elder Germont in a 1935 *Traviata*, it was reported by Anne Stein Roth in the Rocky Mountain News, that, following a hearty outbreak of applause for his "Di provenza il mar," he announced he would sing the Prologue from *I Pagliacci* as an encore.

Bosetti was as startled as anyone at the opening night of the 1949 *Faust* when a woman in grey street clothes broke through the massed chorus ranks to step to the footlights. In the shocked silence following her sudden arrival, she told the audience "We must all say the Rosary together, we must—I've learned a lot since Christmas." Bosetti quickly motioned to members of the chorus who encircled the lady in a great huddle, and moved offstage with her.

The bass hired from The Met to sing Mephistopheles in this production, Wellington Ezekial by name, attended one of Eleanore Weckbaugh's cocktail parties where he learned about the impact of gin martinis at mile high altitude. By the time he recovered, the performances were over, and he had never been on stage, even for a rehearsal.

In the final season of 1951 there was an unsettling occasion involving the Violetta of the *La Traviata* then being performed. She was Emilia Vidali of Italian-Latin American origin, an ample woman with a temperament to match, intent on being the flighty Violetta of Act I. At the end of Act II she found her exertions in Denver altitude had overwhelmed her ability to proceed. She was too exhausted to die on stage. The audience was informed that Ruth Meinke, the fresh-voiced, pretty young Denver singer and understudy, would be her substitute in the final act.

It turned out that one critic, who shall be nameless, had fled the hall at the end of Act II, the terror of yet more violent vocalizing and giddy laughter driving him to such desperation. Only by a chance reference to the morning paper's review did he learn the denouement, and thus was able to salvage his review. It is said that never afterwards did he depart a performance until the very end.

Ruth Meinke had been very appealing as Violetta and her performance, along with that of young George Van Gorden as Alfredo and the fine Germont of Richard Dworak, had presented a delicate and intensely affecting final scene. Ruth Meinke was recalled by the audience again and again.

This was the first Denver appearance of Dworak, a local attorney, whose splendid voice and sure instinct for character was to enrich the Denver operatic scene until the early sixties in such roles as Don Pasquale, Rigoletto, Tonio, and Gianni Schicchi. Bidu Sayao, the diminutive Brazilian soprano who presented such beguiling characterizations on the operatic stage, came to do Donizetti's *L'Elisir d'Amore* in one of Bosetti's most successful presentations. This production introduced to Denver Roger Dexter Fee, an able singing actor, who had just succeeded Florence Lamont Hinman, on her retirement, as director of the Lamont School of Music at the University of Denver. There were many young singers in the company who would in later years take major roles as their abilities matured.

As Nemorino in that production there was the young Denver tenor Marvin Worden, who had been singing major roles in the operas since his successful 1948 Almaviva in *The Barber of Seville*, his first operatic stage role. In the early eighties Worden recalled to me that having been reared in a Protestant household, he "found it strange to be working in a Catholic organization, but Father Bosetti showed me nothing but kindness." Once, Worden had thought otherwise; in 1947 when offered Parpignol in *La Bohème* he turned it down.

Worden was that rarity, a tall tenor. His knowledge of singing was as good as his production was even. He concentrated on the craft and art of singing so intently that his stage presence was lackluster. He genuinely believed the characterization should come from the singing, and he was not truly interested in the movement or the acting.

In the early fifties Worden went to New York City where he sang at Radio City Music Hall and later in the chorus of the operas then being done on NBC television under the leadership of Peter Herman Adler. After singing in *Fidelio* and *Boris Godunov* for NBC, in 1962 he went to the Basel Opera in Switzerland for three years as a Mozart specialist, doing Tamino in *The Magic Flute* and Don Ottavio in *Don Giovanni*. At Basel he increased his repertory by doing Janacek's *Jenufa*, and he came to esteem this challenge. When the management decided Worden should become a heldentenor and sing *Lohengrin* he returned to Denver to teach and to sing.

Another Denver singer who emerged as a performer in Bosetti productions was Fred Nesbit, who did Marcello, Mephistopheles, Rossini's Figaro, and the elder Germont. His voice was strong and well-used, except when he delved into the deep bass repertory. As the years went on, his performances became better because they were more carefully thought out. In May 1955 he sang a memorable Sharpless. Nesbit worked successfully in real estate and seemed never to desire a professional singing career.

A vivacious and versatile mezzo, Truly Barr Nelson, sang Hansel for Bosetti, and later a Siebel in *Faust*. Later to teach at the Lamont School of Music of the University of Denver, she would enrich a large repertory with contemporary works for faculty recitals.

There was a crisis in 1950 when the local musicians union urged that the stage hands should go on strike. The effort to employ union stage hands was not successful. Bosetti, knowing his limited budget, sought and got volunteer stage hands, all priests and friends, who managed these chores during the *L'Elisir d'Amore* performances.

Despite the faded blonde who hung onto the stage curtain and appeared to be counting the house, despite rickety operatic stage conventions and haphazard staging, these productions had memorable moments with fine voices and satisfactory orchestral playing. Who could forget the classic figure of medieval grace made by Dorothy Kirsten when she came on stage as Marguerite in *Faust*? Or the beguiling, diminutive Bidu Sayao becoming generous after seeming spiteful in *L'Elisir d'Amore*?

Remembering such moments is some of the sublimity of opera, and Father Bosetti worked with all the patience he could find to bring opera to Denver. Raised on the operatic traditions of the late

19th century, he could sustain what he relished. He was always the conductor, always the director of stage action. The results, sometimes undisciplined and bordering on chaos, with little real sense of theater, were common to these traditions. The passing of Joseph Bosetti seemed like a final curtain on the Denver operatic scene.

The Tradition Refreshed

With limited resources, Father Bosetti had provided entirely suitable leadership, gauging astutely the proper element of star power as he presented standards of operatic fare. John Newfield would engineer a major, well-considered effort to utilize modern influences in opera, and draw on the best singing and dramatic talents in Denver. The excitement of fresh creation would come to Denver operatic activities, and with it the prospect of bringing Denver a permanent company.

It had been three years since Father Bosetti's final production in 1951 when a group of local singers who had been active with the Denver Grand Opera Company banded together to do opera performances. Antonia Brico, the conductor from The Netherlands, leader of the Denver Businessmen's Orchestra, who was dedicated to making room on conducting podiums for women, expressed interest in such a project. Earl Bach of the theater department at Loretto Heights College also was eager to be involved.

Calling itself the Greater Denver Opera Association, the group announced a double bill of *I Pagliacci* and *Gianni Schicchi*, to be done in March 1954 at the Auditorium Theater. Although the Leoncavallo work had been done several times in Denver, the Puccini was a Denver premiere. There was hope in modest yet fresh plans.

Those fine baritones who had enriched so many Bosetti performances, Richard Dworak, Harold Alexander, and Fred Nesbit took turns as Tonio and as Gianni Schicchi in three performances. Alexander was set to open as Tonio but illness took him out of the performances, so Dworak as Tonio and Nesbitt as Schicchi sang three performances each in as many nights.

The backers learned right off that the support of the Catholic Church and its charitable wing had assured a significant financial base for Father Bosetti's efforts. Losing the support of Church-oriented social figures like Eleanore Weckbaugh made this new effort very difficult. Opera was now on its own, and there was a problem in building the necessary core of support. The Denver establishment was not there at the outset nor at the close.

When *Rigoletto* was staged in October 1954 at the Tabor Grand Opera House, its excellence made a strong case for local opera. Operatic hopes soared with this cogently performed, ably sung presentation. Its conductor, Rudolf Fetsch, had little experience as an opera conductor but he was a thorough musician who knew voices. He had taught in Japan prior to World War II, and subsequently arrived in Denver to teach and to coach singers.

Edwin Levy mounted the production, drawing on stimulating experiences in staging operas by Paul Hindemith, Gian Carlo Menotti, and George Antheil at the University of Denver. He had come from the University of Louisiana in 1946, where he had studied opera production with Pasquale Amato, the great baritone. At the University he had been a prime factor in the national prestige its theater department was achieving.

When Levy directed Antheil's *The Brothers* in 1954 at the University of Denver, Richard Dworak was in the cast, and he shared the lead role with Harold Alexander. Levy wanted to move away from the melodramatic character of the opera. Together, they realized the jester as a human individual rather than a warped monster. Both gave disciplined, affecting performances.

From nowhere Mariko Mukaida emerged with exceptional vocal abilities. She was a lovely Gilda. William Black, a young army captain stationed at Rocky Mountain Arsenal, gave youthful vigor and vocal reliability to the Duke, while Donna Bricker Janzen was a saucy Maddalena, and Apostol Pelargidis a larger than life and sardonic Sparafucile.

In February 1955 Humperdinck's *Hansel and Gretel* was done at the Tabor. Regrettably, there were almost no funds for the scenic elements so crucial to this opera. The antiquated backstage was dirty, dismally dark, and depressing. Kathryn Kayser, a noted director of children's theater at the University of Denver, gave an able version of the opera, which suffered from the slow tempos taken by conductor Antonia Brico.

Witchcraft was in the practiced hands of Violette McCarthy, choral director at East High School, who had appeared in many Bosetti offerings. She demonstrated real feeling for the ghoulish as she skittered gleefully amidst the gingerbread children. At one performance, Hansel and Gretel were so engrossed in their singing that she had to commit herself to the oven at the climactic point.

Denver's very first domestic *Carmen* was staged at the Tabor in May. Robert Tillotsen's production was energetic but somewhat incoherent. He considered the great second act quintet to be the occasion for unbridled slapstick. Richard Dworak as Escamillo was required to wear a motorcycle belt and do a backflip, and emerge upright to sing a high F!

Tillotsen rehearsed with reference to charts which indicated where cast members should stand. George Van Gorden recalls that he could not make head or tails of these charts, which told where his Don Jose should stand. He observed to another cast member, "This looks like a plate of spaghetti."

Marie Mauro, a singer of unfulfilled promise, managed a quite competent Carmen in one cast while Laura Grauer, though insufficiently animated, put her rich mezzo to pleasing use in the other. The cast of the alternating *Carmen* began its rehearsals at 2 a.m. following opening night. One of the two Micaelas was Helen Dedrick, who began her musical life as a double bass player with the Denver Symphony. She concluded there were more interesting challenges in singing. She had a charming presence and grew in artistry through hard work.

In the meantime yet another German musician, conductor Walter Herbert, arrived in Denver. He had conducted in Czechoslovakia; at Bern, Switzerland; at the Leipzig opera; and ultimately at the Vienna Volksoper, and had come to the United States, glad to have a teaching job at Mills College. He was able to get into the San Francisco Symphony as violist, and his abilities on the podium were recognized in 1942 when he conducted both *Die Fledermaus* and *The Bartered Bride* for the San Francisco Opera.

Herbert's operatic involvements spread, and from 1950 to 1954 he was general director of the New Orleans Opera. In 1955, while still active in Denver, he founded the Houston Grand Opera, which he led until 1972. From 1965, when he became music director of the San Diego Opera, until his death in 1975, he worked to establish what has become another fine regional company—Opera South in Jackson, Mississippi, an all-black company, which he founded in 1970.

Herbert conducted only five productions in Denver between 1955 and 1957. His term as music director of the Greater Denver Opera Association was made outstanding by the force of his musicianship, as well as by his all-embracing attention. Herbert never interfered with stage action. His domain was that of the orchestra and the singing. Clearly, he had hopes of developing a dual-city conductorship, with Houston the principal city and Denver a growing center. That Herbert obtained for his opera orchestra the first chair and other Denver Symphony musicians was a fortunate development. Their unmistakable authority and desire to play under such an experienced and knowing conductor produced professionalism in the opera pit. The best in local orchestral playing, including the full seasons of the Denver Symphony, was heard under Herbert in the Strauss *Salome* as well as in the Puccini *La Bohème* and *Butterfly*.

When *Madama Butterfly* was done at the Tabor in December of 1955 it made an advance over all previous local opera. Stage director Edwin Levy and conductor Herbert restudied both the look and the sound of the opera with the aim of extracting what in the opera was believable and of understating or eliminating much that was implausible. Enthusiastic audiences attended the two performances and came away extolling the almost overwhelming beauty and talent of the production, particularly its Cio-Cio-San, Tomiko Kanazawa, a professional who came to Denver, bringing her own beautiful wardrobe, as an ideal Butterfly.

Mario Lalli, Pinkerton of the production, had arrived in Aspen in 1954 with his partner Tish Kllanxjha, where they opened an Italian restaurant devoted to opera. Lalli sang and was joined by many of the young singers studying at the Aspen Music School. The house pianist was a sixteen-year old piano student of Rosina Lhevinne at the School named James Levine.

Lalli later moved his restaurant to Denver where it became very popular as Mario's, because of the excellent talents to be heard there. Mario's was popular with touring professional singers who gathered there after performing at the Auditorium Theater. In 1978 Lalli sold the restaurant, Kllanxjha having opened his own restaurant at Larimer Square, and moved to Palm Springs where he established another voice-centered restaurant. Lalli's sweet, vibrant tenor and jaunty demeanor were highly effective. He sang no other roles in these productions but he left a mark through his generosity to young talents, many of whom he personally aided, as well as by his own singing.

Robin Lacy's delicate, uncluttered setting for *Butterfly* was ideal for Levy's efforts to clarify detail. Instead of having Cio-Cio-San and Suzuki litter the stage with flower petals in the flower duet, Levy directed a scene in which the two singers gathered boughs of blossoms which they then arranged into traditional flower arrangements. Herbert's sense of the musical drama in the Puccini score made the production soar. Many felt that at last, opera had arrived in Denver.

The good fortune of Herbert's Denver presence soon was amplified in the fall of 1955 by John Newfield. This brilliant Austrian was director of the Aspen Opera Workshop at the music school, and brought his extensive background to Denver to test the waters. For five seasons, Newfield led the Denver opera scene with a rare intensity, turning these years into a fulfilling period of operatic activity, one which he filled with imagination and style.

Newfield had had a career of great depth in opera. A native Viennese, he studied with Max Reinhardt at the Vienna Academy to become one of his many assistants, working in Salzburg on Reinhardt's famous *Faust* and *Jedermann* productions, and on *King Lear* in Vienna.

In 1935 Newfield had worked at the Vienna Volksoper with Walter Herbert, who was then Opera Chief. At the Volksoper there was an extraordinary staff. The assistant choral director was Kurt Herbert Adler, who went to the San Francisco Opera and remained for 24 years. The rehearsal pianist was Laszlo Halasz, who founded the New York City Opera. On this staff Newfield was assistant stage director. He and Adler were Teaching Associates in opera at the Vienna Conservatory. In the mid-thirties there had been efforts to stage opera with minimal productions. An assemblage of talents whose co-principals were Paul Csonka and Rudolf Bing, worked with great charm and skill to develop productions suitable for touring. Newfield was principal director. An associate of impresario Sol Hurok heard the ensemble in Europe and on her return to America made a point of recommending her discovery to Hurok. As an outcome, Hurok presented the Salzburg Opera Guild in an American tour in the winter of 1937-38 when *Cosi fan tutte* was done in Denver. The other operas on this tour consisted of *The Coronation of Poppea*, Milhaud's *Le Pauvre Matelot*, Ibert's *Angelique*, and Rossini's *The Marriage Merchant*, many of which Newfield presented during seasons of chamber operas in Denver. Among the principals were Dezso Ernster, Falstaff of the 1953 *Merry Wives of Windsor* at Central City, and Herta Glaz, Met singer from 1942 to 1947, who was active at the Aspen Music Festival in the early 50s. Several years later Newfield made a second Denver visit as an assistant stage director with a Strauss *Gypsy Baron* company sent out from the New York City Opera.

Newfield's first production for the Greater Denver Opera Association was Mozart's *The Marriage of Figaro*, done in January 1956 at the Tabor.

Newfield had come to know a young American baritone named Norman Treigle who was just getting started at the New York City Opera. Treigle went on to establish himself as the preeminent American singing actor of his generation. His first major success at the New York City Opera was Handel's *Julius Caesar* with Beverly Sills, to be followed by Boito's *Mefistofele*. His early death from cancer was a tragic loss to American opera.

Treigle was signed as Figaro, and Newfield was delighted to have this "thinking baritone," as he called him, on hand for a production he devised with him in mind. Figaro was "the attacking underling," the rebel among aristocrats with a revolutionary message. Treigle's light-footed approach to the character had the further benefit of a fine, warm baritone, handled with remarkable grace.

Peggy Bonini was the other hired professional, an adroit Susanna with a winsome stage presence and a pleasing soprano. Denver singers of varied experience and abilities sang other roles, ranging from the particularly effective Cherubino of Ruth Baker to others with potentials still to be approached. Again, Helen Dedrick, the onetime double bass player, attracted with her beauty and vocal promise as the Countess.

The stage was very animated. Newfield accentuated the humor of the piece which an English-sung text underscored. Newfield had William Black play Don Basilio with a "swish" which bothered Black's wife, a proper Army officer's wife, who in private urged Black to sidetrack the comic affectation.

Rudolf Fetsch conducted. Newfield always regarded him as a perfectionist who could not resist informing a musician when he hit a wrong note. Fetsch did not follow discretion but frequently lost patience, and correction of the obvious followed. Despite this, Fetsch was not a greatly effective orchestral disciplinarian, and there were more ragged moments in the orchestral playing than were ideal.

Newfield's most difficult musical problem was that of convincing Fetsch to do something Newfield wanted. Fetsch would never fail to pick up a change once Newfield had explained its importance, and would remind Newfield if he failed to recall exactly what he wished.

In March 1956 the group took on Strauss's *Salome*, one of opera's most controversial works, which oddly was on a double bill with Act Two of *Swan Lake*. Community prudes were inevitably vocal in their outrage at this offering. Director Edwin Levy and conductor Walter Herbert aimed to create afresh and avoid cliche and stereotype. These two worked well as a team and with Robin Lacy's fanciful setting the work's violent mood was dominant.

Levy had not reckoned with the stubborn Salome, Brenda Lewis, who had done numerous performances for New York City Opera. Her lurching, excessive performance was what Levy and Herbert wished to curb. She resisted all urging to restudy what she had set out as her plan. Her performance was thus kittenish rather than tigerish. She refused to make use of a dramatic stairway on which she was to have danced.

There was greater theatrical success with another innovation. Rather than fuss with a paper moon over the Tabor's stage, Levy and Lacy placed the moon, which is addressed in the opening scene, as an invisible element over the audience. This moved the action to the front of the stage for an improved coherence.

The respected Met veteran Frederick Jagel was a malevolent Herod, and Violette McCarthy as Herodias gave a performance of burning intensity.

In *Salome* the orchestra is of prime importance, with savage intensity and sweeping strings. The attention Herbert gave to the mighty roar of this score was a major achievement, made possible by having the services of nearly the entire Denver Symphony. These musicians were thrilled to be performing with so authoritative a conductor as Herbert.

Having proved its strengths in operas by Mozart, Puccini, and Strauss, it was time for the Greater Denver Opera Association to undertake the sine qua non of opera, the great Verdi. In April 1956, *La Traviata* was offered with Licia Albanese, Toscanini's favorite, who had been featured in his famous radio broadcast performance. This was the first of the Newfield-Herbert collaborations, and would be done at the Tabor, where by now the company felt quite at home. Considerable improvement in backstage facilities and in the lighting aided the effort to present attractive productions.

Audience interest was growing with the continued opportunity to see opera and hear what made it grand. Local singers were being more appreciated as experience settled them into greater efforts to better their work. It was quite a coup to obtain Licia Albanese as Violetta, a gracious lady, whose elegance and authority suffused the enterprise with these qualities. Though she was the imported guest-artist, she rehearsed and performed with a sense of pleasure in working with local artists of such diligence and ability. She wondered about her young Alfredo, William Black, and asked Newfield, "Do you think we match?"

In February, Black had won the regional Metropolitan Opera auditions, and this confidence gave him more freedom and vocal richness than ever. Richard Dworak brought his concentrated musicianship to the role of Germont pere, which he made more than usually credible. Both Black and Dworak responded warmly to the Albanese presence, and a rare magic occurred in performance.

In 1981, when I last visited with Newfield, he spoke of Dworak as the finest talent he worked with in Denver. Herbert recognized his superior musicianship, and was very patient with him but was unfailing in correcting any slips from the score. For the first time there was a thoroughly trained chorus, made up of seventy voices which had worked for six weeks and sang very well.

Newfield did not know at first how he was going to use so large a group on a not-too-large stage. The logistics problem was the major one. Verdi provided seven measures to get the chorus off stage, but to Newfield the chance of a traffic jam seemed likely. He designed his own sets, and for Act I devised a series of French doors at stage rear, leading to a rear ballroom into which the chorus gracefully and quickly moved at the crucial moment.

How to keep the chorus from being wooden was another problem. Newfield devised a method of enlivening the chorus by giving each member a small character role which gave these individuals something to think about that was not too demanding. A woman would involve herself in a very slight flirtation with a bearded bass, another relationship between a tall tenor and a plump mezzo would take place. These relationships brought life to the stage without overwhelming it.

There was one determined soprano who always managed to get into the front row. She was not that same Jeanette MacDonald-like blonde who got into the front row of Father Bosetti's productions, where she always seemed to be counting the house. Newfield dealt with this problem by placing her further back in the chorus but she always drifted forward. Friends would tease Newfield by telling him that "we noticed your tootsie was there."

Rehearsal schedules were always carefully and precisely set. Newfield was guided by one rule—"let's take the very first step." He believed that the rest would follow logically, and Newfield would relax because of having a general program. He would say "Tuesday, 6 p.m., blocking of Act I, Scenes 1-4." He would add, "Just traffic." In 1981 he told me, "If I have one talent it is to interpret music in terms of dramatic action."

While Newfield set the stage, Walter Herbert was concentrating on the music. He was a highly competent musical director whose complete assurance gave confidence to singers despite his not-too-warm personality. The impact of such strong leadership meant a *Traviata* which set a new standard for quality in Denver opera annals. The two Tabor performances were nearly sold out, which meant a total audience of perhaps less than 3,000. Audiences relished the care and authority of the production with enthusiasm.

In mid-May a drive began to raise $250,000 for the Greater Denver Opera Association over three years. A 1956-57 season of *La Bohème, The Barber of Seville, Die Fledermaus,* and *Faust* with Norman Treigle as Mephistopheles was announced.

Newfield passed the summer of 1956 in Aspen with the opera workshop, directing Adele Addison and students in a first performance of Seymour Barab's *Chanticleer*, along with Rossini's *The Marriage Merchant*, both done in the venerable Wheeler Opera House.

On his return to Denver, Newfield announced the establishment of Opera Workshop '57 with a board of directors including Dworak, Jack Olson, and Apostol Pelargidis. Forty singers were involved in this effort to support ongoing productions of chamber operas to point up the quality of singing and production in the fully staged offerings.

In October Newfield was named managing director of the Association with the responsibility for directing and designing the four principal productions. Season tickets for these would be available at a $13.50 top.

At the end of November 1956, *La Bohème* was performed in the renovated Auditorium Theater. When the hall had opened with the Denver Symphony under Saul Caston's direction the different sound was thought to be an improvement. Later familiarity proved otherwise. The group seemed to be moving ahead with this well-attended *Bohème*. A strong cast was led by the lovely Eva Likova, the lone guest artist, as Mimi, and William Black as Rodolfo.

Dworak sang Colline, Fred Nesbit was Marcello, and Jack Olson was Schaunard.

Newfield admitted to having borrowed the idea for his Act I setting from a New York City Opera production in which an outside staircase to the garret provided a perfect spot for Mimi and Rodolfo's soaring duet at the conclusion of the act. There were problems in balancing voices and orchestra, but Walter Herbert led a strong production.

Early in January 1957, *Die Fledermaus* had its first Denver performance with some unplanned drama. Thomas Lloyd Leech of the New York City Opera had to be flown into Denver to replace Thomas East, Eisenstein of the cast, when he was slightly injured in an auto accident. With little time to prepare his stage business or adjust to the altitude, Leech got through the part without tuning in on the stylish ensemble Newfield had worked to set.

Jean Fenn, a soprano of great beauty and charm, who had sung Rosalinda on television with Cyril Ritchard, came to do that role. Newfield took endless pains with the chorus in devising its movements in Act II. Apparently he had success because Campton Bell, the demanding chairman of the theater department at the University of Denver, later told Newfield "they all looked Viennese." Fetsch conducted this extravaganza. Second act divertissements included the sextet from *Lucia*, hilariously spoofing operatic pretensions.

Newfield and Herbert were in peak form in March for *The Barber of Seville*, with Hugh Thompson guesting infectiously as Figaro. Betty Jane Townsend, a Denver soprano, was in her best spirits as Rosina, and Apostol Pelargidis was a giddy Don Basilio. The work of Rudolf Fetsch in preparing the chorus was of significance in attaining high levels of performing.

Early in the spring it was announced *Faust* would be postponed until the fall because of "conflicts in Norman Treigle's bookings." No rescheduling was ever announced. With the failure to raise the three-year funding, the end came to the ambitious, yet sensibly guided, effort to develop local opera resources and build audiences.

John Newfield's Greater Denver Opera Association was gone and with it the only organization with a strong orientation to the local opera community. The association took a long time dying, and it was not until the fall of 1958 that checks gathered during the fund drive were returned to their donors. Herbert's American achievements of renown, the establishment of first the Houston and then the San Diego Opera companies, were still ahead of him. Newfield remained in Denver to add a bright dimension to local opera over the following two years through development of an innovative chamber opera program.

As Alex Murphree, music writer at The Denver Post, who had called Newfield "the Victor Borge of Denver," would later write, "It looked for a while as though donors might save the enterprise, but apparently too many thought the movement was already stone cold dead in the market. A failure, though, hardly inspired any one else to try. Meanwhile let it be recorded that the Greater Denver Opera Association achieved some praiseworthy productions and really deserved a better fate."

1956 La Traviata production by John Newfield.

*Rudolf Fetsch
Pianist and Conductor*

*John Newfield, Director
and Walter Herbert, Conductor*

A Little Chamber Opera

Just because opera had always been done in traditional ways it was now up to John Newfield to find other ways of creating valid operatic experiences. Working at a fever pitch to establish the Greater Denver Opera Association, Newfield had kept his imagination sharp. With that group's demise, there were substantial resources to draw on for a new enterprise.

This other way would turn out to be opera in miniature, chamber opera as it is called. In 1936 and 1937 Newfield had been associated with the Salzburg Opera Guild whose deft performances relied on vocal quality, stylish movement, and minimal production elements. Now he would implement a similar design in Denver. It was as Denver Lyric Theater that this group came to be known. Its nucleus was Opera Studio '57, which Newfield formed on his return to Denver in 1956 from a summer in Aspen. This stimulating concept made the years of 1958 to 1960 good ones for opera in Denver, providing a showcase for some exceptional talents who shone under Newfield's provocative direction.

International House at 16th and Logan streets, former home of William Fisher, the co-founder of Denver's great Daniels and Fisher department store, was designed to bring together for social interaction those many nationalities represented in Denver. For these purposes it had taken over this great home, with a small ballroom-hall. In this hall, seating no more than 125, including a small balcony, singers had no need to strain to project, which meant a natural attitude could be held. Acting could be more stylized, lyrics in English would be easily understood. Timing and style would be the hallmarks of these productions.

In the spring of 1958, Newfield approached Blake Hiester, then president of the organization, and wondered aloud if an evening of short operas might be welcomed. Hiester was an opera buff and had sung in the chorus of Father Bosetti's Denver Grand Opera, and was to figure sympathetically in efforts to get opera going in Denver. International House was indeed interested.

Newfield went next to the Colorado Federation of Music Clubs which was to hold its annual meeting in May 1958. He offered to entertain the meeting with some short operas. The Clubs had budgeted $40 for the evening's entertainment, and this seemed just the thing to them. Newfield thought that small amount would about cover costs but he had larger aims in view.

The Music Clubs program consisted of Pergolesi's *La Serva Padrona* with Richard Dworak, Cecilia Kovalevsky, and David Shapiro, the peak of the entertainment. There was also Donizetti's *Rita* with Eric Davis, Patricia Brown, A. Paul Ballantyne, and Lehman Engel's *Malady of Love*, with Helen Dedrick, Lore Jacobs, and Ballantyne.

The success of the performance gave Newfield the courage of his convictions. The group incorporated itself as Denver Lyric Theater, and offered two free performances of the Pergolesi and Donizetti works at the end of September. Guests at the free offerings were invited to subscribe to four evenings of chamber opera at International House. The promise was for intimate stagings with emphasis on singing and acting. The response was so favorable that the equivalent of two full houses was immediately sold out. Newfield's previous work guaranteed novelty and assurance, positive elements on which to base such a program.

Richard Dworak, the amiable and highly proficient baritone was involved both in artistic and organizational concerns, representing the new group in both legal and financial matters. Though Newfield recognized Dworak's excellence in such major operatic roles as Germont pere and Rigoletto, he believed him most of all a truly great basso-buffo singing actor. His performances as Don Pasquale and in *An American in Boston* proved Newfield's point.

Another Denver-based career was about to take off with Warren Gadpaille, a bright young psychiatrist who had done major roles with the New Orleans Opera Company. He was a New Orleans native who had gone on stage when he was nine to tour with a mandolin band. While in high school he performed at the famous La Petite Theatre de Vieux Carre. At Tulane University he joined a very active opera workshop, and upon completion of his undergraduate studies he played more than fifty performances with the New Orleans Opera.

At International House, Newfield's fine-edged sense of humor provoked Dworak and Gadpaille into jaunty, well-sung performances, and they became mainstays of Denver Lyric Theater. Their professionalism set the tone for high style rooted in character and voice.

Many promising singers welcomed the opportunity to take part in these productions. In this small auditorium, Eric Davis made his sweet tenor ring romantically. Another tenor, William Appel, was a voice teacher at the University of Colorado in Boulder, and he was unusual in possessing a rare sense of comedy. Such was Appel's talent that Newfield urged him to become professional. He later took a doctorate at Indiana University, then spent a season with the Vienna Volksoper but chose not to continue. He went on to become a successful stage director and conductor at Western Michigan University at Kalamazoo.

Delores Snyder was a gifted, beauteous soprano whose few performances were outstanding. Newfield recalled her as prudish, but he was able to draw sophisticated acting from her by reassuring her that action or attitude was important. Offstage she retreated into a shell of complete modesty. On stage, she was the passionate smoker, Suzanne, and the vivacious Norina to perfection.

William Covington, baritone student at the Lamont School of Music of the University of Denver, aspired to a professional singing career and his youthful spirits and musical intelligence delivered a series of amiable performances.

All kinds of pretty girls dressed the stage, and in this house little makeup was needed. Their beauty came through. Betty Jane Townsend and Helen Dedrick were known from full-stage productions, and there were Cecilia Kovalevsky, Janet Fee, Sally Scaggs, Norma Lynn Read, and Jeanne Kostelic, a talented, beguiling assemblage.

Newfield and the pianist, Rudolf Fetsch, worked to create an ensemble. There was no room for an egocentric performer, no star turns. The lightness and deft timing seemed almost too good to be true. Newfield was careful to select works to reflect the buoyancy of the company.

Early in December 1958 there were four offerings of a double bill of Von Suppe's *The Beautiful Galatea* and Arthur Benjamin's *The Prima Donna*. The sparkling ensemble captivated the audience. Dworak, Gadpaille, and Appel were in comic fettle to make the Benjamin work fresh and funny. Cecilia Kovalevsky, Pat Brown, and Beverly Warner provided musical charm. Lively performances by Gadpaille, Eric Davis, Helen Dedrick, and Tom East helped make the Von Suppe enjoyable.

In February 1959 a double bill of Ibert's *Angélique* and Offenbach's *RSVP* pleased audiences, the Ibert with its comical cavorting and the Offenbach, when it stopped talking, with its facile Offenbach tunes. *Angelique* incidentally had been one of three short operas which the Salzburg Opera Guild had performed in Denver when Newfield was part of its staff.

In April there were Seymour Barab's *Chanticleer*, which Newfield had directed in its premiere at the Aspen Music School, and Douglas Moore's *Gallantry: A Soap Opera* in which an uncharacteristically mute Newfield appeared. The season concluded in May with Wolf-Ferrari's *The Secrets of Suzanne* with Delores Snyder and Dworak, and Mozart's *The Impressario* which left people wanting more real Mozart.

Not until December 1959 did Denver Lyric Theater sing again, and then it was a strong double bill of Rossini's *The Marriage Merchant*, another from the Salzburg Opera Guild's Denver trio, and Menotti's *The Old Maid and the Thief.* The Rossini's fine cast included Gadpaille, Betty Jane Townsend, William Covington, and Tom East. Covington scored strongly in the Menotti, with Sally Scaggs, Beverly Warner, and Helen Dedrick.

A triumphant *Don Pasquale* was the first full-length opera done by Denver Lyric Theater at International House. Dworak, Gadpaille, and Delores Snyder were in top billing and fine trilling. There were six packed performances, and it was filmed by Channel Six, the Denver PBS station, and telecast as recently as 1980. My review in Cervi's Journal referred to this production as "the brightest gem in its bejeweled crown," and my enthusiasm continued, "It was the peak of local opera endeavors."

April brought Darius Milhaud's *Le Pauvre Matelot*, yet another of the productions offered in Denver by the Salzburg group. This somber opera introduced Elizabeth Scott, who had been a Robert Shaw Chorale soloist, in her lone Denver effort. Jerry Lepinski, who went on to found the Classic Chorale, made this his first operatic performance in Denver. Donizetti's *Rita* filled out the bill with a strong cast including Jeanne Kostelic, Cecilia Kovalevsky, William Covington, Frank Howard, and Richard Hilty.

In his search for fresh material, Newfield found gold in *An American in Boston*. Charles L. Holt had turned the popular

German operetta *Der Bettelstudent* into a satire on Boston during the American Revolution, even incorporating Paul Revere's ride. Dworak as a blustering British general, Gadpaille as a prison warden, along with Appel, Delores Snyder, and Linda Stormont, John Newfield's charming wife, all responded brightly to Newfield's direction, with Fetsch guiding things musically. Audiences were wildly enthusiastic. I wrote that it was "musical theater at its most joyous... a triumph of irresistible proportions."

In the summer Newfield took on the staging of *The Barber of Seville* at the University of Colorado with William Appel conducting. Covington was Figaro; Eric Davis, Almaviva; Ann Rothget, Rosina; and Russell Hillock, Don Basilio. This, it turned out, would be Newfield's final endeavor in the Denver area.

In January and March 1961 Newfield visited the Stonybrook campus of the State University of New York for interviews and in September 1961 he was named Chairman of the Fine Arts Department. In 1966, he became chairman of the Theater Department. He retired in 1974, vacationed for a year in Austria, and in 1975 retired to Lindsborg, Kansas.

So completely had Newfield dominated the Denver opera scene that at his departure it was immediately apparent a large operatic void had opened up. As director, producer, costumer, designer, and lighting expert, Newfield had done everything possible toward the establishment of an opera company except for what might have been impossible: the building of a shock-proof organization.

Despite dedicated supporters, it would be nearly two years before another sponsor would attempt to produce opera in Denver.

Newfield had not cared for the Denver social-cultural situation as he tried to build an opera company. "I am proud of many things," he told me, "I was able to arrange with the Denver Theatrical Stage Employees Union No. 7 to have two stage hands and one electrician at International House, quite an unusual situation. Later, in 1960, I was made an honorary member of the Union by the stage hands and properties crew of the Post-sponsored summer light opera in Cheesman Park."

"In Denver" he continued, "they had a horrible situation, such as is often found in the Midwest, where society women supported by disinterested but supporting husbands, controlled the city's culture. This was the origin of Central City, controlled by mediocre-minded society people who had money. I always fought to get these people to give up the provincialism—that everything from the East is good, and everything from anywhere else is not. Who would have thought in 1960 that a real public for opera and ballet and symphony would grow here? Now we have councils of art that support the arts nationally and state-wide though right now (in 1980) they are in trouble."

"I believed that a company of singers could be made to gamble on the possibility of having an opera company. We do put the cart before the horse in opera by having creative human beings who have not been trained to act and thus move on the same level of importance as those who are trained singers. This contradiction is disturbing. I acted out a lot for our singers, and always told them 'Don't misunderstand—I don't want you to imitate me—do it your way.' The confidence of actors and singers is much more important than the vanity of my conception."

In retirement, Newfield worked in Vienna on a study of medieval history, the subject of his University PhD thesis. In March 1980 he was 80, and observed his birthday with another extended European visit. In May 1981 he had visited some Denver friends, and I was able to spend some time with him as he reflected on his six Denver years. In April 1987, while mowing his lawn, so that he would be free to listen to the Saturday afternoon broadcast of *Parsifal* from the Metropolitan, he fell dead of a heart attack.

Richard Dworak and
Betty Jane Townsend in
The Barber of Seville, 1957

Helen Dietrich and
Eric Davis in
The Beautiful Galatea, 1958

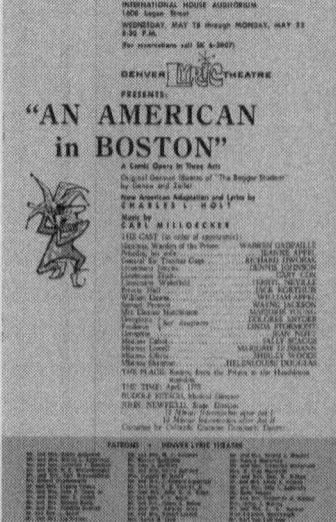
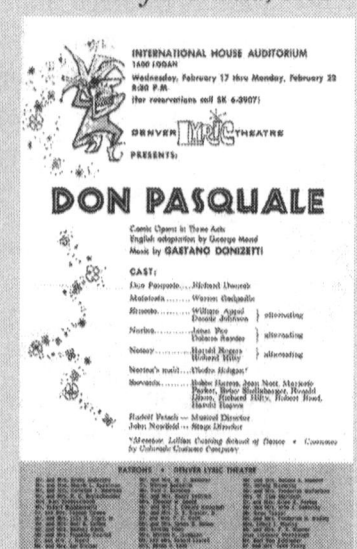

Poster for "An American
in Boston," 1960

Poster for "Don
Pasquale," 1960

The Dutch Tornado

As long as Denver Lyric Theater had limited financial resources, no serious search for a new director could reasonably be carried out beyond the immediate Denver area. Whoever would take on the leadership in producing opera would have to be someone already in the area. On their shoulders the future would rest. In October 1961 the search produced Arthur Schoep, an Iowa native with a Dutch background, whose gusty temperament entitled him to become known among the area's opera singers as the "Dutch Tornado."

A naturally gregarious and commanding bear of a man, Schoep had expected his future to be that of teaching music in public schools. While studying at the Eastman School of Music he was led to opera, and encouraged to attend Tanglewood, summer home of the Boston Symphony Orchestra, where he attended opera workshops directed by Boris Goldowsky of the New England Conservatory of Music.

Goldowsky was then widely recognized as a leader in the academic opera scene as much for his passion for opera as for his experience. As he worked with Schoep, Goldowsky recognized his musicianship and enthusiasm. After 1956, Schoep became a close associate of Goldowsky, going on tour with *The Barber of Seville* in which he performed as Dr. Bartolo, and on occasion stood in for Goldowsky to conduct.

Schoep recognized his need for greater schooling, and applied for a Fulbright award which took him to The Netherlands where he studied contemporary Dutch music. Here he was introduced to the musical life of his ancestral country. While there, he offered recitals of American song and on one occasion took part in a radio performance of Menotti's *The Medium*.

Schoep's interest in opera took an intellectual bent, as was shown in 1961 by his work on both English libretto adaptation and the staging of Paisiello's rarely performed *King Theodore in Venice,* presented in New York during the Eighth Congress of the International Musicological Society. *Theodore* was considered a significant presentation of a forgotten opera. It included in its cast Eric Davis of Denver, then studying at Juilliard, and later to be a Goldowsky singer.

At the University of Colorado in Boulder, Schoep earned a Doctorate in Musical Arts in Voice. During a regional Bach Festival he sang in the *Magnificat* and later joined Saul Caston and the Denver Symphony Orchestra for the national concert premiere of the Richard Strauss *Daphne,* then little known. Schoep's experience with Goldowsky and his general breadth of musical knowledge suggested to the Denver Lyric Board that he could be the one to lead the organization in a new phase.

Dissatisfied with the limitations of the stage at International House, Schoep looked around for a theater of more conventional attributes, one which could house a larger audience and pump up larger box-office receipts. At Pulliam Auditorium at Colorado Women's College he found what he thought would work, despite noisy seats, crowded backstage facilities, and a repressive academic atmosphere.

It was March 1962 before Schoep was ready to roll with his initial offering, a double bill of Donizetti's *Il Campanello* and Martinu's *Comedy on a Bridge*. The music and voices pleased the small audience. There was strong pianistic support by James Moon, who had served as the rehearsal accompanist on the *Daphne* presentation. In the Donizetti, Warren Gadpaille was a source of amusement as he impersonated an Italian singer, an old gentleman with a fantastic catalog of drugs for a miscellany of ailments, and a rake.

Schoep wasted little time getting into production once more. In May he opened a double bill including *The Meeting* by Jan Meyerowitz with a libretto by Dorothy Gardner, and Chabrier's *An Incomplete Education*. The former dealt with Emily Dickinson and Thomas Wentworth Higginson, the man of mystery in her life. The great poet, noted for cryptic verse, seemed lost in the effusive world of opera, and this wordy, complicated piece failed to flourish. The bill did end on a welcome, jovial note, however. Chabrier's opera gave Marvin Worden a good role to mark his return to Denver after a twelve year absence. There was also a comic role for the indispensable Warren Gadpaille.

Schoep's eagerness to move from the diminutive and towards the grand was sparked by an opportunity to program *The Marriage of Figaro* in February 1963 with the Denver Symphony Orchestra as the first staged opera offered as part of the regular subscription series. Schoep conducted and staged the production at Phipps Auditorium where there was no orchestra pit and only a very shallow stage. A reliable orchestra and several singers of promise suggested that opera might again be on its way.

Again, it was Gadpaille as the Count who, with aristocratic effect, carried the performance. The balance of the cast showed its inexperience with these musically sophisticated materials. Schoep's direction painted in broad, comic strokes. Like his mentor Goldowsky, he kept the performers busy. Henry Lowenstein of the Bonfils Theater saw to it that the stage was attractively set.

In November Puccini's *La Rondine* was done at the Auditorium Theater as the first of five productions Schoep would offer with

Ross Reimueller conducting and Schoep now concentrating on the staging. Schoep and Reimueller had been at Tanglewood together where Reimueller had been doing advanced work under Goldowsky at the New England Conservatory of Music after finishing work at Oberlin College. At Tanglewood he was involved in a workshop presentation of the little-known *La Rondine*.

Schoep now recalled Reimueller's intense admiration for this opera, and was guided to offer this production as much by Reimueller's liking for it as by the idea of doing what would be a Denver premiere of an unknown work by a very popular composer. Reimueller came to Denver as musical director, his first professional engagement, for room, board, and transportation. I visited with Reimueller when he was in Denver in 1982 on tour with a road company of *Evita*. He recalled how, at Tanglewood, Puccini's music for *La Rondine* affected him so much he "absorbed the music like a sponge."

Though it was thoroughly prepared, the production needed individuals of sophisticated demeanor to bring conviction to its story of a demi-mondaine. The dramatic tone of the opera quite escaped Schoep. There was not a naughty or frivolous moment to be seen.

Much more was expected when Mozart's *Cosi fan tutte* had its first ever Denver production in November 1964, more than a year after the Puccini, and much more would be demanded of singers and musicians. Reimueller returned to conduct, with Schoep directing, and Henry Lowenstein making silk purses out of the sows ears the company's budget allowed.

Gadpaillle proved again his indispensability to Denver opera, and Larry Day from Colorado State University was a suave Don Alfonso. There was charm and able singing from Donna Bricker Janzen as Dorabella. The dazzling Mozartean vocal requirements were beyond the balance of the cast. Reimueller's work was proficient but superficial. Schoep's staging was unduly broad.

Later Reimueller recognized that he had prodded the orchestra excessively while preparing the *Cosi*. Upset with him, they balked at his demands. When he returned for *La Bohème,* he cultivated a better relationship with the players, and believed the hurts from the *Cosi* were eased.

The *Bohème* in March was a Denver Symphony concert event at the Auditorium Theater, with Schoep on stage as landlord Benoit as well as director. His busiest moments were backstage during Act II as he endeavored to make a relatively small chorus approximate the population of Paris by rearranging costumes and movement. "We need another procession," he is said to have called out to a group just coming off stage. "Take off that hat, change shawls, change wigs, change your make-up, and get back on stage as quick as you can" were his instructions in this extemporaneous episode.

The drama soared with youthful fresh spirits, with the lovely Mimi of Jeanne Kostelic and Marvin Worden's well-sung Rodolfo. Gadpaille's Marcello was not up to his standard. Smaller parts were done by Denver singers familiar enough with the material to convince as Bohemians. One unfortunate decision was that made by Schoep and Reimueller to place the orchestra backstage—a futile effort to conquer the unwieldy acoustics of the hall. Despite amplification, the singers were overpowered for the orchestra too was amplified.

By now the character of Schoep's work was becoming evident. There was careful preparation of the music and stage action. Schoep could take young singers with basic intelligence and little talent and make them appear fairly convincing. He demanded his singers learn what to do, but he kept things neat and tidy in return. He could use humor if he believed it would point up the action.

Stuart Steffen, who sang in the chorus of *Cosi* and *La Bohème* prior to singing Barbarina in the 1966 revival of *Figaro*, recalled Schoep as a "warm, hard-working person who expected much from the singers, many of whom would not and could not learn and remember the music. He made a strong effort to use what was available in Denver."

Schoep maintained his father-son relationship with Goldowsky, and brought him to Denver for an area opera workshop. During difficult rehearsals, it was Goldowsky who smoothed the waters whenever Schoep lost his temper.

Schoep took the responsibility of building an opera company seriously, which was not easy to do in Denver. He was always being pressed by voice teachers to use their students in major roles but these teachers would not press these students to enter into Schoep's established company.

As costs rose, it became apparent that Schoep would have to conduct some of the performances. Financial support from the community still was sparse. This unfortunate piling up of responsibilities produced predictable results. Those experienced singing actors like Warren Gadpaille went their own ways. The taste and talent they had acquired benefited the productions and did not subtract from Schoep's energy.

In December 1965 Patricia Brooks came to sing in *Lucia di Lammermoor* as the first of several guest artists. At Central City in the previous summer she had been hailed for the fine quality of her coloratura as Rosina and Lakmé, as she had been for various performances at the New York City Opera. As a performer, Brooks showed a dramatic understanding of exceptional sensitivity combined with fine singing abilities. An appealing stage presence, she made the central role of Donizetti's opera more than usually coherent.

Marvin Worden brought pliant vocalism to Edgardo, but acting did not interest or stimulate him. He made the singing predominant. But the stiffness of his performance was a drawback for the singers with whom he shared the stage.

Schoep was both conductor and stage director for this production. Brooks and Schoep were at arms length in the preparation of this production. She wanted slower tempi as well as more "give" in the orchestra. Schoep could not see things her way. He could not bend to see things in a freer, more flexible manner. Brooks was completely professional on stage and expected high standards for this production. When her costume was returned from being pressed before the opening performance, Brooks was shocked to see wrinkles. The pressing had been done with a small iron, and there were creases and odd shapes in the gown. Brooks let Schoep know of her displeasure. The Denver Lyric Theater was very much a local effort and had not been able to approach professional standards. The Denver folks were learning the problems of dealing with guest stars.

Another broadly conceived *Figaro* was offered in April 1966, with Robert Hale as the jaunty Figaro. Hale came from New York City Opera where he was considered among its most promising young singers. In the 1980s Hale was ranked high among Wagnerian basses. Gadpaille repeated his high quality Count and Stuart Steffen was a standout as Barbarina. Otherwise the casting brought singing as tentative as it had been three years earlier.

In December, Reimueller returned to lead Gounod's *Romeo and Juliet*, another opera on the Denver Symphony schedule. Schoep was stage director with Henry Lowenstein's attractive, well-lit Gothic arches in a unit set. Gwenlynne Little, a young Canadian soprano who had worked with Goldowsky, was the Juliet to Marvin Worden's Romeo. Together they captured a good deal of the opera's romantic character, though neither displayed sensitive acting skills. She was pretty, moved well, and projected an ardent feeling. Worden worked at his acting. The costume department came up with a tunic for Worden so tight he was unable to raise his arms to reach the balcony where Juliet stood.

The Auditorium Theater was very nearly filled for *Romeo and Juliet*. Reimueller worked for balance of orchestra with voices on stage, and managed well even though voices were miked. The difficulties of opera in the Auditorium Theater were always a major problem. This production marked the solidification of the Arthur Schoep era—careful preparation within the moderate means at hand, solid rather than brilliant craftsmanship, and in general a sincere but wooden effort to bring opera to life.

The April 1967 production was *Tosca* with Maria di Gerlando as Floria Tosca, Richard Fredericks, now at New York City Opera, as Scarpia, and Worden as Cavaradossi. Ten years earlier Fredericks (then Richard Schleffel) was a student at the Lamont School of Music of the University of Denver, and sang a lead in the American premiere in Denver of George Antheil's *Venus in Africa*. He too was a prime artist at the New York City Opera. Maria di Gerlando had been an appealing Saffi in Central City's 1957 *Gypsy Baron*.

Good musical momentum in this performance under Reimueller was aided by Fredericks' forceful performance and the volatility of di Gerlando's Tosca, despite her losing the fine luster recalled from Central City. Worden was unable to bring the needed drive to his role. Schoep could not resist the opportunity to sing the Sacristan, which turned out more sprightly than the overall production, which did not sustain its passionate aims.

The Artistic Committee of the board met frequently to evaluate proposals for various productions. Though yeoman efforts were made to bring Schoep's attention to new repertory he would come to a meeting and declare "these operas we can't do." His cut-and-dried decision had been made before the meeting. Schoep's disposition was Dutch, and he tended to be dictatorial because it was difficult for him to delegate authority. Often he was off in one direction when the board was heading in another. He did not win or sustain support. Board members believed he failed to consult them because he felt that he alone had the wisdom to arrive at a proper decision. This had the effect of walling him off from potential opera supporters.

According to Reimueller, Schoep's belligerence turned off those who had their own deep-felt ideas of what should be done. Schoep had modeled himself so completely on Goldowsky's explosive and domineering manner that Reimueller believed these were the only terms with which he could function.

However, there were no union problems in the Schoep years. Salaries were sent to stars well in advance of performance, and financial matters were in generally good control. *Tosca* had increased indebtedness, however. Prior to its production, the board had begged Schoep to perform the work as a concert opera but he would not hear of it. The board felt no obligation to reason when Schoep had been hired to carry out its policies. In the end the question was whether a director of Schoep's temperament was what was required. The Denver Lyric Theater had no need for a prima donna. It seems there were more exciting moments at board meetings than in performances. This did not lead to a strong base for continued opera activity in Denver. There was "never enough time, never enough money, never enough help," as it was put by a longtime supporter of Denver opera.

During the summer of 1967 Schoep was invited to a teaching position at North Texas State Teachers College, so *Tosca* was his farewell. Schoep's salary was not large, and he may well have burned out as an opera producer on a skimpy budget, getting much criticism and little praise. Schoep had been a hard worker in the cause of Denver Lyric Opera.

Romeo and Juliet

The Conductor and The Soprano

After Arthur Schoep's departure for Texas in 1967, the board of what was now Denver Lyric Opera gave serious consideration to two conductors as a successor. One was Sarah Caldwell, free-lancing in the years before she established her adventuresome company in Boston. At this time she was seeking to place her talent for incisive musical direction and imaginative staging in an environment where it might find nourishment. She flew into Denver for interviews which were held in the Stapleton Airport coffee shop because she required an immediate return flight for an engagement. There was a minor crisis when the rotund Miss Caldwell could not fit into the coffee shop booths where the board members were awaiting her. Nor after hearing of Denver opera prospects could she fit Denver into her operatic future.

Norman Johnson, candidate number two, wished to come to Denver. A recognizable Colorado presence while serving as Assistant Conductor at the Central City Opera since 1962 and Associate Conductor since 1965, he was a Central City regular through 1970. It made sense to him to move to Denver. Educated at Juilliard, and a former director at Peabody Institute at Baltimore, he was well-schooled and experienced as an opera conductor. So it was Johnson who came.

He was not the only one in the family who lived in the world of opera. Mrs. Johnson was known professionally as Matilda Nickel, and she had sung small roles at Central City in the 1964 *The Lady from Colorado* and in both *Lakme* and *Manon* in 1965.

Johnson immediately chose Verdi's *Il Trovatore* to open the 1967-68 season. He was so eager to get things going that details were neglected, and the production arrived on stage before it was ready. Dennis Rosa, who had directed some opera workshop productions at the Peabody Institute, was named stage director for this production. He had staged only these few operas, and was at sea with the Verdi melodrama.

The frequent swirling of capes suggested cape practice day at the bullfighter's school. Ludicrous overacting by the principals marked this production. The steep slope of the raked stage made the men seem bow-legged. Too many scenes sagged from being dramatically inconclusive. An awkward English translation was a further burden.

Lovely singing by Janet Stewart as Leonore compensated in part for her weak acting. Robert Cunningham, a Longmont contractor who had taken a liking to the operatic world, delivered a passable Manrico, encased in an ill-fitting costume. Vernon Skari, Littleton high school wrestling coach, came to the Denver area with opera experience in Minneapolis, and was immediately cast as the Count di Luna. He suffered from a cold during the run of the opera. There was ample heat in Sharon Evans Greenawald's Azucena. Greenawald was so nervous that backstage after her first scene she went into hysterics because of cracking on a note. Stuart Steffen had to pick her up off the floor of her dressing room and get her composed.

The Barber of Seville in April 1968 told a happier tale. Johnson polished the orchestral playing and rehearsed the cast thoroughly, pacing the production smartly, and appreciating the musical wit throughout. It was the best opera production Denver had seen since the Newfield-Walter Herbert *La Traviata*.

The *Figaro*, Calvin Marsh, came from the Met, where he was well regarded, and he had done good work at Central City. He was, however, undergoing stress. After a substantial singing career, including seasons at The Met, he was now going through a religious crisis, and had come to believe opera was trivial and perhaps sinful. Though preoccupied, he was always professional in his work at this time.

Stuart Steffen was the belle of the occasion in her first major role as Rosina. She beguiled the audience as she would Denver opera audiences for many years to come, even as she worked behind scenes to establish ongoing opera in Denver.

Ralph Herbert came from the Met to direct and to sing Dr. Bartolo. His incessant joviality, funny stories, and observations bolstered the performers' spirits and an energetic performance resulted.

The 1968-69 season would include the first fully-staged Denver appearance of Mozart's *The Magic Flute* and also *Madama Butterfly*. In the late 60s the taste for Mozart operas was still growing, and although both *Figaro* and *Cosi* had been done in Denver, as well as at Central City, this was a bold step. In addition there would be a chamber opera production at Pulliam Hall.

It was thought the time was ripe for a fresh production of the *Flute*, a work of incomparable beauty, and that is what was hoped for. The eternal bugaboo of local opera—no budget—made it necessary to scrimp on visuals. A series of steps and platforms with a screen at the rear for projections had to suffice. Narrow steps made it difficult for singers to stand in secure comfort. This distraction led some singers to stand sideways. On the small-sized screen, the attractive projections made little impact. The black curtains at the sides were what people saw. This set the tone for a gloomy, awkward performance.

John Olon-Scrymegeour made this one of his two Denver stage-directing efforts. Without funds for imaginative sets or costumes, there was little grace or grandeur. It was a very static evening. The lack of theatrical animation was compounded by the auditorium's poor acoustics. Johnson had made the decision to microphone and amplify the singers. The system was, however, poor, turning the singing into hooting which negated sensitive orchestral playing.

Able singers participated but they were trapped both in the sound system and on the steps. Marji Tucker showed a darting, dazzling coloratura as the "Queen of the Night." There was vocal refinement in Janet Stewart's Pamina but again, her acting scores added up to zero.

David Holloway, a baritone who sang at the Met in the 80s and on the international circuit, was a lively Papageno. Marvin Worden had not recovered from a flu bug that was going through the company. A wag referred to "The Magic Flu." And Sharon Greenawald again had hysterics.

The first of four principal roles Matilda Nickel would sing with the company was *Madama Butterfly*. Mrs. Johnson was personally gracious and without airs. It seemed she was interested in what had been done and was being done in Denver musical theater. Tilda, as she was known, had studied in Europe on a Fulbright grant, and returned to sing at Central City when she met Johnson. Her director would be another former Central City singer, Adelaide Bishop, well remembered for her charming Norinas and Adeles in the early fifties. She had now shifted to the field of stage direction.

As Cio-Cio-San, Matilda Nickel seemed vocally miscast. Tight singing and swallowed vowels made it hard to enjoy her singing and to understand her. Dramatically, she seemed more like Puccini's Musetta than a winsome, fragile Butterfly. A poor English translation was of no help.

Robert Cunningham was a generally consistent Pinkerton, with Sharon Greenawald a quite affecting Suzuki, and Denny Boyd an able Sharpless.

Bruce Jackson did a particularly good set, and elements of the stage direction were on target. The chorus moved clumsily, but Japanese-born Kuniaka Hata, the production's Goro, newly arrived in the voice faculty of the University of Colorado at Boulder, brought some authenticity with his suggestions.

Denver was extra-sensitive to the idea of a conductor featuring his wife as a singer in performances with whatever group he might owe his responsibility to. Saul Caston had presented his wife Selma in several performances with the Denver Symphony Orchestra, and many had frowned on this.

Both the company and the board were dismayed by a prominence which was not thought to have been earned. Had Matilda Nickel been a grasping, calculating person, the situation could have been handled. As it stood, it seemed impossible to address. Inflexibility on Johnson's part, possibly related to the Matilda problem, impeded the development of Denver Lyric Opera.

In February 1969, chamber performances of the Jack Beeson setting of William Saroyan's *Hello, Out There* were done at Pulliam Hall, along with Russell Smith's musical setting of James Thurber's *The Unicorn in the Garden*. The casts included David Holloway, Stuart Steffen, Jack Olson, and Mary Beth Trout.

The 1969-70 season had been planned to include *Carmen, Salome,* and *The Daughter of the Regiment. Carmen* was another Adelaide Bishop production. It was rigid, musically dull, and employed amplification. The movement ran to ludicrous excess with Sofia Steffan, no relation to Stuart, who acted like a middle-aged, broad-beamed flirt. Her tone was ripe, but the singing was uneventful.

The Don Jose was Tom East, who since working with Newfield at International House, had gone to Germany for studies. His uptight manner and lack of theatrical energy compromised the fine ring of his best singing. Frederick Burchinal, then a student at the Lamont School of Music of the University of Denver, made his first Denver appearance in the small role of Morales. He was destined to sing at The Met, San Francisco, Chicago and in Europe. The effort to do *Carmen* was considerable, but nothing happened to kindle the Denver operatic energies.

In February 1970 *Salome* with Matilda Nickel was done. In this production she was a long way from the theatrically insensitive performer she had been in *Butterfly*. Under Sean Barker's knowing stage direction she moved with feline grace and was subtle in her responses to Herod and Jokanaan. One was almost ready to be converted when she sang softly, but then the voice was thrust forward in harsh over-brightness and textual unintelligibility took hold.

In a continuation of the aberration of placing the Denver Symphony at the rear of the set, from where it was amplified, the brilliant instrumentation of Strauss's music was veiled and sounded like a 35-piece orchestra. This downgrading meant the vocal lines received an eccentric and unintended emphasis.

Howard Fried was a commendable Herod, Benjamin Rayson was a satisfactory Jokanaan, and Donna Bricker Janzen was the Page of Herod. Bruce Jackson's richly textured setting was effective.

The Daughter of the Regiment was canceled, a decision "reached reluctantly by the board, which felt that cancellation was the wise answer, rather than the incurring of a deficit which might make the next season financially impossible." In trying to stay alive, touring productions of *Hello, Out There* and *The Telephone* were sent to Loretto Heights College and to Sterling, supported by the Colorado Council on the Arts and Humanities.

Financial considerations for the short term ignored the need to develop a coherent dependable schedule of productions. No plans for a fall production were made, but at The Third Eye theater on Broadway, Johnson conducted from the piano for a surging production of Menotti's *The Medium*.

With Third Eye director Jean Favre—known in the theatrical world as Joey—to bring the grand *guignol* elements of the melodrama to explosive intensity, this was a smashing success. Mary Beth

Trout as Madame Flora wept real tears and became deeply involved in her torments with the result that she was exhausted by the end of the short run. Stuart Steffen was a delectable Monica. This was vivid musical theater, opera at its most effective, and a succes d'estime, catching the mood of the play in forceful playing devised by Favre, whose lighting and setting furthered the impact.

In January 1971 when an opera was done, it was carried out as though whatever the company might have done or would later do would be judged on this single effort alone. *The Crucible* by Robert Ward from Arthur Miller's drama won its 1961 Pulitzer Prize for music because it actually improved on the original text by tightening and cutting the verbiage, and finding a tough, lean structure. Ward's music complemented the text effectively and although the music lacked high imagination, it made gripping musical theater. The lines of ascending tensions made it an unqualified success.

Johnson led the players from the Denver Symphony in a stirring performance with no nonsense about where the orchestra should be—in the pit. Again there was, regrettably, amplification of voices. A stark setting by Judith Haugen was borrowed from the St. Paul Opera, and the fine textures of costuming were developed by Judy Graese and the Colorado Costume Company.

A strong cast of local and imported singers, all at their best, showed the power Miller had unleashed, as well as what director Jean Favre's comprehending stage direction could achieve. Before the cast went on stage for rehearsals there were readings at which Johnson played through the score, and the music was studied and discussed as nothing else in Johnson's term had been.

Favre aimed for tight ensemble and to establish a firm discipline among his cast. He worked against the grain of certain individuals, and some thought he was callous in his personal relationships. One singer believed he made a special effort to be obnoxious in order to establish this discipline.

Julian Patrick had already created the role of George in the Seattle premiere of Carlisle Floyd's *Of Mice and Men*, a role which had given him national publicity. A powerful singing actor, as John Proctor, he gave what Glenn Giffin of The Denver Post called "one of the best operatic performances one will witness in Denver." Though he had not previously sung Proctor, it was a fully-studied, fully-realized portrayal. In addition, Patrick's strong feeling for the work was a coalescing factor which led to the well-integrated playing of the entire cast.

Nancy Williams, a Goldowsky academy graduate, who had sung Maddalena in the 1963 *Rigoletto* tour with Sherrill Milnes, sang Elizabeth Proctor with acutely projected understanding of the role. She made a strong case for American singers. Despite weak enunciation, Matilda Nickel showed her ability to take good direction and flesh out a role. As the unhinged, provocative Abigail, she flailed about in wild movement, making ghastly vocal sounds to characterize the bedeviled. Other professionals in the cast hewed to a high level. Denver singers blended into the overall excellence with a dedication that spoke well for the nonprofessional talents available to Denver opera.

The following production of *Rigoletto* in March 1971 was Denver Lyric Opera's best work in the standard repertory to date. Benjamin Rayson had been an able Jokanaan, and at Central City he had done the Count di Luna, Scarpia, Jack Rance, and Marcello. He was a dependable baritone who had gotten a start in Europe, but never really made it in this country. He was last heard of as a member of the quintet in the original production of Sondheim's *A Little Night Music*. As Rigoletto he was a reliable but uninspired jester, something of a disappointment.

It was Marji Tucker, the pretty coloratura from Albuquerque, as Gilda who made the music take flight, and with this performance she became a Denver favorite. Without a strong Duke, this opera goes downhill quickly, and Richard Knoll, despite a pleasing middle register and good looks, could not carry the load. Donna Bricker Janzen was a strong Maddalena. Good stage direction by Jean Favre proved his value to Denver opera. Bruce Jackson gave unifying visual strength in his designs.

During the summer of 1971 a flyer was mailed out to subscribers promising all sorts of innovations for the coming season. The piece referred to its "14th season," something of an exaggeration, although John Newfield had indeed set up Denver Lyric Theater in the summer of 1958, fourteen years earlier. The continuity that was implied had not existed.

Innovation Number One was a puppet opera. Aware of the popularity and novelty of the Salzburg Marionette ensemble, which had been in existence for five decades, the management decided to mount Haydn's *The Man in The Moon* as its own puppet show. Elton Norwood's popular puppet theater provided the venue, and the performances were done at his theater on West 29th Avenue in North Denver.

What was planned as the most ambitious effort yet took a nosedive on New Year's Eve in the performance of *Colonel Jonathan The Saint* by Dominic Argento, directed by John Olon-Scrymegeour, also director of the disastrous production of *The Magic Flute*.

It was Olon-Scrymegeour who had proposed this work as one suitable for production. It was a student work by Argento, set in post-Civil War times, and was subtitled, A Comedy of Reconstruction in Four Acts and an Interlude of Waltzes. Its production by Denver Lyric Opera would be the world premiere. Johnson sent out a letter to subscribers inviting support for the production which was further described as a "big romantic opera with graceful tunes" that was "amusing and moving." It turned out Johnson was too easily won over. There were waltzes, cakewalks, and some fake Negro spirituals, but these accessible elements did not relate to the dramatic unfolding of the opera. There was nothing like a bouncy, sentimental romance.

The book was a thicket of verbosity, impossible to perform. Words could on occasion be distinguished but the themes and relationships were wrapped in an impenetrable fog. Nothing concrete ever seemed to take place. There were many production problems. Robert Darling designed a beautiful spiral staircase as the principal setting but it had not been completed by opening night. A large offstage orchestra was called for but at the Loretto Heights Performing Arts Center there was no place for it. Also, a large off-stage chorus was searching for a place to stand.

In the performance there was applause for a florid aria for elderly Aunt Allegra, done by Stuart Steffen. In later years she recalled the spoonerism which tripped her in rehearsal when she was meant to be singing about the Palace of Fashion but heard herself singing about the "Phallus of Passion."

Aunt Allegra was supposedly convinced that Colonel Jonathan of the title resembled the dead husband of her niece Sabrina. When Steffen asked composer Argento about this, he answered that he did not how Allegra got that idea. Steffen then made up her own justifications but never explained them to anyone. She considered director Scrymegeour to be a disaster from all viewpoints.

Argento told Steffen she might "take a high C—if you like." Argento seemed to make an effort to be considerate of the singers, and Johnson also was cooperative in keeping from the cast the criticisms he was receiving from the board. But within, all the singers knew disaster was impending.

Matilda Nickel played Sabrina, widow of a Confederate soldier. As indicated, her Aunt Allegra believed Jonathan to be a reincarnation of this figure. Because of the musical setting of the text and the singer's poor enunciation there was no understanding of the words, nor could she find any velvet in her voice.

As a newcomer on the tenor scene, Mallory Walker was eager for new challenges. With a reputation building, he came upon Colonel Jonathan as a challenge requiring all his abilities. He expressed himself as thrilled to do the role, but a virus settled in his throat, and he was unable to sing the dress rehearsal. He was involved in many scenes with Matilda Nickel but was unable to penetrate the isolation in which she moved on stage. He was unhappy not to establish rapport with so important a cast member.

The role of Captain Mullikin was small, but it was a key role, and Archie Drake, popular with the Seattle Opera Company, was brought in for the role. Drake was an old Navy hand, and he lightened the tension of rehearsals during breaks with robust Navy patter songs. He kept real tension-breaking laughter present.

An audience dressed to celebrate New Year's Eve gathered expectantly for the first performance. It sat in increasing bewilderment, believing it inconceivable that there would not suddenly be a burst of life and the opera would get going. Only the Palace of Fashion aria raised the frigid temperature.

The reviews were harsh. In The Denver Post, Glenn Giffin ascribed to the work "all the hallmarks of juvenilia" and he called it "a paste-up job, with parts working well but on the whole undistinguished—at that, it's not such an obvious put-together as the libretto. Here is the real problem." Giffin also referred to the "arch and irritating prologue."

Thomas MacCluskey of the Rocky Mountain News observed that the evening had "all the gaiety of a funeral" and offered his own subtitle, "a dirge of lethargy in four dreary interludes (it seemed that long) with an interlude of nondescript waltzes." MacCluskey also noted the only comic incident was the "unfortunate accident in which Mallory Walker sang the latter portion of the final act with only one quarter of his mustache. The balance dangled from the right corner of his mouth." He also quoted an observation that he had overheard, "I didn't know they were going to do it in slow motion."

Stuart Steffen had a dress made for the New Year's Eve gala which was to follow the performance. The party turned out to be a wake, she recalled, registering deep disappointment for all the fruitless efforts of cast, opera boosters, and all concerned. The board believed it had received damaged goods, so great was the difference between the promise and the unedifying reality of the production.

The final season offering was *Don Pasquale* in April at the Auditorium Theater. Donizetti's perfect comedy sparkler was done with zest by a cast thoroughly and brilliantly prepared by Jean Favre. Everything was done with high humor, with Spiro Malas as Pasquale, Marji Tucker a fetching Norina, Julian Patrick in fine voice as Malatesta, and William McDonald an agreeable Ernesto. Ensembles were stylish, Johnson's orchestra responded with polished playing from the pit, and Johnson skipped the usual voice amplification.

This occasion drew lots of smiles, a happy note amidst so much regret. In The Denver Post, Glenn Giffin wrote that "These four principals whether in solo or in ensemble were so well matched that their like is unlikely to be seen soon," but he also observed there was a small house.

On balance, Johnson lacked consistency in the preparation process. When singers got over their heads he seemed unable to assist them. With *The Crucible* he was ideally teamed with Favre, with the largest number of professional singers Denver Lyric Opera had employed in a single production. Too rarely could he get the best singing from his local casts. When things went well as they did for *The Crucible, Rigoletto,* and *Don Pasquale,* the cohesion and musicality was impressive. When Matilda Nickel was trying to do a role for which her inexperience and vocal problems promised trouble, everything seemed to go downhill.

Johnson never saw himself as a stage director. However, as artistic director, he was ill-prepared to establish styles of movement and production elements. He seemed not to know how a stage should look. He wanted the singers to watch him, and that was his overriding wish.

During the life of Denver Lyric Opera under Johnson there were six stage directors in eleven different productions, among which only Jean Favre stood triumphant. He alone brought success to Johnson's work.

Johnson was socially reticent, a very shy man who could never get out and persuade, yet on the one occasion he made the effort, he oversold. Unlike John Newfield, he had no outgoing personality to carry the organization through rough times.

Singers and orchestra members demanded high standards of singing and playing, and although Johnson did not spare himself, he failed to win them with an essential warmth and openness. Thus many hopes were dashed. In the final year, a majority in the board of directors decided to pay Johnson but a small portion of what he was due. He did not receive the $10,000 that was due. By 1971, the organization was $43,000 in debt.

In November 1972 it was announced that with Norman Johnson having moved to the East Coast, future opera productions would be done under the auspices of Denver Opera, with Brian Priestman, conductor of the Denver Symphony Orchestra, in charge, and with an entirely new cast of characters on the board. That plan expired as soon as it was announced. It would be more than a decade before a major effort to establish opera in Denver would be made.

A guild was founded in 1965 by Helen Burns and a group of dedicated women to help support Denver Lyric Theater. When the company changed its name the guild, accordingly, became the Denver Lyric Opera Guild. Although the final curtain came down on the Denver Lyric Opera Company seven years later, the guild did not succumb. It continued and thrives today, keeping to the original purpose of "encouragement and support of young singers and the continuing education of the members in the appreciation and knowledge of opera." When the Junior League of Denver relinquished sponsorship of the Metropolitan Opera Regional Auditions in 1972, the Guild assumed responsibility. In 1984, the DLOG inaugurated its own competition. The Guild also generously awards vocal scholarships to students at Colorado colleges and universities and supports young singers of the Opera Colorado Outreach Artist Ensemble, the Central City Opera apprentice Program, and Opera Theatre of the Rockies.

Symphonic Overtures

For several years the Denver Symphony Orchestra management toyed with the idea of doing opera. The wife of Saul Caston, conductor of the Orchestra from 1945 to 1964, had sung in Philadelphia and wished to continue her singing career in Denver. In the winter of 1948-49 Caston scheduled *Aida* for a concert opera presentation featuring Selma Caston as Aida. Frederick Jagel came in from The Met for Rhadames, the lone import for this ambitious performance. Denver singers took on other roles, with Fred Nesbit as Amonasro and Robert Busch as Ramfis, two pleasing light baritones in heavy roles. There was no pretense of this being drama or spectacle. This was an oratorio.

The following season *Samson and Dalilah* was done, also an unstaged presentation. Gladys Lansing was a very reliable Dalilah. She and her husband, Robert Lansing, had been in the Metropolitan Opera chorus, and moved to Denver after World War II to become active in choral and operatic endeavors. Marvin Worden impressed with the potential of his Samson. These two productions were part of the regular DSO season, and did not attempt to build audiences for opera.

In July 1950 a record-breaking audience overflowed Red Rocks Amphitheater for Helen Traubel and Lauritz Melchior with Caston conducting the DSO in highlights from *Tristan and Isolde*. According to reports, over 10,000 attended, each paying $2. Again, there was no effort to stage the presentation. It was, however, a rare and wonderful but purely musical event.

From 1947 until its 1962 demise as a performance site for classical music and symphonic pops, Red Rocks was synonymous with great music. Such artists as Marian Anderson, Lily Pons, Rudolf Firkusny, Van Cliburn, Yehudi Menuhin, Jarmila Novotna, Jerome Hines, and Dorothy Maynor drew vast audiences to this awesome natural amphitheater.

The vision of George Cranmer, who developed the site with forces from the Civilian Conservation Corps, was that one day Wagnerian opera would be done there as an extension of the primal "Ring" settings. Cranmer always hoped to provide auspices for such performances. Was there a comparable audience to support staged opera on a regular basis? This eternal question was in part answered in July 1957 when a fully-staged production of Wagner's *Die Walküre* was given at Red Rocks.

The plans for *Die Walküre* were grandiose. Herbert Graf would come to stage the opera. No operatic stage director stood higher internationally at that time than Graf, renowned at Salzburg and at The Met as at San Francisco, and, of course, at Central City, Colorado. In 1941 Graf had been enticed to Central City to do *Orpheus and Eurydice*, and in 1946 when opera was resumed there, Graf returned for *The Abduction from the Seraglio*, a preparation for its successful first performance at The Met where Eleanor Steber repeated her Constanza, which had charmed at Central City. That year he also had done a popular *La Traviata*. In 1947 Graf staged *Fidelio* and *Martha* and in 1948, *The Tales of Hoffman* and *Cosi fan tutte*. His final Central City production was *Carmen* in 1954.

Caston would lead *Die Walküre* as his first complete Wagnerian opera. Much local interest attended this ambitious undertaking. The horsey set was delighted to care for the Valkyrie Mounts, and the Colorado Mountain Club assisted the Valkyries in their climbs up the great Ship Rock. Attendance was only fair, nothing like the turn out for Melchior and Traubel. The DSO at that time contained about 70 musicians, too small for Wagnerian duties. Shortly before performance time it rained, and in the damp night air the strings could not carry their weight, so the rich Wagnerian tapestry remained filmy. The standards of singing were disappointing, and the acting was uneventful. Only the Wotan of James Pease, a 1952 Figaro at Central City, loomed as substantial. Inclement weather for the second performance reduced attendance, and rain following Act I canceled the remainder of the opera.

There was a more successful revival in 1958 with a larger orchestra, improved weather, and a stronger realization of the problems of out-of-doors opera. In The Lively Arts I noted that "it was clear that great pains had been taken to offer a satisfactory performance." According to the program, the production was "staged" by Herbert Graf, who however was not in Colorado that summer, and "directed" by Hans Busch, who happened to be in Colorado for Central City productions of opera's "ham and eggs," *I Pagliacci* and *Cavalleria Rusticana*.

James Pease again came from Hamburg to do Wotan, which though youthful was lively, "a trifle gay for Wotan," I wrote, commending his "excitement and fine tone." Tragically Pease died a few years later, before establishing himself among American singing actors of distinction, as it seemed he was destined to be. Margaret Harshaw again was Brunhilde, this time anchored by chains to a huge rock, against the battering of the winds. Her work I described as about as good vocally as it was awkward dramatically. Heidi Krall returned for Sieglinde, this time quite expressive and lustrous of voice. Albert da Costa, then hailed as a promising heldentenor, was back for Siegmund. He was much more at ease in this second go-round.

Among the Valkyries were singers noted in the area musical community for singing of quite different character. They included Cecilia Kovalevsky White, and Beverly Warner from Denver Lyric Theater at International House, Truly Barr Nelson from Denver Grand Opera, now teaching at the Lamont School of Music, and Mary Lou Nesbit, Beverly Christiansen, Lucille Lynn, Martha Miller, Norma Lynn Read, and Joanne East, all singers whose names would appear in the annals of Denver musical theater.

For 1959, it was decided to do Puccini's then little-known *The Girl of the Golden West,* from Belasco's romantic melodrama, with Graf returning to stage the opera, Saul Caston conducting his first Puccini opera. What made it workable was that Eleanor Steber would come to sing Minnie. So far as it can be determined, Steber had never before sung the role, nor had Dr. Graf staged the opera. Eleanor Steber relished the role of the Bible-reading, bar-tending Minnie, and she found the zest to enliven the part, although she seemed to disdain Minnie's religious sense. Privately, she complained of Caston's musical support, but even more was worried about the dryness of the air.

The English adaptation had its hilarious moments, and the efforts by Puccini to sound "American" led more to laughter than to dramatic ends. Brian Sullivan was well cast for Dick Johnson. He had sung for Dr. Graf in Central City's 1947 *Fidelio,* and more recently, in 1949, had been singled out for attention in Kurt Weill's *Street Scene* on Broadway. He had sung both at The Met and in San Francisco. His tenor voice had enough ring in it to ride over the heavy orchestration, but he too complained of the dry air. Sadly, Sullivan met a tragic end in 1969 in the waters of Lake Geneva when he drowned himself in a frenzy of despondency.

William Chapman made Jack Rance, the opera's one credible individual, quite convincing. There were such excellent Denver singers as Richard Dworak, as Jake Wallace, the balladeer; William Appel as Nick. Mike Livingston as Billy Jackrabbit, and Truly Barr Nelson as Wokle were two curious Italianate Indians. They all brought credit to the Denver vocal scene, and to the Denver

Lyric Theater, where all had gained acting and singing experience. Caston's inexperience with Puccini's special musical idiom proved crucial. Again, the orchestral sound evaporated into the night air, unmarked by the requisite musical insights.

Of the opening night, Alex Murphree wrote in The Denver Post, "it started out as a blustery night, with a gale roaring over the audience from the back, sending bottles spinning from the stage bar, and generally making a mish-mash of the proceedings." Murphree observed that the sound was poor, and that at the opening performance, "the lighting design was incomplete." Time Magazine described the performance as having all "the flamboyance of a wide-screen Western." It also reported such rehearsal difficulties as the sudden deadening of conductor Caston's earphones, Steber's "walking out of the dress rehearsals after trying to sing over howling winds, and the chorus of miners, recruited from local choirs and glee clubs, groped for entrance cues." In The Lively Arts I wrote that "Herbert Graf's stage direction made no effort to turn the production towards dramatic logic, but moved performers for effect. The miners are a bunch of pink lemonade cowboys for whom little can be done. When they enter singing 'Hello' and little else except for an occasional 'Give me some whiskey' there is little a director can do."

In May 1958 George Cranmer had flown to Germany to visit Wolfgang Wagner, grandson of Richard Wagner, and at that time the major force at Bayreuth. Cranmer persuaded Wagner to come to Denver and study Red Rocks and recommend specific renovations which would make it a usable operatic stage. Wagner brought with him Dr. Werner Gabler, a Bayreuth sound engineer, and together they studied the situation and made recommendations. Stanley E. Morse, architect on the structural drawings for the first phase of Red Rocks construction, under its original architect Burnham Hoyt, drew up suggestions. The essence of these plans was "to conserve sound energy" and avoid the use of amplification. Together with the great Ship Rock at the rear of the stage, the two new massive side walls would issue a natural flow of sound.

Each of the two walls would contain dressing rooms, and were surmounted by light towers, which, when implemented by a modern electrical system, should permit extraordinary lighting effects. The fore-stage was pushed forward almost to the front row of the amphitheater. The pit was covered with louvres which could be controlled in good weather to direct orchestral sound back to the sound-board rock wall, and in rainy weather to protect the orchestral instruments. The pit was designed so that the conductor stood atop a series of risers, as at Bayreuth, with the orchestra surrounding him in descending fashion, and it was based on recent studies in the Bayreuth pit.

These improvements were made prior to the 1959 Red Rocks season, with the exception of the "tulari" sounding boards and advanced electrical systems. Both Wagner and Gabler preferred a narrow stage width for practical purposes but Morse fought for what he believed was required—a wider area which would maintain the impact of Red Rocks spectacular natural beauty. As I wrote in The Lively Arts "For Cranmer, Morse, Wagner, and Gabler, the project has been a challenging one indeed. For Morse it has been a 'religious endeavor,' and it seems certain that these improvements, made at a cost of $175,000, are some of the best investments in Denver's future that have been made."

Regrettably, the newly designed "tulari" baffles were not in place for *The Girl of the Golden West*, so most of the sounds drifted off into the night sky. In heavy irony, after this production, when Red Rocks was at last ready for staged opera, no more opera was done. As always, there were no funds.

No true test of the completed work was ever made, and the realization of Cranmer's dream, which seemed at the time possible, never took place. Since then the "tulari" baffles have been destroyed, along with installation of lighting equipment for highly amplified rock presentations. Classical concerts at Red Rocks are now, at best, once or twice each summer.

Until March 1962 when Caston led *Daphne* by Richard Strauss in its second, unstaged American performance, Saul Caston led no opera in his remaining years. This was yet another oratorio line-up of local singers, part of the symphony season, with no consideration given to staging of it. In a Red Rocks setting it would have been perfect, at least visually. In reviewing *Daphne* for Cervi's Journal, I wrote "With all credit to conductor Saul Caston, the local singers, and the orchestra, the stamp of final authority was not there, chiefly because German is a language foreign in every way to most of the singers, and because the orchestra was at times uncertain of the difficult score." Though Arthur Schoep's enunciation and singing I found "outstanding" and noted that "his was a performance of style and energy," I believed a more fervent musical cultivation was required in concert performances of opera.

When Vladimir Golschmann led the Denver Symphony from 1964 to 1970, he made no effort to present concert opera. In 1968 opera again was contemplated and Harold Farberman came to Denver as a guest conductor for "highlights" from *La Traviata*. Again the singers were lined up for a stilted concert performance with no effort by the singers to characterize or relate. Phyllis Curtin, Frank Poretta, and Dominic Cossa were gracious performers but not actors.

Golschman's successor, Brian Priestman, led a generous surge towards opera. In 1972, the Denver Symphony went so far as to announce a five-year agreement between the symphony and the Denver Opera Association, after Norman Johnson's departure from Denver Lyric Opera left an operatic void. Agreements were worked out between members of the boards of the two organizations for a plan that a spokesperson euphorically termed "probably the most outstanding development in revitalizing opera in the Denver Metropolitan area." The Denver Opera Association was led by Tony De Marino, and Rike Wooten headed the Denver Symphony group. David Kent was the orchestra manager at that time.

It was agreed that Denver Opera would pay $25,000 to the Denver Symphony for services which included those of Priestman as conductor, the orchestra for rehearsals and one performance, plus preparation of a brochure, and other publicity efforts. The Denver

Opera Association would pay singers, provide settings and costumes, Auditorium rental fees, and payment for ushers and programs. It was freely estimated that if the auditorium were sold out for one of these performances, it still would cost over $40,000 to produce. This was a gift horse into whose mouth no local organization would be tempted to gaze. Beyond the announcement of this agreement, no word was again heard from the Denver Opera Association.

A staged production was promised for March 1973 when the '72-'73 DSO prospectus came out, but in fact it turned out to be only semi-staged. Because of Priestman's lively involvement in more than strictly musical elements, this partially-staged *La Boheme* in March 1973 was a pleasant surprise and an admirable event. It was like nothing the Denver Symphony had done previously. There was a high energy level and considerable imagination in the effort. There were pieces of furniture on stage, but more importantly, the singers knew how to move and use furniture as well as how to react and respond to one another. The lovely Joanna Bruno captivated as Mimi, and John Walker was a youthful, ardent Rodolfo. The brilliant Brent Ellis was a zestful Marcello, and Karan Armstrong was a gloriously impudent Musetta. Except for Armstrong, these singers were schooled at the Santa Fe Opera, and showed attention to their singing.

Die Fledermaus, semi-staged in December 1973, was a vocally and instrumentally spirited production even if having DSO musicians in the background was somewhat prosaic. Phyllis Curtin as Rosalinda, Kenneth Riegel as Alfred, Thomas Palmer as Eisenstein, Elaine Bagnios as Prince Orlovsky, and Carol Wilcox as Adele made a charming cast, and again Priestman invested his personal energy with generosity, and this was no static event.

A fully-staged production by the DSO of *La Traviata* took place in April 1974. It was a comedown from the previous year's *La Boheme* and also from *Die Fledermaus*. The long-awaited fully staged production was downhill all the way. Somehow Priestman found himself consulting with the Department of Theater and Speech at Colorado State University for guidance in producing opera. Dr.

Porter Woods was enlisted as stage director, and Robert Braddy executed submarginal sets and lighting. What occurred was an academic workshop production on a low budget with a soprano who turned Act One into The Opera Star Visits the Servants' Ball. Such was the Violetta of Mary Costa, a once-admired soprano with the San Francisco Opera, who arrived with a truckload of costumes gaudy enough to suit Las Vegas. The chorus was drably costumed, flimsy settings threatened collapse, and the mixture could not breathe. Giuseppe Campora had recorded *Madama Butterfly* with Renata Tebaldi, but two decades later the perceptible thinning of his tenor could not be rescued by sensitive phrasing. Only the strong baritone of Louis Quillico showed the promise he eventually would fulfill.

In July 1974, Franz Allers, leader of *My Fair Lady* in its first year on Broadway and in its original recording, highly regarded as a conductor in the musical theater, came for a concert version of *The Merry Widow*. The singers who caught the Viennese lilt so well were Lorna Haywood, Ryan Edwards, John Walker, and Claudia Cummings, charmers all.

Cosi fan tutte was the next concert opera. The men, stronger than the women, were John Walker, Brent Ellis, and Theodore Lambrinos, while the women were Patricia Wells, a bit short of style, Olivia Stapp, and Judith Haddon, both of whom were too young in experience to explore Mozart's sophisticated roles.

Again, with the CSU people in tow, Priestman chose to stage *Carmen* in February 1975. Apparently believing that what transpired with *La Traviata* was only a miscalculation, the CSU people devised a treatment of bullfight as rodeo, with Escamillo a champ rider, and Priestman took it on. Mayor McNichols of Denver was enlisted to do a walk-on as the Alcalde, and Rosalind Elias, who had proved herself a fine singer on many occasions, was the Carmen. She brought more temperament than this amateurish production could handle. Despite her stylish singing and energy, the acting was conventional, and in the end, flat. Except for the youthful promise of Carol Wilcox as Micaela, the other singers were poor. But in this farcical concept, what did it matter whether anyone sang well or not?

Priestman contemplated the staged disasters, then moved ahead with plans for yet more concert opera. These were, by and large, well prepared versions without pretensions of being fully staged. Their modest claims were well received, kept financial problems away from the doorstep. By drawing on Priestman's excellent directorial talents they achieved a good deal.

Tosca, though dramatically wrong for concert opera, since full staging is an imperative for so theatrical a work, somehow came to vibrant life in the stunning, animated Floria of Karan Armstrong, Musetta of Priestman's 1973 *Boheme*. Glade Peterson was a heavy-voiced Cavaradossi, and the familiar Theodore Lambrinos missed the sensuousness in Scarpia's villainy. Originally Frederick Burchinal, a onetime student at the Lamont School of Music whose professional career was starting to mount, had been signed for Scarpia, but he had to cancel, with Lambrinos a late-moment replacement. Many local singers appeared to good advantage in this May 1977 presentation, among them Herbert Eckhoff, Dennis Jackson, Thomas Haddow, and Scott MacAllister. The Adams State *a cappella* choir sang.

For subscription concerts in April 1976, Priestman programmed Act One of *Die Walküre* with the promising Johanna Meier as a glowing Sieglinde, James McCray as a not too impressive Siegmund, and Arnold Voketaitis a strong Hunding. Priestman got an excellent sound from the orchestra.

In Priestman's term at the Boettcher Concert Hall he did only one concert opera, Rossini's *La Cenerentola*. Priestman presided at a harpsichord where he conducted as well as played for the recitatives. Shinja Kim was admirable as Cinderella, with Janice Hall, the greatly talented young singer from Aurora, and Victoria Vergera as the two comic sisters, less funny than they should have been because of clumsy costuming and insufficiently comic movement. Brent Ellis had to cancel and Lawrence Cooper came in as Dandini at the last moment, and was quite effective. Spiro Malas gave a light touch to his work while tenor Enrico de Giuseppe was inconsistent. My review in the Sentinel papers noted that "opera is still an unresolved puzzle at Boettcher. Concert opera is going to have to be restudied before more heavy investments in its cause are to be made there."

So, what was accomplished with these concert operas? Without the distraction of sets and costumes more attention could be given to vocal and instrumental writing. Audiences could learn how the great operatic composers accomplished many of their most exciting scenes. The magic that made involvement so heady was in the music. But opera is theater; it is staging, acting, and singing coming together. Someone attending one of these performances would scarcely know what opera was all about. Some pleasing singers in entertaining evenings carried it off, but it was not opera in the true sense. It was the barest of substitutes.

Priestman would have relished a chance to stage opera at Red Rocks, and wrote to me in November 1974 that "I would love to take up Mr. Caston's successes in 1957-58 with Wagner opera but financial circumstances at the present mitigate against such a program." The prevailing economic situation seemed to remove any hope of opera returning to Red Rocks. It had become clear in a time of rising costs and changing tastes that opera was not the primary responsibility of a symphony orchestra unless an operatic program were heavily endowed for that purpose.

Central City Opera House Association
and the Denver Center for the Performing Arts Present:

La Bohème

(IN ENGLISH)

Opera in Four Acts by GIACOMO PUCCINI

Libretto by GIUSEPPE GIACOSA & LUIGI ILLICA

By arrangement with Belwin Mills Publishing Corporation

English translation by RICHARD PEARLMAN and FRANCIS RIZZO

With the DENVER SYMPHONY ORCHESTRA

Conductor
DAVID EFFRON

Stage Director
BODO IGESZ

Sets Designed by
JOHN WRIGHT STEVENS

Costumes Designed by
SUZANNE MESS, for Malabar Ltd.

Lighting Designer
ALAN CORDIAL

Chorus Director
DUAIN WOLFE

Principal Accompanist
SUE MOHNSEN

Accompanist
JUDITH HUNT

Scenery provided by
Metropolitan Opera Studio

CAST
(in order of appearance)

Marcello, a painter	Ryan Edwards
Rodolfo, a poet	George Shirley
Colline, a philosopher	Gary Kendall
Schaunard, a musician	Thomas Jamerson
Benoit, a landlord	Herbert Eckhoff
Mimi, a seamstress	Benita Valente
Musetta, a girl of the Latin Quarter	Ashley Putnam
Alcindoro, an admirer of Musetta	Herbert Eckhoff
Parpignol, a toy vendor	Robert Marinoff
Customs Guards	Thomas Haddow, Keith Tackman

Time and Place: 1830, Latin Quarter, Paris

ACT I — A Garret in the Latin Quarter
ACT II — A Square in the Latin Quarter
INTERMISSION — 15 minutes
ACT III — D'Enfer Gate, City of Paris
INTERMISSION — 15 minutes
ACT IV — The Garret of the Four Bohemians

First Performance: Teatro Regio, Turin, Feb. 1, 1896

The use of cameras and any kind of recording equipment is strictly forbidden.

The performance will last 2 hours, 50 minutes.

La Bohème, 1976

Opera Goes To College

College is where arguing and learning should go hand-in-hand. In the academic arena, the old dissonance over the primacy of drama or music in opera can be openly addressed. The enrichment of repertory through imaginative presentation of new works at the University of Denver in cooperation with the Lamont School of Music and the Department of Theater gave a very spirited life to the post-World War II Denver cultural scene. Selective opera productions stressed the theatrical in opera in a view now accepted as contemporary. In the Little Theater in the Marjorie Reed Hall, seating 235, provocative performances were mounted. There were times when it would be filled for each of three performances. Despite good attendance, these were far from being mainstream efforts.

By 1947 the Theater Department was outstanding in its personnel. Its chairman, Campton Bell, was a Colorado native whose PhD. thesis on Denver theater from 1881-1901 confirmed his knowledge of Colorado theater history. He was Chairman of the School of Theater, which became a department in 1942, and which he led until his death on December 7, 1963. Only two times during his tenure did he direct productions. His imprint was on the repertory, acting style, and the affirmative character of the department during all these years. In the lobby at intermissions, Bell stood like a tall but very human praying mantis, making dry observations with a solid glint of wit, trying not to show offense when faced with commonplace comments. His mind was fine. He kept considerable reserve on his emotions. Anything he commented on was carefully considered, and he was always observing and listening intently. He believed students lacked the maturity for Chekhov, Ibsen, or German expressionists, and while he was in charge, their works were never done. He loathed dramas which dwelt on self-pity, and he protested their consideration. He built a strong department and gave it credence.

Edwin Levy came from Louisiana State University where in the opera workshop he had worked with the legendary baritone Pasquale Amato and noted conductor Louis Hasselmans. Levy knew and enjoyed both spoken and musical theater. It was natural that he would take the helm for musical productions at the University. Martha Wilcox and Dulcy Amter truly created the dance department which gathered strength under the energy and discipline they imparted. At the newly established Department of Radio and Television, Russell Porter was a chairman with extensive theater experience and a bemused view of that world. Kathryn Kayser had been a classmate of Porter's at Kansas State Teachers College in Emporia, and he recommended her to Bell, who brought her to Denver where her reputation for theatrical skill soon was established. Porter had come to the University in 1946 where he was welcomed by Bell, who had attended Northwestern about ten years after Porter. When Bell died, Porter succeeded him as chairman.

Porter had transferred to Kansas State from Sterling College after affirming his sense of social justice so firmly in a student newspaper editorial that he got into trouble with the authorities. As an English major, he worked more in poetry than in theater, but during summers he began touring with a company known as the Gilson Players, founded by Professor Franklin Gilson, who directed plays that went into various Kansas high schools for one-night stands. In this company, Professor Gilson's daughter Mimi was a standout with her witty nature, sparkling eyes, and fine acting ability. Porter was so impressed he married her. She sparkled at the University of Denver Theater as *The Madwoman of Chaillot* and in Anna Cora Mowatt's *Fashion*.

The first of many novel musical theater productions at the University was the Virgil Thomson-Gertrude Stein *The Mother of Us All*, staged and designed by Roi White, a graduate student, in a combined effort of the Lamont School of Music and the University of Denver Department of Theater in July 1948. This novel presentation set a high mark. Steve Dahlby in the Rocky Mountain News hailed the work as a "highly entertaining and strangely moving theater piece." White found its key in "the irrational but controlled mood of the piece." The staging and singing opened windows to new ideas.

In August 1949 a double bill of Hindemith's *There and Back*, or *Hin und zuruck* in the original, and Menotti's *The Old Maid and The Thief* was done by Edwin Levy. The conceit of the Hindemith, in which the action proceeds to a critical point at which it returns over the same ground with incongruously laughable consequences, was smartly caught by the performers. The Menotti stands as one of the most popular of his many operas, and Levy and an able cast delivered a bright performance.

Over the next few years such distinctive one-act operas as *The Jumping Frog* by Lukas Foss and the Czech, Martinu's *Comedy on a Bridge* were done by Levy. In August 1950 Levy and Waldo Williamson as music director offered Denver's first performance of Benjamin Britten's *Albert Herring*. This production set a high note of comic response with its challenging, brilliant score. Richard Dworak was heard for the first time in Denver, as the Vicar, and George Van Gorden was an expert Albert. This opera became a true staple of 20th century opera at the University of Denver where it was repeated in 1969 and again in 1978. When *The Jumping Frog* was done, the orchestra was so ragged at the opening that Waldo Williamson stopped the orchestra just after the start and spoke to the audience—"With your permission we will start again." Later, asked by Russell Porter if this were part of the show, director Levy responded, "It is now."

Another significant regional premiere was given the following August when Menotti's *The Consul* was performed memorably. Kathryn Kayser devised a series of powerful sequences which combined with the score to leave a mighty impact. So popular was this production that it was repeated several weeks later for three more performances. Menotti had proved so successful at the University that it was no surprise when rights to *Amahl and the Night Visitors* were obtained, and it was done in the old neo-Romanesque Buchtel Chapel at the campus. Kathryn Kayser directed and Rudolf Fetsch was musical director for the enthusiastically received area premiere.

The University of Denver Theater Department did a number of original musicals but *Silverheels*, done in May 1954, was a good deal more than operetta. Its story followed the Colorado legend of the mining camp girl who sacrificed her beauty to attend ailing miners during a smallpox epidemic. In love with a miner, yet pockmarked, she vanished to reappear on a nearby mountain, as a barely visible figure, named in her memory, Silverheels. There was theatrical energy in Kathryn Kayser's affectionate stage direction. Russell Porter's book and Waldo Williamson's music had charm and feeling. Williamson had been involved in several Central City productions, including arrangements for Robert Edmund Jones's *Central City Nights* in 1935, and writing incidental music for *A Doll's House* and *Ruy Blas*. An interesting cast included Roger Dexter Fee, the newly arrived Director of the Lamont School of Music, William Black, the opera singer from the Army, and Sandra Caldwell, a charming light soprano.

When Kurt Weill's *Down in the Valley* was done in 1953, Hans Heinsheimer, of Schirmer's music publishing house, was interested in seeing how this Schirmer property would be produced. The thoroughness of its musical preparation and Levy's energetic stage production impressed Heinsheimer so much that he recommended to American composer George Antheil that his new opera *The Brothers* be done in Denver. When Virgil Thomson reviewed a Stokowski performance of Antheil's Fourth Symphony it was headed, "Our Musical Tom Sawyer." Thomson thought Antheil "extravagantly gifted but imperfectly trained." He was known as America's "Bad Boy of Music," and that is what Antheil called his autobiography. At one time he was thought to be the heir of Stravinsky, and still later to be the heir of Shostakovich, but he was an original.

As long ago as the late twenties in Paris, Antheil had discussed with James Joyce the idea of an opera based on the Cain and Abel theme. It stayed as a kernel in Antheil's mind for a quarter century, and although *The Brothers* was not that particular opera, it evolved from thinking associated with it. It now set the action contemporaneously, touching on Communism and the Korean War. In writing to me about the opera prior to its production in July of 1954, Antheil wrote that it "dealt with indifference to individual anguish and its terrifying brutality." Later he told of the evolution of his feeling about melody; once melody had been "a naughty word." Now it was an idea he welcomed. Following the premiere he told me "It is exactly as I imagined it."

For students to have the privilege of working with Antheil was a peak academic experience. His volatile background made it difficult for him to comprehend the working of the orchestra whose instrumentalists were unpaid students, working hard, long hours on a complex score. Because of this, conductor Williamson could not exact an ideal accuracy of playing from the students. Part of the ongoing problem the department had with the Lamont School was the feeling that instrumental standards were not sufficiently rigorous, and not at the higher level of vocal training. The opera was in good hands vocally and dramatically with Susan Mancourt Downing, a Denver-born soprano who studied in Italy and had returned calling herself Susanna Mancorti, and with Richard Dworak and Anthony Samarzia.

My review for Opera News said that "The music which Antheil has written for this narrative is melodious and dramatically expressive. In creating tension, Antheil uses dissonances, breaking them with tuneful music for moments of reminiscence. The music builds tension, slackens, builds again, keeping a growing intensity that creates absorbing musical theater."

It was December 1955 before another serious work was undertaken, and this was Daniel Moe's *The Coventry Narrative,* presented by the Denver Symphony Orchestra as a pre-Christmas program. Because of the reconstruction on at the Auditorium Theater the orchestra was performing at the Tabor Grand Opera House. Moe conducted the work, which was more a tableau-cantata than opera. As director of the Lamont chorus, Moe brought authority to the choral portions and interesting style to the vocal lines.

Meanwhile George Antheil was busy. In the spring of 1956 Edwin Levy visited his friend Elaine Perry, the producer, a daughter of Denver native Antoinette Perry, after whom the Broadway Tony award takes its name, and suggested doing an operatic double bill of *The Brothers* and an opera yet to be written by Antheil. Thus came her commissioning of Antheil's new opera, which turned out to be *Venus in Africa*. Antheil had been thinking about this opera, and though he had done the libretto for *The Brothers,* he felt too close to the origins of the new work to prepare an adequate libretto for it. Antheil had observed the work of Michael Dyne on television and had been impressed, and on this basis he suggested that Dyne be chosen.

It turned out, in one of those endless coincidences, that Dyne was a close friend of Elaine Perry, which seemed to erase any doubts she might have had on the project. When the work was done Antheil was described by Mrs. Antheil in a letter to me as feeling "that this little romantic fantasy is one of his most integrated operatic works as far as words and music are concerned." A Denver premiere was set for May 1957.

Prior to the opening, during winter and spring, Antheil was absorbed writing more than two hours of music for Stanley Kramer's film, *The Pride and the Passion,* an adaptation of C.S. Forrester's *The Gun,* starring Cary Grant, Sophia Loren, and Frank Sinatra. Antheil had done three other Kramer films. This turned out to be an artistic disappointment whose grandiose manner turned off audiences, so it was a financial loss.

The background of *Venus in Africa* is given in Antheil's *Bad Boy of Music*, where he tells of a time in the distant past when he traveled to North Africa with a young woman following a spat with his wife, Boski. In a letter to me in May, Antheil enlarged on this incident. After having a big fight with Boski, who then returned to her family in Budapest, George "alone and lonely, wandered into the Louvre and came to the statue of Venus de Milo. Being in a strange mood, I made a silent prayer before the Goddess of Love to please help me make a decision. Venus had probably had few prayers made before her throughout the centuries, and she must have liked this one, for directly after I left the Louvre, I met a lovely, red-haired girl, born she said, in Macedonia. I forgot all about Venus, the Louvre, and spent the rest of the afternoon wandering about with her. How it happened I do not know; but that evening I was on the train with her to Marseilles, and from there we took a boat to Tunisia. We had very little money, so we constantly had to have the same hotel room, the same bed, but she would never allow me to make actual physical love with her. She gave no explanation except that 'If I did, I would die.'" After a month of such life, she urged that he reconcile with Boski.

"I decided to write this opera one day," Antheil continued," after having heard a Mozart opera (comedy) all the way through. I had just come from a rehearsal of one of my own operas which, in contrast, seemed ponderous and belaboring the point. 'Oh, if I could only write an opera in the medium of today with that divine lightness!' I exclaimed. And that's where it all began—well, we shall see soon whether I came anywhere near it. I'm sure that insofar as staging is concerned, a production, Ed [Levy] and Camp [Bell] will present it superlatively. But the stage itself is the final test."

Again it was Levy directing and Williamson conducting, with Robin Lacy doing the set and lighting; the same team as on *The Brothers*. The previous summer Levy had shared directorial responsibilities for *The Ballad of Baby Doe* with Hanya Holm at Central

City in its premiere. He was glad to be working on a solo basis, especially to be directing another Antheil piece.

Venus in Africa turned out to be a tantalizing sequence of incidents in a richly lyrical flow. The music seemed to stem directly from the characters and the action. Levy and Williamson made the most of the opportunity. A strong cast gave musical life to the production with the lovely Winnie Magoun (now Hartman) as Venus. The young baritone named Richard Schleffel, who went on to the New York City Opera in 1960, changing his name to Richard Fredericks, gave musical life to the opera. *Venus in Africa* was done by the St. Paul Opera in the early 1970s when Levy went there to stage a production with professional singers, including Alexandra Hunt as Venus. By now the University of Denver was getting a reputation for taking on bold challenges with commendable results.

The following winter in Hawaii, Bell learned from Mexican conductor Carlos Surinach that Paul Bowles had made a musical version of Garcia Lorca's *Yerma*, for which he was seeking production. Bowles had received attention for his music for Orson Welles's 1935 highly-praised production of Marlowe's *Doctor Faustus*. He also wrote incidental music for the Broadway production of Tennessee Williams's *The Glass Menagerie*, which critic Stark Young called "strangely beautiful and strangely right."

While living in Algiers, Bowles continued to search for musical styles and was thus led to Spanish music. The idea of adapting a work by Spain's foremost modern playwright appealed, and many other matters made the project worth doing. As Libby Holman, Rose Bampton, Angna Enters, and conductor Carlos Surinach came into the picture, Bell became interested in doing *Yerma*. However, by 1958, the wonder that would be evoked by such names had drifted away. They were figures of the thirties and forties, names only in a past tense, no longer vital talents.

Libby Holman had gone from torching Johnny Green's *Body and Soul* in the thirties to popular revues like *Three's A Crowd* to an innovative Arthur Schwartz-Howard Dietz 1937 musical, *Revenge With Music*. Her sultry vocal style intrigued audiences of the thirties. She now fancied herself a vocal stylist, and seemed not to have problems imagining herself as a beauteous young woman who is unable to conceive. During rehearsals, the awful discovery that she was incapable of singing on key or of dramatic projection shocked Bell and the DU staff. At the opening night, the audience sat astounded at the incompetence of her performance, her toneless, leathery singing and dramatic isolation.

Angna Enters' production was hardly better. Had it demonstrated a strong concept, the disaster might have been lessened. Her wispy efforts came to nothing in a production without focus. The presence of the fine Rose Bampton in a tiny role seemed to have thrown the direction off. The possibility of devising for her a grand-styled earth mother characterization was an unexplored option. Of course, during the intermission, everyone pointed at her husband, noted Metropolitan Opera conductor Wilfred Pelletier, and his friend, Walter Toscanini.

The one sure element of the production was Bowles' attractive instrumental writing, well prepared by Waldo Williamson, with Surinach taking over for the three performances. In The Lively Arts I wrote: "The music of Bowles charmed with its lovely exotic timbres, its unique woodwind plus cello plus harp instrumentation. He is a writer for theater, capable of mood-stirring entre-actes. There was a lovely scene in the second act for the women at their wash, and in the final scene, the off-stage male chorus has exciting material. Of the songs that Libby Holman sang it can only be said that until they are truly sung, judgment will be hard. There was a richness of imagination in the music which nowhere else was sensed." This *Yerma* was far below the standards established by the staff of the Theater Department, and never again would the rein of responsibility be so lightly regarded.

When Normand Lockwood came to the University of Denver in 1961 as composer-in-residence, he was known in advance as a man jovial and creative, and of high imagination in his music. He had written for the full spectrum of instruments and many vocal combinations. As a musician who had studied with Respighi in Rome under a Prix de Rome, and in Paris with Nadia Boulanger, he was a heady addition to the University. Lockwood was born in 1906 in Manhattan. His father, Samuel Pierson Lockwood, a violinist, was named conductor of the University of Michigan Symphony in 1908. There, Samuel Lockwood joined his brother Albert, who headed the piano faculty. Normand grew up hearing music, string quartets in which his parents were first and second violinists. He recalls a Grieg quartet which became involved in a childhood nightmare. Sweeter melodies drew him on.

He made an early decision to compose. He studied piano, finding a means to the end of composition. Like so many young Americans, he had found study with Nadia Boulanger provocative. Her ability was above all, he recalls, that of "instilling in a composer the ability to be aware of his own music—to become self-aware, to help him find himself, and to determine the core of his music."

Lockwood's music does not easily categorize. He is a man of the 20th century with roots in the 19th century which give him a conservative bent, but that is where the mainstream of American music of the 20th century exists. He once told me of the then-new sounds which established his view of 20th century music, sounds heard as he was growing up, and they included *Sea Drift* by Delius, the *Mother Goose Suite* by Ravel, and works by Debussy and Holst.

Before coming to the University, Lockwood was asked to work with Russell Porter on *Land of Promise*, a "dramatic portrait of Rocky Mountain Methodism," done in May 1960 at the Auditorium Theater with Levy as stage director, Roger Dexter Fee as musical director, and sets and lighting by Robin Lacy. Porter's book made a strong thrust towards pageantry, with a large cast of singers and actors representing John Calvin, Martin Luther, and Thomas Jefferson in this "oratorio in action" as it was termed. With its contrasted great intellects and noble spirits, Lockwood saw the opportunity for music he then described as being "as disparate as Byzantine and plainsong," and it did have an emotional resonance uncommon to pageantry.

"A constant change and flux are necessary in a pageant, even more than in opera," he told me in 1960. "I have tried to use common musical language in an uncommonplace way. There are some innovations but I try to underplay these. Innovations wear out so fast. I never cease to wonder how the novel becomes the accepted order of things. It's hard not to run a gimmick into the ground. A composer must from time to time do something radically different."

Another Porter book served as Lockwood's first true opera for the university. This time it was an adaptation of Porter's poem, "Early Dawn," which had been staged as a spoken work at the university in the summer of 1957. Campton Bell had urged Porter to do this dramatic poem as an original drama for the Civil War Centennial Year. Its subject of a single family's relationships put the root conflicts of the war in microcosm.

Early Dawn was a worthy effort with many textual niceties, and its effective story line provided several levels of interest. The score responded with a strong texture to Porter's ideas. Some thought it overlong, and there was criticism that the musical balance was disturbed by the need for certain passages to be spoken rather than sung. Genvieve McGiffert's first stage singing was in this work, although she had worked at the University in spoken theater. She would become a key individual in later university operatic efforts. Peter Paul Fuchs made certain the choral portions received their due. However, an outdoor presentation made amplification necessary, which hindered balances.

In August 1962, *The Wizards of Balizar* by Porter and Lockwood was done, this time indoors. Drawing on Arabian Nights lore, Porter found a slender story about a tailor who becomes a wizard in order to please his shrewish wife. When his best efforts succeed beyond his expectations he realizes the power within him. The orchestration was for thirteen instruments. Its pungent theatricality was colorfuly carried out by Kathryn Kayser. Robin Lacy provided a charming set.

In December 1962, Lockwood and Porter turned up with *No More From Thrones*, a one-act play with musical interludes, suitable for the Christmas season. Porter's thoughtful way with words and Lockwood's sensitivity to the text made this a pleasing collaboration.

Still to come was *The Hanging Judge*, most ambitious of all these collaborations. Originally it was called *Inevitable Hour*, the title still preferred by Lockwood. Subtitled *An American Opera of the Western Frontier in Three Acts*, its origin was in the Sand Creek Massacre of 1861, where Denver militia killed Indians southeast of the city. This production was the major event of the University of Denver Centennial Program, and was given at the Auditorium Theater on March 6, 1964. In a program note, Porter and Lockwood denied any historical intent, wishing to remove the work from historicity, saying "The events depicted are the purest fiction." They were playing off history, not in its midst. A clarification and strengthening of performance would have taken place had there been funds to hire professional singers. As it was, local singers took the roles, much to their credit. Stan Burk, a second in the February 1964 Metropolitan Opera auditions, played the lead while the hard-working Truly Barr Nelson played his wife. Roger Dexter Fee and Sharon Marie Evans, (later Greenawald), handled other roles. Edwin Levy directed a large cast. Some thought a libretto of more direct nature would have clarified the action. There was too much musical splendor in the opera for it to be filed away without further reference. There had been a point in this artistic relationship when Lockwood observed to Porter, "Every time you write four words I have to write a page of music."

The next Lockwood opera to be done was *Requiem for a Rich Young Man*, a comic satire done in November 1964 for a Denver meeting of the National Opera Association. It is the most often performed of the Lockwood operas, later done in New York by the After Dinner Opera Company. Donald Sutherland, the late professor of Classics at the University of Colorado, wrote a sophisticated book which relished its slyly comic turns. The satirical libretto pointed out that a young widow can be merry if she lets money be the balm of her sorrow. Lockwood's pointed, clean-textured music provided amusement with its quotations from Wagner and Menotti. The Menotti quote actually was from Verdi by way of Menotti. Kathleen Knight, the beauteous Miss Colorado of 1964, was a charming widow.

Henceforth Lockwood would devote his musical energies to writing incidental music for the University of Denver Department of Theater. Among works he provided with music are *The Bacchae*, *The Emperor Jones*, *The Crucible*, *The Mandrake*, for which he set to music songs by its author, Machiavelli, *A Midsummer Night's Dream*, and *Macbeth*. Lockwood's music is vigorously diverse, including such very recent works as a harp concerto, a choral work employing string quartet and handbells, and a work for the Colorado Children's Chorale. To his 95th year he wrote every day.

When Genevieve McGiffert became director of the Lamont opera program the emphasis at the Lamont School made a marked shift to performance. She was a thoroughly trained theater person, at home on both musical and spoken stage, and could conduct ably as well as direct stage action imaginatively. As always, there was the question as to whether or not any single individual should embody both responsibilities. One or the other always seemed to suffer.

The production of *The Merry Wives of Windsor* in April 1965 showed that Genevieve McGiffert was going to provide opera as good as her available forces would permit. Her first effort featured Lamont director Roger Dexter Fee as Falstaff in the Nicolai treatment of the Shakespearean comedy, and it was impressively thorough in details. Next was Carlisle Floyd's *Susannah*, and this movingly integrated production was followed by a *Cosi fan tutte* with charming comic spirit.

Herbert Beattie, of New York City Opera and Central City, came in February 1968 for a lively production of Douglas Moore's *The Devil and Daniel Webster* on a double bill with Menotti's *The Old Maid and the Thief.* Beattie's vast experience enabled him to draw the student performers to a high level. The Menotti was attractively done.

Again in 1969 it was *Albert Herring* time, but in 1970 with a production of Puccini's *Il Trittico* the emphasis was on grand opera. Frederick Burchinal in a commanding performance brought splendid energy to *Gianni Schicchi,* underscoring the importance of schools like Lamont in preparing talents like Burchinal for professional careers. A singer at the Met, San Francisco, and in 1991 with the Deutsche Oper am Rhein at Dusseldorf, he has had a major career, primarily in such great Verdi roles as Rigoletto and Posa in *Don Carlo.* In this full Puccini evening, Jennifer Mills' soprano evoked tender sentiments in *Suor Angelica* but *Il Tabarro* remained earth-bound.

In 1971 it was again *The Consul.* In 1972 the multi-narrative opera struck again, this time with *The Tales of Hoffman,* a perhaps overambitious effort in which the demands exceeded vocal abilities, but it was a handsome production. Rossini's *La Cenerentola* in 1973 boasted expert singing by June Rauschnabel but was otherwise weakly cast.

When Genevieve McGiffert moved to the East Coast in 1973 a new team came on consisting of Ron Worstell as stage director and Vince LaGuardia, Jr., as musical director. At the Corkin Theater at Colorado Women's College, where voices rise into the loft, Mozart's *La Clemenza di Tito* was done in 1974. Again June Rauschnabel's talents were evident, as were those of Irene Van Ham. Though too difficult for a student production, it was an effort in new terrain.

In 1975 it was *Madama Butterfly,* in 1976 another *Cosi,* and then that most deceptive of operas, *Carmen.* Seeking a large hall for expected crowds, the University rented the Cherry Creek Center for the Performing Arts. There was some luster in Betsy Hoover's voice and Glenn Giffin in The Denver Post found that there was "enough fire to give the eternal gypsy heroine a believable stage life," and elsewhere called the production a "most credible performance." Jack Morris of the Lamont vocal faculty lacked vocal heft for Don Jose but Patricia Baxter Wright had a beguiling Micaela soprano. This was the first operatic effort by Harry Ritchie, then Chairman of the Department of Theater. While Vince Laguardia, Jr. conducted well enough it was a very tentative performance. Lewis Crickard's settings lacked his customary polish, and the action did not relate to the ruins of Seville depicted. Ritchie determined the work would escape the mundane, but his own dramatic logic warred with the libretto.

In 1978 what else should one expect but another revival of *Albert Herring*. In 1979 there was a miscalculated *Don Giovanni*, far beyond the singers' capabilities, and in 1980 a curious double bill of *Gianni Schicchi* and *The Medium*.

In 1981 it was different, with Stravinsky's tricky *The Rake's Progress*. As the lone operatic production in the city in the season of 1980-81, it drew attention. Lewis Crickard designed handsomely and David Fennema as stage director worked hard on style. "Freeze" openings were devised for each act, and they were the most novel aspect of the staging. Once the "freeze" thawed, there was much very fussy movement.

David Gordon, guest tenor, came from Chicago Lyric Opera to sing Tom Rakewell. His acting was ineffectual and his tenor had too short a range. Graduate student Steven Taylor, later an active participant in Opera Colorado productions, displayed instinctive theatrical talents as Nick Shadow. His baritone was lighter than desirable but he demonstrated promise. Carolyn Nava was an engagingly funny Baba The Turk. In 1982 it was *Die Fledermaus*, which was popular, well cast, and lavishly produced.

The contradictions of academic opera lingered. The need to stage productions that were financially rewarding contested with the need for students to be challenged by true experimentation. It was the standard repertory which they really needed to know.

The opera department at the University of Colorado in Boulder had been relatively inactive, but with the presence of the nationally recognized Cecil Effinger as Professor of Composition, it was clear this department would consider some new directions. During his high school years, Effinger played oboe with the Denver Civic Symphony. Regarded in Denver with awe, he attended Colorado

College in Colorado Springs where he was active in the college band. In 1942 while in the Army at Lowry Air Force Base, where he conducted the 506th Army Band, and while commuting to Fort Logan, where he had additional duties, he wrote his Opus 1, *Two Motets for Male Chorus*.

Following Army service, he returned to Colorado College to teach and compose. From 1946 through 1948 he was music editor and critic for The Denver Post, following which he took on teaching responsibilities at the University of Colorado in Boulder, and also continued to teach in Colorado Springs. In the early 50s he took time to invent the Musicwriter, a typewriter for writing music, and presently concentrated his teaching in Boulder.

Among his many orchestral compositions were what he called a "little" symphony; a choral setting of Thomas Hornsby Ferril's poem, *Words for Time, Variations on a Cowboy Tune*, and *A Child is Born*, a Christmas cantata written and performed in 1953. Saul Caston, conductor of the Denver Symphony Orchestra, was proud to program these Effinger premieres, an almost unprecedented association of composer and orchestra.

Effinger's first opera, *Cyrano de Bergerac*, was done in 1965 in an adaptation by Donald Sutherland. Produced by the College of Music of the University of Colorado at Boulder, it was conducted by Andor Toth and stage directed by Rolf Sander, with professional baritone Kenneth Smith in the lead, and Shirley White, a university graduate and a mezzo-soprano active in Denver musical affairs, as Roxanne. The opera was rich in musical idiom, drawing on Baroque brightness with contrasting alarums of percussion and brass. A final scene with interweaving, shimmering strings reflected the tragedy of the misplaced, romantic hero. The opera was revived in 1968 with some revisions that tightened its drama. Herbert Beattie not only caught Cyrano's exuberance in his performance but gave valuable directorial advice. Valerie Goodall, a CU alumna, came from Vienna, where she was having a successful operatic career, to sing Roxanne. Abraham Chavez was the conductor of this excellent performance.

In 1976 Effinger turned to Colorado and the Victorian eccentric, Isabella Bird, for *The Gentleman Desperado (and Miss Bird)* with a book by Donald Sutherland, and commissioned by the Centennial Commission of the University of Colorado. Isabella Bird was a popular travel writer who turned up in Estes Park in the 1870s where she met Jim Nugent, a mercenary, ruffian, occasional trapper, cultured man of mystery with a melancholy streak—a man curious enough to beguile Miss Bird. Both Effinger and Sutherland were drawn to these individualistic characters and were grateful to Colorado historians Marshall Sprague and Louisa Arps, as well as Longmont playwright, Anne Matlack, for steering Miss Bird in their direction.

Similarities in Nugent and Cyrano were noted by Effinger and Sutherland; Cyrano was disfigured by his great nose, and Jim by the deep bear scratches which cost him an eye. Both were poetically inclined, well-schooled men who lived far below their potentials. In the background was the struggle between the English-born land barons of Estes Park who wanted to raise cattle along the Front range and maintain private game preserves in the mountains. The native-born farmers wanted water rights and good fences for their acreage which adjoined the cattle spreads. Lord Dunraven figures in the opera as one who wishes to have Estes Park as his private game preserve. He paid squatters $25 to homestead in Estes Park by which he meant placing four logs in rectangular position. For him, this amounted to homesteading.

Sutherland had been drawn more to the Victorianism of period speech than to the direct exposition required by opera. Many conflicting emotions passed within the action, and in the end there were too many contrasts to permit an ascending interest. There was much attractive, fresh music. Effinger realized there were imperfections in the book but nothing could be done with it, as Sutherland, who became tragically ill in the course of the writing, died in December 1979, a short time prior to its scheduled opening. The idea was good but the execution was disjointed. In the Post, Glenn Giffin blamed its failure on the fact that "someone who has a firm sense of what a show can and can't do should have had over-all controls."

It is the obligation of such academic departments to bring challenges to the students, and both of these university departments were surely other than ordinary in their programs. Although it is never a foregone conclusion that such vital traditions as these departments supported will last, a very imposing suggestion of what those traditions might be continues to exist.

Exotic and Irrational

THE HANGING JUDGE

AN AMERICAN OPERA OF THE WESTERN FRONTIER IN THREE ACTS BY

NORMAND LOCKWOOD, *Composer*

RUSSELL PORTER, *Librettist*

Musical Director and Conductor, GENEVIEVE McGIFFERT

Staged by EDWIN LEVY

Settings and Lighting by ELDON ELDER

Costumer, JACK VAUGHN

Raleigh . . .
Shannon . . .
Elder Webb . .
Elizabeth Shannon
Bardwell . . .
Rheba . . .
Townspeople .
  Gerald Finley,
  Lincoln, Micha
  Bailiff, Veryl
  Green, Alice G
  Susan McCarth
  Leone Young

THE DENVER POST Thurs., Jan. 27, 1977   23

Entertainment and the Arts

ELABORATE DU STAGING

'Carmen' Brings Life to Program

By GLENN GIFFIN
Denver Post Music Editor

After a fallow period the University of Denver's opera program has bounced back in full force with the most elaborate production it has attempted in years.

As its vehicle, the theatre department in conjunction with the Lamont School of Music took on Bizet's "Carmen." While this could hardly be called adventurous, it does challenge everyone concerned. Between Ronald Wersteld, music director, and Harry Ritchie, stage director, a most creditable performance emerged with only minor problems.

In the title role came Betsy Hoover, whose mezzo soprano voice projection, a smooth and plea tion and enough fire to give gypsy heroine a believable sta this is a concept of the char must grow some to commen and dominate the action witho

INDEED, IN THIS produc Don Jose who provided the dramatic sidelights. Facult Jack B. Morris Jr. took th played it as a very young, ve ed and withal vulnerable man painful attention to duty in th spilling over into the second, j ing depth to the personage ar of comedy, as well.

For any tenor Don Jose is signment. Morris has the rol his voice though occasional s be detected.

Micaela, no matter what t says, is a voice, not a charac production I've ever seen thi true, and it held true for Pat Wright. The character is so b can do anything with it but si one can—as Miss Wright did, easy soprano.

The remaining solo roles these. There is the officer Mo ard Aulie, not too steady voca ing night) and of course Esca reader (Matthew Smith, giving role the presence but not the itative voice necessary). Fr Mercedes, the gypsy compan men, had Van Ann Moore

'CARMEN'

Opera in four acts by Georges Bizet (in English), musical director, Ronald Wersteld; stage director, Harry Ritchie; sets by Lewis Crickard; costumes by Marcia Whitney, Vincent La Gaurdia Jr., conductor. Additional performances Friday at 8 p.m. and Sunday at 2:30 p.m., at the Cherry Creek Center for Performing Arts.

CAST
Micaela .... Patricia Barker Wright
Don Jose .... Jack B. Morris Jr.
Carmen .... Betsy Hoover
Frasquita .... VanAnn Moore
Mercedes .... Nancy Ross Klingman
Escamillo .... Matthew Smith
Morales .... Richard Aulie
With supporting soloists, chorus and orchestra.

Ross Klingman in the roles and providing a bewitching performance of the fortune telling scene.

IN MOVING to the Cherry Creek Center for Performing Arts, DU finally

---

THE RAKE'S PROGRESS

Musical Director and Conductor   Ronald Wersteld
Stage Director   David H. Bonumo
Stage Designer   Louis Crickard
Lighting Designer   Brett B. Rich
Costume Designer   David McCart

THE CAST

Tom Rakewell   David Gordon*
Anne Trulove   Cynthia Herzong
Trulove   Arte Marchand
Nick Shadow   Steven Taylor
Mother Goose   [illegible]
Baba the Turk   Carolyn Nava   *Lisa Peters*
Sellem   William Strong
The Keeper of Bedlam   Jonathon Wolf

CHORUS of Whores, Roaring Boys, Servants, Citizens, Madmen.

Charlotte Boyd   Heidi Johnson   Kent Jones   Lee Sadler
Shelley Lee Cole   Lou Peters   Roger Longbotham   Tim Throckmorton
Peggy Lee Deever   Marcia Ruth Shang   Steve Lucis   Rick Vaught
Nancy Ealy   Jane Seaman   Tad Lienau   Jonathon Wolf

*Guest Artist-in-Residence at University of Denver

The Opera is presented by arrangement with Boosey and Hawkes, Inc. Publisher and copyright owner

The Synopsis of THE RAKE'S PROGRESS

ACT I: Anne Trulove's father does not approve of the impoverished Tom Rakewell as a suitor. Tom determines to live by his wits and makes a wish for money, summoning Nick Shadow to his aid, thereby beginning a life of moral deterioration. This Mephisto-like character, Nick, serves his new master in the inevitable path through false glory to damnation. Tom's adventures lead him away from Anne to the brothel of Mother Goose and a life of luxury.

ACT II: His second wish to be happy, Shadow interprets this as marriage to bearded Baba the Turk, who, however, succeeds only in boring Tom by her incessant chatter. He claps a tablecloth over her head to silence her. Out of a dream he makes his third wish: a machine to turn stones into bread. Nick supplies it, but like all his justifications, it is a fraud.

ACT III: Now Tom, bankrupt and loveless, must pay his soul in debt to Shadow. Shadow gives him another chance—to guess three cards; but even though Tom succeeds, his evil genius cheats him again, taking away his sanity. Anne visits him in the madhouse, but it is too late. In an epilogue, all the principals sing the moral: "The Devil finds work for idle hands and hands to do."

A Little Yearning

The disbanding of Denver Lyric Opera in 1972 had caused disturbingly little concern among supporters of local opera. There was no question that these supporters gave more enthusiasm than money to the cause. Raising money was arduous. Building an audience without the stars and productions that money could buy was a further hazard.

There would always be someone courageous enough to try a first season. In the early 1950s there had been the Capitol Opera Company, developed by Bob and Gladys Lansing, which offered such operatic might as *The Magic Flute*, *Aida*, and *Il Trovatore* on the tiny stage at the Barnes School of Business auditorium, with piano support and casts consisting of high school and college age singers as well as young working people.

In the wake of Denver Lyric Opera's demise there was Opera West and there was Opera! Opera! Opera!, and some years when the only opera in town was at the University of Denver.

It was in these years that more and more of those with a relish for opera found it easy to go to New York or San Francisco for world class productions. With its increasingly provocative productions, Santa Fe was just down the way. Central City was a reliable player at the operatic tables. Packaged tours to the major domestic summer institutions as well as to Vienna, La Scala, and London were available at the push of a button. No one thought Denver could ever match what was seen on the great international stages. At least no one speaking out.

At the Denver Symphony, Brian Priestman continued his appealing, if sketchy, concert operas. Fleeting moments of opera would come and go but a groundswell for opera did not exist. Until June 1976, when an evening of operatic excerpts was done by a group calling itself the Denver Opera Repertory Company, opera had been asleep four years. Nicholas Laurienti was the instigator of this group, and a believer.

Laurienti had attended Juilliard and in Denver was nominally conductor of the Mount Carmel Concert Choir, out of which the Denver Concert Chorale emerged. With some Chorale soloists, Laurienti began a workshop for singers who had operatic interests. By the spring of 1976 he and his singers were ready to perform.

The initial offering consisted of *Lakmé*, Act I; *Turandot*, Act II, scene 2; and *Adriana Lecouvreur*, Act II. These works required musical sophistication. The surprising thing was the amount of potential shown by such singers as Jennifer Leigh, Janice Matisse, and DeRos Hogue. Anne M. Culver in the Rocky Mountain News noted that "opera from Denver may be in its infancy but it's alive and squalling." Glenn Giffin in The Denver Post called the evening "a splendid job all around." Again there was hope for a company that might succeed.

There was talk of *La Traviata*, and in November it was done with Beverly Christiansen Fernald as Violetta, DeRos Hogue as Alfredo, and Vernon Skari as Germont père. The three performances were well attended by receptive audiences despite such production problems as those which forced Robert Wells to turn over stage direction to a high school student one week before opening, due to his own theatrical involvements.

By February 1977, Laurienti was going full steam and ready, so it seemed, to take on another Verdi, this time *Il Trovatore*. As conductor, Laurienti obtained a robust sound from the pit orchestra, and he got some fair singers to take parts. Vernon Skari, a wrestling coach with aspirations for the operatic stage who had done the Count di Luna for Denver Lyric Opera, repeated his rather basic characterization. Janice Matisse was always energetic but her gypsy dowager seemed dramatically wide of the mark. DeRos Hogue, a good-looking young architect from Colorado Springs was vigorous to the point of pushing. It took most of the evening for Anita Alexander to get her voice in focus.

In June 1977 it was *The Merry Widow* with Dennis Jackson, director of the opera workshop at the University of Colorado in Boulder, showing a jaunty, convivial professionalism as Danilo. Jennifer Leigh was the Hanna, and she knew how to phrase to evoke style. Laurienti relished the Viennese atmosphere and tempos. With a handsome finale, costumed in black and white, this may have been the best of the Laurienti offerings.

In the mind of every opera producer there swims the notion of doing the great *Carmen* he has been destined to create. Or is it the resident mezzo-soprano who nourishes this idea? *Carmen* it was, right on the heels of the University of Denver presentation in the same theater. These two may have set local *Carmen* productions back for all time.

Janice Matisse delivered a rich mezzo sound and flamboyant acting but lacked the crucial violence of Carmen's spirit. So the richness and conviction in her singing went for naught. The loose, ill-proportioned production was marked by freeze-frame scenes and a complete absence of character motivation throughout.

The second of the four operas in this ambitious season was *Rigoletto* with an outstanding Gilda from Beverly Christiansen Fernald, who continued to justify this group's activities. Her delicate vocal colorings, and the purity of her tone along with graceful stage movement brought authority to the stage. She had graduated in both voice and violin from the University of Denver's Lamont School of Music, was a Metropolitan Opera audition winner, and had gone on to study in Aspen with Jennie Tourel and Hans Hotter. At New York City Opera she sang a Rosina and a Susanna but returned to Denver to teach in the late 1960s.

DeRos Hogue was the Duke, a more competent performer than some professionals heard in the Denver area; but there was a need for intensive voice work to smooth out his production. Even more he needed to find an acting style that would make him comfortable on stage. Vernon Skari as Rigoletto gave emphasis to the wonderful vocal lines and was less choppy than on other occasions. Fred Dransfeldt's stage direction failed to get the traffic patterns right, and the corrupt, decadent court was like a meeting of the River City School Board.

At the peak of Laurienti's ambitions, the Denver Opera Company delivered two operas in tandem in June 1978. Massenet's *Werther*, in a first Denver performance, and the Johann Strauss *Die Fledermaus* were a daunting couple.

Laurienti strongly believed Denver should know *Werther* which had been in the Met repertory until 1910, not to be revived until 1971-72. Later it was done both in Chicago and San Francisco. As Werther, Laurienti cast the promising young black tenor Lionel Stubblefield. For a young, little-schooled tenor with a somewhat beefy voice to try on this poignant, delicate role could only be foolhardy. He lacked theatrical guidance to tell him not to wear his hat indoors. My review referred to him as a "wooden figure in a big hat." There was definite luster and expression in Sharon Greenawald's Charlotte, and young Cynthia Heinemeyer surprised with her captivating Sophie, while Vernon Skari was a capable father.

While *Die Fledermaus* lacked overall musical and dramatic style, there was the charming Jennifer Leigh as an animated, vocally pleasing Rosalinda. DeRos Hogue allowed himself an evening of amusing comic turns. There was an excellent Orlovsky by June

Johnson Marvosh and in the hyper-active ball scene there was a bathtub in which a lady bathed. Haphazard staging of so familiar an opera as *Die Fledermaus*, with complicated movement whenever a simple one was needed, combined to defeat all the individual efforts in these productions.

For 1978-79, a season of *Madama Butterfly*, *The Merry Wives of Windsor*, and *Tosca* was promised. As *Butterfly's* Cio-Cio-San, Irene Van Ham Friedlob demonstrated considerable potential, though in her final scene she forced an unnaturally large sound which went out of control. At the Paramount Theater, home for this season, the acoustics over-stressed trumpets and horns.

In June, Laurienti had better luck with Cynthia Makris as Tosca. The singer had just completed a master's degree in voice at the University of Colorado in Boulder where she had sung Donna Anna and Cio-Cio-San among other roles. Subsequent to the *Tosca* she attended the American Institute of Musical Studies in Graz, Austria. At the end of summer she signed with the opera company at Enschede, Germany, and a year later signed for two years with Freiburg. Her current repertory includes Macbeth, Lulu, Tosca, Turandot and Aida in Germany, Austria and Finland.

Makris possessed an amplitude of temperament, with unusual warmth and conviction in her singing. The Cavaradossi was a little known professional, Frederick de Marseille, who brought a big, smooth tenor, if rather casual acting abilities to the part. The always available Vernon Skari did Scarpia with a rather low degree of intensity. Laurienti was stimulated by Makris to strong musical effect, mastering the Paramount's acoustics with a richly textured orchestral sound, which caught a good deal of the Puccini score.

In a small stage setting which very nearly lost the opera in the vastness of the Paramount, Nicolai's charming *The Merry Wives of Windsor* had a mostly satisfying performance. In spite of a heavy-handed Falstaff by David Anderson, the production was jovial. Jennifer Leigh again infused a Denver Opera Company evening with her pleasing singing, and Shirley White was an adept, attractive Mrs. Page, in her first and only local stage work. Thomas

Halvorson, a regional Metropolitan Opera auditions winner showed as Ford why he was thought to have such promise. His firm, warm baritone was impressive. In the end, his business involvements prevented him from taking his singing career seriously.

At the end of the season, Laurienti announced a massive operatic schedule for 1979-80. There would be Laurienti's first *Bohème*, with Jennifer Leigh and DeRos Hogue. Verdi's mighty *La Forza del Destino*, the ham-and-eggs double bill of *I Pagliacci and Cavalleria Rusticana*, and it was further announced that "the Denver Opera Company would present a guest artist in the title role of *I Pagliacci*" (sic). Later in the season *Il Trovatore* with Beverly Christiansen Fernald and Janice Matisse would be revived.

Since the Paramount had worked reasonably well in the just completed season, that would be the site for the new season. That it was centrally located was about its sole claim to being used. The stage had no depth, there was no proper orchestra pit, and backstage facilities were as primitive as those at the Tabor had been twenty years earlier.

Season ticket prices were announced, in a range of $19.80 to $39.10. Later, the *Trovatore* was replaced on the schedule with *Naughty Marietta*. Plans called for a concentrated series of intermixed performances in February, March, and April but in January before the season had begun, Laurienti resigned, stating that "it is increasingly apparent that the broad base of financial support does not exist in Denver for the Denver Opera Company." Further, he wrote, "after many hours of soul searching and praying over the Christmas season, I have decided to remove myself from a situation that appears hopeless."

Later he told John Ashton at the Rocky Mountain News that "Basically we have tried for four-and-a-half years to accrue funds for what can be called a partial season. We do have our supporters, and they're very dedicated. But it's just that the big money people are not so free when the talent is, quote, local. That problem was our single most troublesome area of battle. We tried to get people to see that the talent here is as good as it is anywhere, but we had a hard time getting people who write the big checks to come out and see us—see how good we were."

Laurienti told Ashton that there weren't enough volunteers to get the big financial support. At one time, a Comprehensive Employment and Training Act (CETA) grant had been made so that there could be an eight-member paid staff, with a publicity person, business manager, and a marketing and development expert, but the CETA funds were then cut back, and the Denver Opera Company was back in the doldrums.

"The audience is there," Laurienti insisted, "and if we had the money to stick it out, I'm sure the audience would continue to build. There's a real possibility in this town that there's just too much to support," referring to the Denver Symphony, Denver Art Museum, and other fine arts organizations.

In the summer of 1979 the Denver Opera Company had a $40,000 indebtedness, which sounded like a replay of the old Denver Lyric Opera at the end of the Johnson period. Most of this was for the rental of the Cherry Creek Performing Arts Center. Though efforts were made to resolve this problem, little headway was registered. When the five large business supporters withdrew, the end was nigh.

Laurienti had been involved in fund-raising, personnel problems, the CETA grant—all the things which stagger the artistic director whose concentration always is under attack. He told Max Price at the Post, "The thing I have done the least amount with is the music. I must return to that which I do best."

A year without opera was anguishing to Laurienti, who tried a pop singing career briefly, and though continuing with the Denver Concert Chorale, he found time on his hands, and singers eager to perform with no place to carry on. In February 1982, Laurienti announced plans for the New City Opera Company, based on his experiences with the Denver Opera Company.

"If you can't pay, you can't prosper," so he would present opera with a focus on music and singing rather than the costly trappings of fully-staged opera. Fiscal responsibility would be stressed. He told Glenn Giffin at the Post, "the whole concept is not to do anything until the money is there." He also spoke of a desire to perform Carlisle Floyd's *Susannah* or some Monteverdi.

By this time Central City had announced a plan for a Denver winter season, and already Nathaniel Merrill was firming out plans for Opera Colorado. It appeared there might be full-time opera in Denver. Giffin asked Laurienti why, in view of these announced plans, there needed to be a new company, to which he responded, "Because they're international, I think that Denver needs or will support an international company, and it's going to be either Opera Colorado or Central City, and quite frankly I don't care which it is, because I would like to see an international company here. But I still think that there needs to be something on a regional level. Essentially, in an international company there isn't going to be a whole lot for the people who are here to do."

Performances so low key that they were hardly visible were done by Laurienti at the Denver Botanic Gardens but major fundraising efforts by Opera Colorado and Central City dimmed prospects for the New City Opera Company.

Laurienti was right in believing a regional company should exist, and when Harriet Lawyer-Duvallo's Opera Fair presented Purcell's *Dido and Aeneas* at St. Paul's Lutheran Church there was a memorable example of imaginative but not elaborate staging.

There was a compelling theatrical flair to this baroque masque, with its waving banners, ascending Cupid, all fused with a blending of color, movement, and music that was truly operatic. The senses were excited by the abilities of a young and attractive cast with the lovely Lydia Ko, a Korean soprano, as Dido and the virile Thomas Allen as Aeneas. Charming performances by Anne Achenbach, Janet Wentland, Ruth Seeber, and Rebecca Young were further enticements. Jurgen de Lemos, principal cellist of the Denver

Symphony and leader of the Arvada Chamber Orchestra, led a carefully prepared performance.

Lawyer-Duvallo's stage direction was the best operatic staging since Jean Favre's 1971 *The Crucible,* and it demonstrated how greatly imagination could supplant heavy sets. Nothing could replace good singing and musicianship, but fresh ideas of movement and decor could work wonders. Lawyer-Duvallo was a strong-willed woman who relished her independence, though she did not follow this production with the expected offering. Her tragic murder by young thugs on a Denver street ten or so years later was a terrible blow to the Denver artistic community.

These had been rough times for opera in Denver. Those who put themselves forward to develop opera were always too busy to notice that the stragglers behind them were hardly evident.

120   Allen Young

Cynthia Makris

Opera In-the-Round

Audacious in placing *Aida* on the tiny Central City Opera House stage, vividly imagining such familiar works as *Don Giovanni* and *Il Trovatore*, Nathaniel Merrill left the impression of a man intensely dedicated to his work. Those who recalled the high level of achievement by Merrill at Central City responded positively to the May 1981 announcement that Merrill had formed Opera Colorado to produce opera-in-the-round at the Boettcher Concert Hall starting in 1983. "I feel an urge to do opera in a new and different form," Merrill told the press. "What we'll be working with is a new kind of scenic concept which for better or worse is being called scenic ambience rather than setting," he further explained. It would be some years before Denver realized what a bolt of electricity Merrill's decisive move sent through the Denver music community. Single-handedly, Merrill brought major opera to Denver.

His imagination thrived on the challenge of opera-in-the-round. "Instead of having stars projected against a canvas backdrop, the stars could extend over the whole auditorium, over the people's heads, thus amplifying what Boettcher does well anyway, which is to bring people, the public, into contact with the singers." And indeed, at the close of the first act of the opening production of *Otello* the stars did come down to illuminate Otello and Desdemona and captivate the audience.

Not only was Boettcher a challenge to Merrill's imagination. There was a problem in that settings could not be fastened either to the stage floor or the plaster fascia around the hall. Settings might be "treated as mosaic... might be treated in many different ways, but practically from an acting view, there will be a platform arrangement which I hope can transform itself from act to act with things which telescope or go into one another, or flow over one another like staircases which nest together."

Locally and nationally, funds to accommodate a $1.7 million budget for the first season of two different opera productions in an unspecified number of performances would be required. With $400,000 due to come from ticket sales, a substantial campaign would have to be carried out. A large budget was required, for, as Merrill also told the press, "a company of international stars is the only way I see that opera can survive in Denver," adding that such stars as Placido Domingo, Sherrill Milnes, and Shirley Verrett were among those who would be hired.

Boettcher's acoustical properties, always in dispute, were discussed by Merrill who said, "I don't think we have an acoustical problem. I think this is a very touchy subject. I think that whenever you have a new hall built, people say 'Oh, I don't like it because the chairs aren't plush' or 'I don't like it because of its terrible acoustics.' I think that too much of that has gone on; and too much of the correction of that has tried to be done by electronic means, and which has probably compounded any difficulties that the hall might have in that direction."

Keith Raether of the Rocky Mountain News was told by Merrill that "the obvious problem with working in the round is keeping the orchestra and singers together. How does the conductor cue the singers when they have their backs turned to him? Opera is not just making high C's sound lovely in some mannered way. It is the thrill that comes from believing in what you're singing."

Opera on the grand scale had not been tried in Denver, though there was a whiff of what might be in the Licia Albanese *Traviata* back in 1956 and the Norman Johnson-Joey Favre 1970 *The Crucible*. These efforts had proved a failure as far as Denver audiences were concerned. All this grandiose talk of major operatic stars and $400,000 in ticket sales and a $1.7 million budget made heady reading for those with memories of past opera companies going "stone cold dead in the market," as in 1957 the collapse of the Greater Denver Opera Company had been described.

Merrill described the potential of Denver for opera, its size, as well as Colorado's proven support for The Met, the Chicago Lyric Opera, and the Santa Fe Opera. A defensive attitude immediately developed among supporters of opera at Central City. To them and their cause Merrill said, "Opera is a funny thing. Opera breeds opera. It feeds on itself. And when you have more opera, the public wants more opera...up to of course a certain point, until you are saturated with opera." Whenever Merrill had the opportunity he stressed his wish to assist the Central City Opera House Association and pledged his support. Furthering these expressions, Merrill emphasized that following the Met's first tour to Dallas, there was a 50% increase in ticket sales for the local opera. A similar tale was told of Washington, D.C. and its opera. The Central City leaders remained skeptical and somewhat fearsome.

Gunther Schneider-Siemssen, noted Austrian stage designer for The Met and the Vienna State Opera, was eager to be involved, and came to Denver. He told The Denver Post's Max Price of his interest in developing a special projection system for Boettcher. "Everything that is missing in the sets will have to be put in by projection. And everything will have to be transparent so it can be seen by everybody." To Price's questions about which operas would best work in the surround situation, Schneider-Siemssen responded that *The Tales of Hoffman, Die Fledermaus, Turandot, Fidelio* and *Lulu* would be among the best.

Details of the initial season were disclosed in September 1981, and the two operas would be *Otello* and *La Bohème*. James McCracken, Maria Chiara, and Silvano Carroli would appear in the Verdi with Carlo Felice Cillario conducting, while Placido Domingo, Ileana Cotrubas, and Allan Monk were to lead the cast of the Puccini, Bruno Bartoletti conducting. The Swiss designer Toni Businger would design the 1983 productions, with Merrill serving both as director. When Businger arrived in Denver in January to explore the house, he told Marjorie Barrett of the Rocky Mountain News, "Boettcher is something very special. It is not like doing an opera in an opera house. There will be so many technical problems in a round house. Right now, I stand at zero." "We will concentrate on the floor and on the people, not the backgrounds," he continued. "We will have one budget for the floor and one budget for each of the operas."

Announcements of board members were looked at with great interest and some skepticism. Robert G. Anderson, a Tulsa oil man and ardent supporter of the Aspen Music Festival, took credit for getting Merrill to come to Denver to probe the potential of Boettcher. Many came for brief stints, but Nellie Mae Duman remained to chair the tenth anniversary observations, while Sonja Mast, Dennis Law, Jill Crow, and Anderson continued through the first decade.

The Denver Symphony Orchestra was signed for a three-year-contract as the official Opera Colorado orchestra. A calendar was set with an English-language *Bohème* with a young Jerry Hadley as Rodolfo to open March 25, with Domingo and an international cast opening April 5.

Merrill explored all his Met connections, and lined up Sir Rudolf Bing, Schuyler Chapin, and Tony Randall for a National Advisory Board. Later Sherrill Milnes, Luciano Pavarotti, and Domingo came to this board. Only Domingo and Milnes ever participated in or observed any Opera Colorado productions.

Benefits became increasingly frequent. At one private party where James McCracken was a singing guest, $100,000 was raised.

For a large affair at the Fairmont Hotel donors were promised such glittery names as Ashley Putnam, Rudolf Nureyev, and Judith Blegen, but were presented with Joan Fontaine, Buddy Ebsen, Estelle Parsons, Cornell MacNeil and his tenor son, Walter. With a goal of $1.7 million to be raised, a "Diamond Circle" ball was held at the Fairmont in November 1982 with tickets for a couple going for $500, single tickets for $300, and an overall goal for this event of $150,000. By this time only $300,000 had been raised.

Tickets for the season went on sale in January, and in the first four days $50,000 in orders was received. This money was directly needed to pay for dampening the reverberation at Boettcher, and for installing platforms and steps below stage for chorus entrances. Now it was said that throat mikes would be needed, that "voice lift" would be used. On one occasion Merrill admitted that the hall was "too live for opera to be ideal" but he believed the possibilities would be balanced out by a "wonderful connection of audience to things on stage."

Although those opposed to music at Boettcher Hall continued their criticism, the majority found voices resonant and exciting there. The logistics problems were enormous. Boettcher's structure required new techniques, so five closed circuit TV monitors were placed about the stage and auditorium, along with other monitors backstage and below stage. To achieve the intensity of stage lighting that was required, a large switchboard with electronic controls was rented. An increase by one-third in lighting potential was being arranged.

Incredibly, by February $1.6 million had been raised, with $170,000 still to be located. Merrill reported that getting the balance of funds was "eminently accomplishable; we know where at least half the money is coming from." By then more than half the tickets had been sold. When funds became tight, the nascent Young Artists Program was canceled; Merrill was determined it would be revived in 1984. Ticket prices reflected the high cost of doing opera. The opening night top was $80 but $8 tickets in the Ring were available for the English language *Bohème*.

There were the casting problems. Maria Chiara had now withdrawn as Desdemona in favor of Pilar Lorengar. Conductor Bruno Bartoletti had to undergo heart surgery, so Carlo Felice Cillario would do the *Bohème*, while Argeo Quadri would come to lead *Otello*. At the very last moment, Gloriosa Caballero withdrew as the English language Mimi, to be replaced by a San Francisco hopeful, Nikki Li Hartliep. From Barcelona, also at the last moment, came word of Barbara Daniels' illness, so Pamela South doubled her Musetta for both sets of performances.

By March, Merrill was telling Keith Raether of the Rocky Mountain News that "I always said in public that it would be a piece of cake, but what else are you going to say? I wasn't sure; you're never sure until you try it. But I have to say now that it is easier than I thought it would be."

Merrill set an impressive rehearsal schedule, with seven orchestral rehearsals for each opera. *Otello* rehearsals would start March 17, and the international *Bohème* would go into rehearsal on March 27. Louise Sherman of The Met musical staff, Mrs. Merrill in private life, had been working since October with a chorus of 116, with Kevin Kennedy of Denver as assistant chorus conductor. Rather than gather all tenors into one stage group, sopranos, baritones, and basses into other stage groups, the singers were being mixed into smaller ensembles which would make more effective dramatic use of the chorus. For Act II of *La Bohème* there would be nearly 180 people, including 50 supers, on stage.

Opera was ever more costly. Out of charter memberships in Opera Colorado, $862,374 was raised, along with corporate and foundation grants. Now it was hoped that as much as $810,000 might be realized from ticket sales.

Opening night, April 4, 1983, came with a tension and excitement far greater than most Denver opera-goers could recall. Expectations were both puzzled and high. What was opera-in-the-round? Would opera work at Boettcher? *Otello's* musical drama surged triumphantly in a production as fine-tooled as Venetian leather. Bolts of lightning struck the Cypriots on the quay. Like leaves in a storm, the mighty chorus was tossed and scattered. *Otello* made his entrance from a portal on Dress Circle One with a squad of flag-bearers. At the end of Act I the starry heavens descended upon Desdemona and Otello in a transcendent blend of sight and sound.

Other visual and aural treats were to come. In Act III, clusters of trumpeters sounded their call from high balconies in the hall. After a brief blackout, brilliant lights revealed the full chorus in stunning Renaissance splendor as the ambassadors were welcomed. Duane Schuler's eloquent lighting met all demands. Richard Lorraine's costumes provided elegant finery.

James McCracken was a powerfully stirring Otello, while Pilar Lorengar advanced from an insecure beginning to the dark pathos of the final scene. Silvano Carroli's razor-sharp and bitter Iago was a characterization of coruscating force. Minor roles were in good hands from Cynthia Munzer's Emilia, Walter MacNeil's Cassio, Stephen West's Montano, all strongly realized.

Toni Businger's scenic design featured bas reliefs of the Lion of Venice empaneled in two facing areas, while a series of hexagonally structured steps at stage center served variously, and with high effectiveness, as quay-side, battlement, fountain, throne room dais, and the final act's bed chamber.

The musical essence was the heart of this production, so tautly and expressively led by the venerable Argeo Quadri. The fine voices were heard without difficulty. The Denver Symphony Orchestra was commendable at its most thunderous and at its most silken. The choral forces in their splendor represented a new level of achievement by Denver singing forces.

Blair Chotzinoff, reviewing in the Rocky Mountain News, wrote "to put it conservatively, the event was a triumph, an emotional blockbuster, a technical and scenic milestone, and a musical and dramatic feast far beyond the scope of anything in the genre ever presented in Colorado. Its effect was visceral. It hypnotized one's involuntary responses. Wonder followed wonder. The grandest of operas is not only possible in Boettcher but it was in this production spectacular, compelling, thrilling—in every response a marvel." "Because of many acoustical cooks," he continued, "or perhaps in spite of them, the voice articulation has become completely natural with orchestra-singer balance perfect."

For City Edition I wrote "Yes, opera works in Boettcher Concert Hall... It worked because Nathaniel Merrill, artistic director, brought together musicians, singers, designers, and other production staff members who created new approaches to the novel demands of in-the-round opera." In the audience were those who pinched themselves, wondering if they were actually in Denver.

Except in its second act, *La Bohème* cannot overpower with color or spectacle. Merrill was judicious in maintaining the intimate proportions of this opera, but that Act II will be long remembered. Following an unusually sensitive first act, the stage was blacked out. Before bringing the lights up, chorus members appeared throughout the house, carrying tiny lamps as they moved towards two bridges over the orchestra pit to cross onto the stage to join other singers and supers on the by-now-lighted stage.

Businger made no effort to dress a setting for the stage, achieving a miracle of color and movement with the use of display carts for the many vendors, each cart lavishly designed. With the panoply of Suzanne Mess's costumes, the stage was a fresh wonder.

This production was marked by the intimacy achieved by the principals. Merrill directed Placido Domingo and Catherine Malfitano in a scaling down of standard gestures, which could not be used because of the nearness of the audience. A fresh impact resulted from the convincing portrayals which resulted.

Merrill's casting triumphed beyond the leads, for Pamela South registered delightfully as Musetta, and Allan Monk charmed with the zest of his Marcello. Lanky, virile Justino Diaz as Colline, amiable Adib Fazah as Schaunard, and the Denver bass Stephen West as Benoit joined the principals to fill Boettcher with a rare ripeness of sound. Later Jack Harrold bounced in as Alcindoro. On opening night conductor Cillario seemed over-concerned that the orchestra might overwhelm the singers. The pallid orchestral support was later replaced with a properly robust Puccini sound.

The English-language *Bohème* brought enthusiasm. Jerry Hadley received acclaim for the fresh ring of his tenor as well as for his spirited acting. Placido Domingo came to hear him, but he was not heard by enough Denver opera goers, for everyone wanted to hear Domingo. Nikki Li Hartliep, who had come in very late to replace ailing Gloriosa Caballero as Mimi, sang sweetly though she was more womanly in her figure than desirable. In this cast Adib Fazah was a resilient Marcello, with Erich Parce and Eric Halfvarson filling out the foursome.

Blair Chotzinoff, reviewing in the Rocky Mountain News thought the Puccini orchestral sound was "not enough to overwhelm the singers, but still too heavy considering the hall's quirks." "Yes, Virginia," he continued, "Boettcher's acoustic gremlins still stalk the premises. When the singers face you and the music is pianissimo, the English text is loud and clear. Only the most skilled diction can hope to cope with other postures."

For Glenn Giffin, *Bohème* was "a triumph on all fronts, particularly Merrill's in-the-round staging. Denver will be talking about this production for years to come. Of the staging he wrote, "one has the feeling of looking over the shoulders of principal characters, of eavesdropping on great events... the voices have been discreetly manipulated through the hall's 'voice lift' which doesn't so much amplify voices as re-direct them. When a singer faces away from any section of the seating, a drop-off of volume is noticeable, but because of the voice lift, reinforcing the voice throughout the hall, most of the words come through."

In retrospect this was an event of historical proportions which proved that opera could be done in Denver on the scale of the great international houses of the world. There was no escaping the cost, just as there was no easy remedy for paying those costs. But Denver opera audiences would always look to this opening season as a time of great fulfillment.

During opera week there were several panel discussions for the International Council of Opera Colorado, the support group of opera lovers from all over. At one discussion of "Scene Design of the Future," designer Peter Wexler criticized Boettcher for its lack of a "sense of majesty," caused largely by "being very aware of people opposite you; you shouldn't ask the audience to count the house." He also regretted the inability of the hall to produce a true blackout. He missed a sense of height, and wondered how scenery could be made vertical at Boettcher, but praised the "strong masculine, brilliant production" of *Otello*.

At another panel, Dr. Marcel Prawy of the Vienna Opera led a discussion of musical values, in which he expressed his belief that in Boettcher singers could be heard only at the expense of orchestral sound, while conductor Quadri thought the sound of the orchestra should be increased. Conductor Cillario was concerned that the singers anticipated the beat, and he urged having an assistant conductor beat time separately towards the TV monitors. Raising the sound of the singers was important, he thought.

Justino Diaz believed it was as important for the singers to hear the orchestra as to hear the beat. Of the playing by the Denver Symphony, Quadri thought it "gave everything it could. We have to take into consideration the hall. I was not too enthusiastic at first, but this increased. The orchestra must be accustomed to play opera."

Towards the end of June, the 1984 season was announced, with *The Tales of Hoffman* and *Turandot* to be featured. Nicolai Gedda was named to sing Hoffman, with Ruth Welting, cheered at the Met for her 1982 performance as Olympia, Rosalind Elias as Giulietta, and James Morris as the four villains. There were rumors Merrill was seeking Michel Plasson of The Met's 1982 production to conduct. Later, Ashley Putnam was announced for Antonia, and Joseph Frank, Susan Quittmeyer, and Stephen West were announced for other roles. Joseph Delacote was named as conductor, and Gunther Schneider-Siemssen to design, with Duane Schuler as lighting designer.

Argeo Quadri returned to conduct the Puccini, which featured Eva Marton as the frigid princess, Vasile Moldoveanu as Calaf, and Diana Soviero as Liu, with Eric Halfvarson as Timur, Erich Parce as Ping, Leonard Eagleson as Pang, Richard Brunner as Pong, and Joseph Frank as the Emperor. For the English language, popularly-priced production, June Fiske would sing Turandot; Edgar Stivan, Calaf; Hei Kyung Hong, Liu; and Stephen West, Timur.

Schneider-Siemssen had designed the critically-favored 1982 Met *Hoffman* production, and while his Denver *Hoffman* was being done, he came to talk about his efforts in behalf of holograms, patterns produced on photosensitive negatives which have been exposed to holography, using lasers to project a three-dimensional image. The designer described and demonstrated ideas he had executed for a 1986 Hoffman for the Salzburg Marionette Opera Theater. It was suggested that Opera Colorado might be the first to employ holograms in its productions, but the extensive work in developing the required very high resolution photographic plates made it clear that 1984 was too early for such experimentation in Denver.

The second season set a new standard of opulence with the extravagances of Offenbach's *The Tales of Hoffman* and Puccini's *Turandot*, productions so sure vocally and dramatically that they continue to rank among the top Opera Colorado achievements.

Eva Marton in opulent voice was a magnificent Princess Turandot, "a legendary voice in complete command of her art," as Glenn Giffin wrote in the Denver Post. Vasile Moldoveanu as Calaf had dignity and vital presence and a fine ring to his tenor, while Diana Soviero brought out all the handkerchiefs for her tender performance as Liu. The chorus filled the hall with rich sounds as it commented on the action. Argeo Quadri was the superb leader of the vastly impressive Denver Symphony Orchestra. Schneider-Siemssen's imperial Peking with its great dragons looming above great red columns showed that indeed vertical effects could be done at Boettcher. Duane Schuler lit this set magically.

The Hoffman was likewise wonderfully cast, even though Nicolai Gedda developed voice problems and canceled. His replacement, Alain Vanzo, showed "an agile lyric tenor with more style than voice and more voice than technique," as I wrote in the Rocky Mountain News. James Morris commanded evil force with a mighty bass-baritone, and Ruth Welting was brilliant as expected as Olympia. Ashley Putnam was a fragile Antonia, and Rosalind Elias a somewhat overdone Giulietta. Susan Quittmeyer very nearly stole the show as Nicklausse, and before the year took more than the show when she married Morris. *Hoffman* was cast in depth, and that made the difference. It was a unique presentation of the original version of the opera, one worth doing for the eloquence of the expanded Nicklausse role.

A Champagne Night of the Stars was notable for Hei Kyung Hong singing "Caro Nome" and Mimi in a second act of *Bohème*, and most exciting with Eva Marton and Vasile Moldoveanu singing the Act I duet from *Tosca*. Attendance was disappointing, demonstrating that people wanted operas, not fragments. Buying and paying for opera on the scale of Merrrill's ambitions threatened but never brought the ultimate danger of bankruptcy. Somehow Opera Colorado weathered the storms. Speaking of Opera Colorado to Eleanor Keats of Muse monthly, Merrill told her "If Denver wants this, here it is. Now, it has to be bought and paid for. If Denver wants to be big time, then this is a project it can't afford not to support."

Budgeted at $1.7 million, with ticket sales of over $600,000, the second season accrued $400,000 in unsecured debts. Ernest Tucker of the Rocky Mountain News had barely finished writing of Opera Colorado's "fear of folding" when an "anonymous donor" pledged $500,000 in a matching grant against the total debt of $900,000. Within five weeks the donation was found to be fraudulent, an extravagant gesture by a floral store employee who claimed to have received a grand inheritance from a lately deceased relative. Later another fellow employee was found to be involved. These two had set up such conditions for the donation as the firing of the entire board and staff, the empowering of one of the two to make all new appointments, the provision of 12 tickets for opening nights, and a free parking space at Boettcher. Opera was showing its ability to attract crazies as well as zealots.

It was thus a matter of relief to Merrill and the board that the gift was shown to be false. When reality returned, there was the $400,000 debt from 1984, $370,000 in guaranteed debts, and $150,000 in revolving credit for day-to-day operations, all of which added up to $920,000 in obligations that would not go away. By September a master plan for dealing with the outstanding indebtedness was assembled though few specifics were made public. The immediate plan was to reduce substantially the cost of the 1985, third season. Canceling this season had been considered but dismissed as non-productive.

In the third season, scaled-down productions of *Tosca* and *Il Trovatore* were set in order to adjust to the $870,000 budget that had been declared the maximum. The singers were not the most exciting available, but were competent. Martina Arroya sang the Leonora of this *Trovatore* in a glowing, opening night performance with the slow-starting Adelaide Negri following in remaining performances. Due to a bronchial infection, Giancarlo Cecchele had to be replaced by an experienced Giorgio Lamberti whose melancholy tone and easy production was welcome. Viorica Cortez was an alarmingly potent presence as Azucena while Pablo Elvira's smooth baritone made the Count di Luna a valuable asset.

There were no funds for a lavish staging, so Merrill went for underplaying the very up-front dramatics of the work. Anton Guadagno supported the singers ably with fine playing from the Denver Symphony Orchestra. The *Trovatore* chorus was oddly seated in straight chairs which gave the performance some overtones of a skewed Kabuki performance. This production served to show that doing opera on the cheap at Boettcher led nowhere.

Next came *Tosca*, with Sylvia Sass as an adequate but curiously-mannered Floria Tosca and Silvano Carroli a lustful, thwarted Scarpia. Tenor Giorgio Lamberti as Cavaradossi seemed tight, his singing on the constricted side. Stephen West had a great success as the Sacristan, and Philip Booth showed power as Angelotti.

The church scene of *Tosca* was fully done, for which the Denver Archdiocese and St. Thomas Seminary provided costuming and other needs. Another adjustment to Boettcher's circular staging was made at the conclusion. Since Tosca could not leap over a parapet onto a mattress, as usually done, and since she must die, it was arranged that a prison guard drop a pistol, which Tosca pounced on to kill herself.

Limiting performances to a two-week period, and cutting the office staff from 11 to five people, Merrill, with the assistance of administrative director Reeva MacDonald, made certain there would be other seasons for the company. She brought a determination and shrewdness to Opera Colorado which had been honed through her experience with Bob Garner and Center Attractions. She was to have ultimate impact on bookkeeping methods and control over expenditure.

The 1985, third season, was a financial success in that it had ended in the black. Shortly before the 1985 season, Anne Randolph, now director of resources for Opera Colorado, reported reduction of the $800,000 indebtedness had been made through guarantees and donations to a "long term debt of $295,000 secured by guarantees, and a short-term debt of $220,000 which we are in the process of paying off."

With a sure-fire billing of *Aida* and *Don Giovanni* set for 1986, things seemed on the upswing, and indeed these offerings sold out 99.9 per cent of Boettcher's capacity. Its grandeur humanized by a powerful focus on the personal drama as well as by strong casting, *Aida* was a great popular success. Glenn Giffin in the Denver Post called the production a "vivid demonstration of what grand opera at its grandest is all about." In the Rocky Mountain News I wrote of the performance as seeming to realize a dream of finding all the best elements for this Titan of operas."

The much-heralded Aprile Millo took the audience by storm with a vibrant, thrilling soprano. Amneris as realized by Viorica Cortez was a poignant figure caught in the web of history. The opera's final image of Amneris lying distraught on the stone door to the crypt as it hung in mid-air was a masterful, riveting touch. Kevin Langan as Ramfis and Stephen West as the King had the strongest male voices and were dramatically vivid. Gianfranco Cecchele as Rhadames was on the pale side dramatically but his singing had good presence, while Pablo Elvira was that unlikely figure, an understated Amonasro, who did bring luster to his singing.

It was the splendor of choral singing by the Opera Colorado chorus prepared by Louise Sherman which gave a special power to the triumphal entry scene, in which the sensual dances directed by Cleo Parker Robinson brought much pleasure. Argeo Quadri again showed the authoritative musical strength he brings to the late Verdi operas. Robert O'Hearn's designs were impressively understated, and thus ideal.

Don Giovanni was a quite brilliant production. I wrote in the Rocky Mountain News that "Merrill's staging achieved striking comedy in vivid interplay. In the world of this opera no one is ever out of the sight of another. These people interrelate on the stage as they would in life."

Casting was strikingly good, with James Morris in sensuous vocal form as the Don, Stephen West, a lusty, imperious Leporello who was sometimes over-directed by Merrill. The women were uniformly good, with Nancy Gustafson a rare Elvira and Susan Quittmeyer delectable as Zerlina. Winifrid Faix Brown, a late replacement for an ailing Ashley Putnam, gave Anna beautifully rounded tone. Walter MacNeil gave polish to his "Il mio tesoro." Julius Rudel led the Denver Symphony in an elegant, scintillating performance, while O'Hearn devised a stunning platform whose floor, under the magic of lighting, was alternately marble and parquet.

A *Die Fledermaus* gala attracted 2,000 to hear a highly abbreviated version of the operetta, while special guests for the party scene included Nancy Gustafson singing a seductive "Vilja," and James Morris singing, as he had for The Met 100th celebration, three songs from *The Man from La Mancha*. Susan Quittmeyer sang one of Nicklausse's arias from Hoffman, and Stephen West chose to sing "Old Man River."

This second effort at such a gala was enjoyed by the audience but could not be justified financially without a completely sold house, so this may have been the last of the great galas, unless there were to be a Pavarotti, Sills, or a Domingo to entice audiences.

Having gone the conservative route in 1985, the board approved a higher budget of $1.4 million for 1986 so long as the certainty of strong box office response existed. Nearly 19,000 people paid $630,000 in ticket sales for this season of four performances of *Aida* and three of *Don Giovanni*.

For 1987 there would be Saint-Saens' *Samson and Delila* and Puccini's *Manon Lescaut*, a quite different set of operas. Jon Vickers came to perform his awesome Samson, giving the opera a mighty focus. His total identification with the role made for strong personal affirmation in a memorable highlight of the first decade of Opera Colorado. Viorica Cortez was back as Delila, breaking through the rhetoric of Saint-Saens' music to create a flamboyant character for whom Samson's resistance would melt. Frederick Burchinal, the Denver-schooled baritone, displayed a fine sheen and dramatic urgency as the High Priest. Kevin Langan brought distinction to the role of The Old Hebrew. Emerson Buckley, who led opera at Central City from 1956 until 1969, including the five Merrill-O'Hearn seasons, conducted in full appreciation of the Saint-Saens music. The full-throated Opera Colorado Chorus prepared by Louise Sherman again took honors.

Merrill had worked with Robert O'Hearn at The Met for their successful mounting of Samson in 1964, and in a totally different venue they again made vivid an opera that is close to oratorio. Of course the destruction of the temple at the conclusion was anticipated, and it was indeed stunning. This became a popular success, selling out for two of its four performances.

Puccini's *Manon Lescaut* was not the stuff of brilliance despite a stunning second act in Geronte's salon. The contingent of lackeys at Geronte's establishment as well as the number of officers who arrived to arrest Manon were laughable. There had been absurdities in the antics of the students in Act I. The third act, with its gangplank pointing to an unknown land, was powerful.

Josella Ligi was not pretty enough for Manon, and nowhere near frivolous enough. It took the first two acts for her to go beyond her dowdy appearance, but she handled her voice well. Vasile Moldoveanu, in his second Opera Colorado performance, was slimly handsome as des Grieux, projecting an image both virile and vulnerable. Erich Parce was an intriguing, dashing Lescaut, and as the gouty Geronte there was Stephen West. Joseph Frank disarmed as the dancing master. Janos Acs led the Denver Symphony in an acute performance.

These operas were staged on a $1,430,000 budget. Ticket sales brought in $565,000, or 91.4 per cent of the budget estimates. For the entire run, houses were at 83 per cent of capacity. Production costs were down by $35,000 from the 1986 productions of *Aida* and *Don Giovanni*.

Opera Colorado was on its way. Triumphs of artistry brought financial panic but determination led to the hard work that would keep Opera Colorado going.

138   Allen Young

Entertainment/arts
Rocky Mountain News, Denver, Colo.

Opera in the round excites Merrill

By NANCY DEAN
For the News

Entertainment/arts
Rocky Mountain News, Denver, Colo.   Thursday, Jan. 28, 1982 — Page 77

Boettcher poses puzzle for costume, set designer

Dramatically...

Announcing Opera Colorado

I am pleased to have this opportunity to introduce you to Opera Colorado. Our plans are exciting, for Denver, for Colorado, and indeed, for the future of opera, as a dynamic entertainment and artistic medium. Opera Colorado is the only opera company in the United States to present opera in the round, and this is made possible by Denver's own magnificent Boettcher Concert Hall.

What's more, the plans for Opera Colorado go beyond our performance schedule to include an educational program, signaling the establishment of a national opera studio to train gifted American singers, a statewide touring program and innovative outreach programs encompassing lecture and chamber concert series.

We are off to an ambitious start, and we are confident that now establish a company of international scope and calibre...
place among the country's most energetic and...
fully appreciate the grandeur and jo...

This is an important...
with two produ...
internation...

It is al...
now will b...
achievement...
furthering th...

Opera C...
forward to yo...

OPERA COLORADO PREMIER SEASON '83

...establish
...provide operatic
...you to participate in
...the entire region.
...entertainment and artistic excellence. We look
...that excellence.

Nath / C Merrill

Nathaniel Merrill
President and Artistic Director
Opera Colorado

Opera in Round Has Merrill Going in Circles

By GLENN GIFFIN

Placido Domingo

Catherine Malfitano

Superstars enchant 'La Boheme' audience

By BLAIR CHOTZINOFF
Special to the News

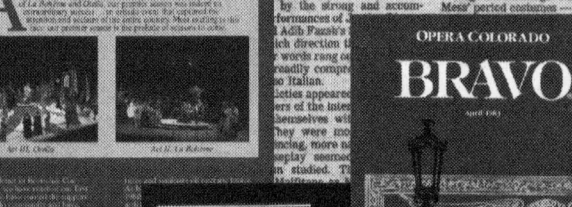

140 Allen Young

Exotic and Irrational

LIVELY ARTS
A City of Theaters
Curtis Street was Denver's Great White Way before the end of the Golden Age of theatre in 1928

ALLEN YOUNG

Denver is no longer a city of theatres. Many of the places where vaudeville, opera, repertory theatre, operetta, musical comedy, burlesque and prestidigitation were performed have been torn down. The few that remain are reminders of the Golden Age of shows. Ticket prices ranged from 25 cents to $1. Among the attractions during the first season were the great soprano, Marcella Sembrich, Eddie Foy and Marie Dressler as "Tillie's Night Mare."

The highlight of 1913 was a performance by the 150-member Chicago Grand Opera Company featuring Tetrazzini as Lucia di Lammermoor and Mary Garden

TURANDOT

Entertainment

Rocky Mountain News, Denver, Colo. Monday, May 7, 1984 — Page 85

'Turandot' full of Puccini's passion

ALLEN YOUNG

BOETTCHER • CONCERT • HALL

IL TROVATORE
Starring: Martina Arroyo,* Margarita Castro-Alberty, Gianfranco Cecchele and Pablo Elvira
Conductor: Anton Guadagno

TOSCA
Starring: Sylvia Sass, Giorgio Lamberti and Silvano Carroli
Conductor: Argeo Quadri

Tosca (in Italian)

Il Trovatore (in Italian)

Exotic and Irrational   143

Robert O'Hearn's sets for "Aida"

The Nile Scene

Amneris hangs on slab above the tomb—Act IV

Merrill Innovations

As Opera Colorado's sixth season in 1988 was about to unfold, a new element, too effective a ploy to skip, had come into being via the Toronto Opera and other companies, including the San Francisco Opera. Supertitles, translations of the libretto as an aid to comprehension of the opera's action, were being used. Projection of supertitles in a circular hall such as Boettcher had never been attempted. It was found that four well-placed screens could carry the translations to the entire audience, in what Nat Merrill was calling SurRound Titles. First to enjoy the fun of supertitles was the double bill of Leoncavallo's *I Pagliacci* and Puccini's *Gianni Schicchi*, and Bizet's *Carmen*. There was irony in commencing usage of the SurRound titles with so accessible a group of operas.

I Pagliacci was to have featured Jon Vickers but a conflict at Covent Garden over rescheduling a revival of Britten's *Peter Grimes* prevented his return. Gianfranco Cecchele was an adequate but not a shining replacement. Cornell MacNeil's first Opera Colorado performance as Tonio was a bravura one, rich in furious drama. Pamela South was the fetching Nedda, and Kevin Anderson was a choice Beppe. However, this production didn't come together, although the chorus and moments of individual singing satisfied. Toni Businger repeated the substance of his *Bohème* Cafè Momus scene, with its vendor carts, this time the carts of the traveling performance company dressed the stage. The effect was flat.

Gianni Schicchi was a different, novel effort. Featuring a host of young Denver singers who impressed with fresh vocalism and stage ability, it delighted the audiences. Stephen West took the lead role with aplomb, commanding the roguish character with his strong baritone, and offered his best acting yet. Among the young local singers were April Gutierrez, a charming Lauretta; Thomas Poole, an able Rinuccio; Catherine Stoltz, Hao Jiang Tian, Marcia Ragonetti, Steven Taylor, Barry Johnson, Ronald Brown, and John Armstrong, together essaying old crones and gnarled old men—all mendacious types—with considerable success. Jean Robertson of the Opera Colorado staff designed a stylish Renaissance bedroom. Janos Acs led the double bill effectively.

Carmen proved a troublesome production. With the Polish Carmen of Stefania Toczyska and the Russian Don Jose of Vladimir Popov, there were bound to be difficulties. There was no artistic unity among any of the principals. None of the leads captivated, though all were adequate. Businger's setting crowded the space with its high steps, and the third act was laughable, with the smugglers peeping out of their trapdoor holes like so many overgrown prairie dogs. Once more *Carmen* displayed the extent of the problems it can offer. So much always depended upon balanced casting of this opera. Not enough thought was given to the difficulties of *Carmen*, which are perhaps as insurmountable as those of any opera. Jacques Delacote conducted with flair but could not bring the principals into harmony with each other.

The seventh season, 1989, was supposed to include *La Traviata* and Rossini's *La Cenerentola*, but before much time was up, an all-Verdi bill, with *Falstaff* replacing the *Cenerentola*, had been substituted. This came about when Cornell MacNeil responded positively to the idea that he sing Falstaff, which he had not done for many years. He moved to Denver to restudy the role with Louise Sherman, but presently developed health problems, so he was obliged to move down and out from Opera Colorado. Giampiero Mastromei was his replacement, a fit Falstaff, often infectious and funny, but not yet ready for a major role. The young lovers, sung by Deborah Cole and Kevin Anderson, all but stole the show with the lyric appeal of their singing. Anthony Laciura and John Armstrong as the two low-comics, Bardolph and Pistol, were singularly deft in their boisterous play.

Pamela South was a beauteous, vocally beguiling Alice, while Marcia Ragonetti was a further delight as Meg Page, with Patricia Spence as a fanny-waving Mistress Quickly but not the "bassa buffa" the part demands. Brent Ellis did Ford's big aria well but otherwise seemed uninvolved. Anton Coppola drew animated, lusty playing from the Denver Symphony and in the final fugato the chorus triumphed. Jean Robertson's designs were uncommonly attractive, and the applause for the oak tree in the final scene was deserved.

The hit of the season and one of the very best of Opera Colorado's productions was *La Traviata*. In its freshly minted, affecting performance, it was a personal success for Merrill and for Diana Soviero, for together they achieved the miracle that opera can be—a touching, intimate experience. In 1984's *Turandot*, Soviero had been an affecting Liu, but here she was a full-fledged artist at the peak of her form, and Denver seemed to be the first to recognize this. She was surrounded by designer Jean Robertson in a delectable evocation of the Paris demi-monde, but she was never overwhelmed with excessive supernumeraries or distracting actions.

In a production that views Violetta with understatement there is not much for the baritone essaying Germont père. Sherrill Milnes took this to his advantage and became a figure of granitic force gradually rising out of his prejudices to see Violetta's sorrow. Marc Shulgold of the Rocky Mountain News wrote of Milnes's characterization as of "unwavering strength and repressed emotion." Walter MacNeil, son of baritone Cornell MacNeil, had sung Cassio in the first season's *Otello* and now, as Alfredo, he was doing a Verdi lead.

He gave a youthful, romantic lift to his singing. There was on occasion a scary pushing for a large sound that blunted the refinement of most of his work. He had already been announced for the 1990 *Faust*.

Despite the presence of Milnes and Soviero this was in no way merely a star vehicle. The company of singers Merrill and Louise Sherman had been fostering was beginning to shine. With singers like Anthony Laciura, Hao-Jiang Tian, and Steven Taylor, there was a solid core of performers.

Janos Acs returned for his third season, leading the Denver Symphony Orchestra in what would be its final appearance in that guise, for in October 1989 the DSO became the Colorado Symphony Orchestra. Acs was by now wholly familiar with the ensemble, the problems of opera-in-the-round, and he delivered an abundantly sensual performance.

With *La Traviata* it seemed Opera Colorado had mastered the unnerving budgetary problems and all their deleterious impacts. Now, creative productions with a flair which commanded the potential of Boettcher were at hand. Merrill no longer needed to cram multitudes of chorus and supers on stage. Again the future seemed without limit. There was still red ink but it was not of catastrophic dimensions.

Having survived seven seasons, Merrill was anxious to test Denver's ability to absorb an increase in the number of productions Opera Colorado could offer. Over the past several years there had been talk of developing a five-year plan which would attract foundations and other sources of support that would enable the company to contract the required singers.

In early April 1989, in a pre-season fundraiser chat with the radio station KVOD's Charley Samson and Opera Colorado's Charles Schneider, Merrill talked about the future and dropped some hints of what was to come in the next five years. He saw no probability of Alban Berg's *Lulu* or *Wozzeck* being done. "It is not pleasant to be alone in Boettcher," he added. *Les Pecheurs des Perles* "would not succeed in Boettcher Concert Hall." *Madama Butterfly* "cries out for Japanese houses and screens. The same thing applies to *Rigoletto*. *Figaro* has problems," Merrill continued, "because in the second act you have to have a locked room, a closet that only has an entrance into that room, and someone has to jump out a window—into the orchestra pit, I suppose. I have difficulty in finding a way to do this at Boettcher, and similar problems in doing the *Barber*." Merrill told Samson there was a consensus that such singers as Placido Domingo, Eva Marton, Nancy Gustafson, Kevin Langan, and Stephen West should return. Merrill also agreed that Alfredo Kraus, Jose Carreras, Jose Van Dam, and Nicolai Gedda should come. Evidence of many hours of negotiating was divulged in Merrill's five-year plan.

Curlew River, one of Benjamin Britten's four "church operas," was to be done in February 1990. In April *Faust* was set with Kevin Langan doing his first Mephistopheles, the Australian soprano Angela Dunning in her American debut as Marguerite, Walter MacNeil as Faust, and Erich Parce as Valentin. Ming Cho Lee was to do his first Opera Colorado sets, and there would be lots of lusty choral singing. *Faust* would be paired with Verdi's *Un Ballo in Maschera*, cast with cosmopolitan flair. The English soprano Josephine Barstow had long been on the list of singers he wished to bring to Opera Colorado. Finally she would come as Amelia. The Romanian tenor Vasile Moldoveanu was to be Ricardo.

A Chinese baritone, Yalun Zhang, had come to Boulder from Beijing to study with Barbara Doscher at the University of Colorado. In Beijing he had sung leads with the Central Opera Company. When Merrill and Louise Sherman heard him they were bowled over by the appeal of his powerful baritone. Although he had done a part in Robert Ward's *Crucible* in a student performance at the University of Colorado he made his professional American debut as Renato.

Others to be involved were Harolyn Blackwell, a fast-rising coloratura then at The Met, as Oscar, and Isola Jones, long at The

Met as Ulrica. Jean Robertson designed the sets for T*he Masked Ball*, as it was being called, and Janos Acs would conduct.

Plans for the 1991 season called for two operas new to the repertory, *Don Carlo* and *The Elixir of Love*. The Verdi cast included Vyachaslov Polozov, Stefka Estatieva, Sharon Graham, Justino Diaz, a member of Merrill's 1963 celebrated Central City *Don Giovanni* cast, Allan Monk, and Dimitri Kavrakos, another of Merrill's favored international casts. The Donizetti plans included Denes Gulyas, Brian Schexnayder, and Stephen West.

Adjacent to the Boettcher Concert Hall, work was under way to create the Temple Hoyne Buell Theatre, a 2,800 seat proscenium theater. Opera Colorado was a major participant in a series of gala opening performances. It planned to present *Otello*, this time with Placido Domingo, Justino Diaz, and Ilona Tokady. Although the opera had figured as the opening opera in 1983, this was to be a new production in a proscenium hall. As a 10th anniversary festivity there would be a special concert in the spring at Boettcher Concert Hall.

The first Wagner from Opera Colorado was to be Die *Meistersinger von Nurnburg*, set to open the 1992 regular spring season, with Stephen West as Hans Sachs. West had done this role to great acclaim at the Seattle Opera during one of several years when he had been encouraged to seek major roles away from Opera Colorado. Among other roles, he had done Don Giovanni for Opera Pacific and Gianni Schicchi for a Met school-touring company. Others in this production would be Ashley Putnam and Eric Halfvarson. Richard Bruner was another protegè being given the major role of Walther von Stolzing. He had been Pong in the 1984 *Turandot* and Spoletta in *Tosca*, and was now thought to be ready for this great role. A revival of *La Bohème* with Diana Soviero, David Malis, Pamela South, and Kevin Langan was set.

Plans for the 1992-93 season included *Rigoletto* at the new Buell Theatre with Yalun Zhang in the lead. Hei Kyung Hong, the Liu of the opening *Turandot*, and now a featured coloratura at The Met, was set for Gilda. Preceding the spring season at Boettcher a double bill of *Gianni Schicchi*, with Stephen West repeating his successful 1988 role, and *Cavalleria Rusticana* with Stefka Estatieva, Vasile Moldoveanu, and Marcia Ragonetti, was to be done at the Buell. The regular spring season pencilled in *Macbeth* with Sherrill Milnes, Josephine Barstow, and Hao Jiang Tian, along with still another opera new to the repertory, Mozart's *The Marriage of Figaro* with Martile Rowland, Harolyn Blackwell, Yalun Zhang, and Stephen West. Presumably Merrill had satisfied himself he could master the staging problems of Act II.

In the 1993-94 season, Merrill made plans for a November production of *Madama Butterfly* with Diana Soviero. The February production of Rossini's *The Barber of Seville* included Ruth Ann Swenson, Pablo Elvira, and Stephen West. For *Der Rosenkavalier,* a dream cast of Ashley Putnam, Susan Quittmeyer, Eric Halfvarson, Harolyn Blackwell and Stephen West was promised. A revival of *La Traviata* with Diana Soviero, Sherrill Milnes, and Walter MacNeil was set as a winning attraction.

This repertory included many of Merrill's favorite operas, operas he had done in memorable fashion at The Met and at Central City, and they would draw on his most creative inspirations. By now certain theatrical devices to bring the action closer to the audience were in danger of becoming cliches. Large groups of singers worked their way from the theater aisles across bridges to the stage. Clouds of smoke would at some point fill the Boettcher vastness. Occasional miscalculations of movement contorted singers, as excessive numbers of singers and supers crowded the stage. The tendency to bring back once admired singers who had gone slack in musical disciplines was detected. Too many singers from Eastern Europe brought sloppy vocalism which pointed up the superiority of the best-trained American singers.

However much Merrill may have wished to have returns by Placido Domingo, Aprile Millo, and Nancy Gustafson, there was increasing use of singers who had grown up along with Opera Colorado including Pamela South, Sheryl Woods, Stephen West, Kevin Langan, Yalun Zhang, and Marcia Ragonetti. The ongoing bugaboo of opera, and not just at Opera Colorado, was the difficulty of holding firm to announced casts. Planning far in advance did not protect contracts. A month prior to the opening of *The Masked Ball*, Vasile Moldoveanu called in to report his indisposition. Bulgarian tenor Zwetan Michailow replaced Moldoveanu as the Swedish king. Also Harolyn Blackwell, having back problems, would be replaced as Oscar by Sally Wolf, wife of Kevin Langan, and a frequent performer at Santa Fe. The *Faust* cast remained intact.

Disclosure of these future plans almost immediately preceded the tradition-breaking performances in 1990 at St. Paul's Lutheran Church of Britten's *Curlew River*, one of the composer's several "church operas." These works of suitably religious subject were designed for simple performance within a church. *Curlew River* required four principals: a tenor to portray a madwoman, made desperate by the loss of her son; an Abbott, a Ferryman, and a Traveler, all the leads emerging from a group of medieval monks who enter in procession to perform a ritual of faith. Britten's music requires seven instruments, including organ. The production was in the Japanese Noh tradition in its staging, and costuming was likewise minimal. It thus appealed to a budget-conscious board. It also expanded Opera Colorado's repertory in a significant direction.

There was a riveting performance at the opera's dramatic center by Douglas Perry, who had sung featured roles in seventeen operas in Santa Fe, where he started out as apprentice. Hao-Jiang Tian distinguished himself as the Abbott, his bass enriched by experience. Scott Root was an impressive Ferryman and James Bobick showed a promising, youthful baritone.

The medieval tone of the music was eloquently established by conductor David Shaw, a Britten veteran who had led the London premiere of *Albert Herring*. The occasion marked his American conducting debut. Though the church acoustics were quite satisfactory, the flat main floor seating broke the sight lines. There were plans for *The Prodigal Son*, another in this series for 1991, to be followed in 1992 by *The Burning Fiery Furnace*, at which point all three operas would be done in repertory. Opera Colorado would have been the only opera house to have done the three.

Faust turned out surprisingly to be a strong, traditional production with an aura of freshness about its familiar lines. The lion's share of the performance was Kevin Langan doing his initial Mephistopheles and luxuriating in the rich opportunity to expand his repertory. Walter MacNeil seemed barely visible as Faust with strain in some of his singing and insufficient focus on his acting. Angela Dunning came for Marguerite, a pretty and convincing portrayal, not brilliant but quite satisfying. Erich Parce was an exemplary Valentin, bold in acting and singing. Marcia Ragonetti was a vibrant Siebel and Patricia Spence's robust mezzo enriched her Marthe. Anton Guadagno brought discriminating energy to his conducting. The overhanging gargoyles in Ming Cho Lee's design brought drama to the stage although for some in the audience design details in the first act scene obliterated clear viewing.

The exciting realization of Verdi's *A Masked Ball* made this a strong season. Merrill recognized that amidst the splendor of the scene this is a tragedy of male arrogance and female passiveness, and his casting gave thrust to this thought. Yalun Zhang made a significant professional debut as Renato, with fine presence and an oak-strong baritone. His riveting presence and the rich sound of his singing compensated for the need for work on enunciation, but his career seemed well-launched with this performance,

Josephine Barstow's Amelia blended forceful singing with lovely soft tones, although several times in stress she missed high notes. Tenor Zwetan Michailov substituting for the ailing Vasile Moldoveanu as Gustavo III had sung in the "Rousse Opera" in Belgrade before going to Saarbrucken. He tended to squeeze out his notes as well as hurry rapid passages, but mostly he landed on the correct notes. His smug demeanor did not help, nor did his toothy grin at the conclusion of each aria. There was distinct pleasure in Sally Wolf's exuberant Oscar, a role she learned only after reporting to Denver for rehearsals. No one missed Harolyn Blackwell. Isola Jones was a harsh, loud Ulrica but Jean Robertson's design for her den, rigged ropes surrounding her in tent-like form, was compelling. Hao-Jiang Tian's Sam had vocal might and Kevin Langan's kid brother David was a modest-voiced Tom. Three Denver area singers, Steven Taylor, Don Renner, and Dan Vines, showed the reliability that led Merrill to use them in small roles. Although Merrill favored cosmopolitan casts, he never neglected local singers.

Fund-raising never ceased. A series of private parties raised $30,000. A Gala Grand Opening of Saks Fifth Avenue in its new Cherry Creek Shopping Center locale, with Martile Rowland and Yalun Zhang raised more. The Bravo! Ball raised $126,000. Approximately $230,000 was raised by the Opera Colorado Guild. A raffle for a Mercedes raised $137,000.

Opera Colorado's ninth season, 1990-91, was a large one which got off to a big start at the end of October with a well-attended recital by Samuel Ramey.

Britten's *The Burning Fiery Furnace* riveted audiences in St. Paul's Church for four performances in February. Again the sightlines prevented satisfactory viewing of what was too good a performance for the improvised theater. Like *Curlew River* it was staged as ritual by hooded monks who proceed to tell of Nebuchadnezzar and the three Hebrews, Shadrack, Meshak, and Abednigo, who deny the golden Babylonian god whereupon they are thrown into the furnace, to emerge whole in the company of an angel.

Douglas Perry returned with his striking presence and voice to portray the king, while Hao-Jiang Tian, baritone James Bobick, and tenor Curt Peterson comprised a strong trio of Hebrews. Scott Root and Steven Taylor were others in the cast. These Britten operas were enthusiastically received by capacity audiences. Merrrill admirably extended the repertory with Britten's operas.

In no time at all, the spring productions, *Don Carlo* and *The Elixir of Love* were at hand. There was a smoldering intensity in *Don Carlo* which made the somewhat sprawling work enthralling. Merrill concentrated on personal relationships and rejected spectacle for spectacle's sake. The remarkable assemblage of singers from everywhere gave it power. There was the Russian Carlo, tenor Vyacheslav Polozov; a Bulgarian Elisabetta, Stefka Estatieva; a Chinese Rodrigo, Yalun Zhang; a Puerto Rican Philip, Justino Diaz; a Greek Inquisitor, Dimitri Kavrakos, and an American Eboli, Sharon Graham, all under the leadership of Hungarian Janos Acs. The one cast change had been the substitution of Yalun Zhang for Allan Monk. The strength of ensemble achieved by this disparate cast was remarkable, and supported Merrill's idea of international casts. The Colorado Symphony brought a splendid sonority to its playing.

After the understatement of *Don Carlo*, it was dismaying to come to the overloaded antics of *The Elixir of Love*. This lovely little work was turned into a lavish wedding cake of excessive population in overdone action. To moderate the excess, there was Sheryl Woods in her Opera Colorado debut, exuding classic vocal purity, musical skills, and a glowing presence as Adina. Tonio di Paolo substituted for a late-canceling Denes Gulyas. At Central City in 1983 di Paolo had done a charming Nemorino but now he was so busy prowling the stage that he could not concentrate on his singing. Even his "Una fortiva lagrima" failed to make the grade. Allan Monk was moved from the Verdi for an ingratiating Belcore. Stephen West was a victim of Merrill's indulgent stage business as Dr. Dulcamara, mugging his way onto stage aboard a Rube Goldberg contraption complete with bells and whistles to delight an easily amused audience. West did handle his patter song smartly and charmed in a duet with soprano Woods.

Richard Buckley, son of Emerson Buckley, who had conducted Merrill's joyous O'Hearn-designed 1961 Central City production, led vigorously but without refinement. Toni Businger was responsible for the heavy rolling stage pieces which cluttered the stage, destroying the light charm which is what this work is all about. Martin Fredman devised the distracting dance interludes.

Almost immediately there was bad news. Placido Domingo had canceled his *Otello*, planned as the company's inaugural offering at the new Buell Theatre. Scheduling conflicts created by the requirements for setting up the mechanics of *The Phantom of the Opera* meant that *Otello* had to be moved up. On hearing this news, Justino Diaz canceled as Iago.

In an interview with the Denver Post's Jeff Bradley, Merrill told him "We think we're disgustingly healthy. Doing opera in Boettcher has been a real eye-opener for everybody. I'm curious to see people's reaction to opera on a conventional stage. Most of our audience haven't seen opera anywhere but in the round. When somebody from Denver called and said 'let's see if we can establish an international opera company here,' I said let's try, and then I fell in love with Boettcher Hall. I had a hunch that if one could do opera-in-the-round—and I had never done one and had never seen one—it could be unique." Merrill continued his musings, "I think if you do opera well, it's always popular. Of course, it's difficult to do it well, and sometimes you can do it badly and get away with it. We've been guilty of that once or twice."

Merrill talked to Bradley about cancellations. "We have the same problem all other opera companies have with leading singers. The fees they charge in Europe are three or four times what we can afford. A normal fee for a baritone in Europe might be $35,000 an evening. Here it's about one-quarter of that."

On the same day an interview with Merrill by Marc Shulgold appeared in the Rocky Mountain News. To Shulgold, Merrill boasted that "We've been in the black for the past eight years, and now, one year earlier than expected, the $1 million debt has been retired." He reflected on the decision to come to Denver. "I was willing to come to Denver. I'd been wanting to leave The Met. I was bored to death—I guess I was having a mid-life crisis. When I arrived here I made it clear that we needed to do something unique. At that time I needed a commitment to do something I didn't know I could do. I wanted a challenge. The old money was against us, so we went for the new money. It took about five years before the theater could work for us rather than our being at the mercy of the theater." Of the forthcoming *Otello* he observed "It's fun to work in a proscenium again—but it's more fun in the round."

Of the five-year plan, he told Shulgold, "I figured someone had to make a statement—'we'll be here.' My first obligation is to stay in business, and my second is to turn people on, to be inventive. In Denver, opera is still a strange, forbidding territory for many people. It will take a while to change."

Reverting to traditional proscenium staging was a challenge after establishing the sense of audience involvement achieved at Boettcher. For the November 1992 *Otello*, Robert O'Hearn devised a massive, rock-hewn wall against which Ray Duffen's lavish costuming was striking. But the conventional theater arrangement put most of the audience at a great distance from the stage, a distance all the more annoying because at Boettcher audiences were accustomed to being close in.

The problems were not only on stage but also in the theater which had been planned specifically for large touring Broadway shows which rely on amplification. When singers were at front stage, voices came through with adequate sound, but as they moved to stage rear, voices became progressively muffled. There were problems in the pit where the brasses overpowered strings. On their own, the strings came over reasonably well. But with a loud, crude Romanian tenor named Corneliu Murgu making a futile endeavor to replace Domingo, Verdi's opera did not work. Murgu had loud notes but no sense of musical line, and certainly no idea of musical nuance. As Desdemona, Fiamma Izzo d'Amico began with a reedy, unsteady soprano which somehow gained in strength for the requisite power of the final act. Allan Monk as Iago pulled the threads of his web of deceit in a fine subtle performance, never overtly villainous but strongly concentrated and admirably sung.

There was a gratifying Cassio by Mark Calkins, lamplighter in the 1987 *Manon Lescaut*, on his way up, while Julie Simson was wholly effective as Emelia. The Opera Colorado chorus under Louise Sherman made its customary splash, and under Janos Acs, the Colorado Symphony did its best in trying circumstances. Nevertheless, the *Otello* production was fated to go flat. The difference between attendance for a Domingo *Otello* and a Murgo *Otello* was that between a rousing triumph and a grave disappointment.

This was not one of Opera Colorado's glory times. And it put a question on the *Madama Butterfly*, *Barber* and *Rigoletto* planned for the Buell. The 2,800 seats in the Buell were not so many more than Boettcher's 2,700 but it was said that the production lost $15,000. Too many tickets had been given away so that there would be a respectable audience opening night. In every way it was, just as Merrill had said, "more fun in the round."

In view of this loss, and with uncertain prospects for *Die Meistersinger*, the three Britten church operas as well as the 10th anniversary concert were deferred. The costs of the three operas were simply too great, and *Rigoletto* at the Buell was another question mark.

Merrill concentrated on the Wagner and Thomas Holliday, who now served as assistant to Merrill, and had directed operas at the Hamburg State Theater and at Klagenfurt, directed the revival of *La Bohème*. The *Bohème* cast was led by Vasile Moldoveanu and Fiamma Izzo D'Amico with Pamela South, Erich Parce, Kevin Langan, Scott Root, upped to his first major role as Schaunard, and Steven Taylor as Benoit. Douglas Perry was back as Alcindoro, with Don Renner as Parpignol. Janos Acs conducted.

Merrill had been preparing for *Die Meistersinger von Nurnburg* for several years. At The Met it had been one of Merrill's most successful productions. As a celebration of ten years of Opera Colorado, it won the highest standards he could achieve. *Die Meistersinger* was that most remarkable of Wagner productions, an all-American one. The exception was in the pit. With uncanny luck, Merrill had latched onto Alexander Sander, an Austrian conductor of vast experience and schooling, a protegè of Karl Bohm. Merrill believed it to be crucial to the success of the production to have a conductor thoroughly ingrained with the Wagnerian tradition. Sander was ideal for the job.

There were problems, Sander told a symposium on the opera late in its run. "It is the most difficult conducting in my life," he said, of leading the performances at Boettcher. He could not hear singers when their heads were turned and could not hear the parts of the chorus at the end of Act II. He was uncertain about Wagner opera at Boettcher but had enjoyed the theater of *La Bohème*. At this symposium, Merrill told how he treated Act I as a prologue to the essence of the opera, the second and third acts. He also gave out a secret of movement. Singers must always turn to their right. He acknowledged that a director cannot radically change his approach to a work he has done in another medium. There were 19 minutes of cuts in the 12 deletions that were made, cuts made everywhere in Europe except at Bayreuth. Sander praised the Colorado Symphony for picking up the orchestral style of the opera quickly, and also praised the American singers.

Stephen West led the cast as Hans Sachs, the longest role in the Wagner repertory, a role he had done at the Seattle Opera with the clear approval of The New Yorker's Andrew Porter. West had been singing Wagner less than five years. Intense study and reflection gave him authority. Merrill had been nurturing West since Opera Colorado began and now both were ready for Hans Sachs. West's outgoing personality and his superbly empowered bass-baritone provided a solid base for building a character of wit and generosity. In his two major arias, West showed a sensitivity to text that resulted in a hallowed kind of communication. He was noble without being pompous, amiable without being a sap.

Richard Brunner was thought to be ready for Walther. He had made a debut at the Vienna Staatsoper in the 1991-92 season, and at Bayreuth sang the small role of Walther in *Tannhauser*. This might be a foot in the door. His sweet tenor had some heft in it but not much could be said for his bland presence. There was an astonishingly professional performance of David by young Curt Peterson who managed to blend fresh acting and buoyant singing to identify with this young apprentice. He is David, and could make a career of doing this role. Ashley Putnam was a lovely Eva, bringing the heroine to fervent life. Her natural beauty, the sympathy she brought to the role, and the strength of her soprano made hers a more than usually effective portrayal.

Julian Patrick, that wonderfully versatile singing actor, showed a comic sense which shaped Beckmesser into a figure of propriety so extreme that it was absurd and funny. His singing was true and pointed with a strong satirical edge. His natural flair for musical theater made his work a deep pleasure. Patrick had been in and out of Denver for many years. In 1970 he had done a noble John Proctor in *The Crucible* for Denver Lyric Opera and in the following year a rascally Malatesta in *Don Pasquale*. At Seattle in 1969 he had created the role of George in Carlisle Floyd's *Of Mice and Men*, which he then recreated at Central City in 1970. Now he was making a specialty of Beckmesser. In 1988 he made his Met debut as Alberich in *Das Rheingold*. The following year he returned to The Met for another Alberich, doing the same character in *Siegfried* and *Gotterdammerung*.

As Pogner, Eric Halfvarson enriched the production with the sonority of his bass baritone. There were other stalwart Mastersingers by such Opera Colorado regulars as Hao Jiang Tian, who also did the night watchman, Don Renner, Dan Vines, Scott Root, Steven Taylor, and Thomas Poole. As replacement for Partricia Spence, Julie Simson was a reliable Magdalena.

Merrill's direction worked for intimacy among the personages of old Nuremburg, and the grace of movement devised for the singers brought the audience into a vanished, picturesque world. Designer Toni Businger created this world with such details as the ornate crest of a church, a magnificent tower in the square, based on an actual Nuremburg tower, signs hung high denoting the various town crafts, which were adorned with flowers for the final scene. This scene was a triumphant blend of music, color, and movement, with processions and hailing multitudes of chorus and dancers, a festive occasion that symbolized the achievement of ten years of opera on a scale unprecedented in Denver.

In its foray into the Wagner repertory, Opera Colorado had been successful beyond its dreams. Approximately 150 seats remained unsold for the opening. For the second performance 2,400 seats were sold, 300 unsold. The cost of mounting so big a production was high, particularly for a five-plus hour opera. The orchestra was paid on the basis of two services for each performance, which pushed the cost high.

It may have been that the waves created by the gigantic vessel of Wagner's opera capsized Puccini's evergreen but fragile *Bohème*. Its pallid Mimi was Fiamma Izzo d'Amico who was in advanced state of pregnancy. Vasile Moldoveanu was unwell and far below his usual fine standards as Rodolfo. It was left to reliables like Pamela South, Erich Parce, and Kevin Langan to carry the performance. As subsidiary figures, no matter how skilled their performances, a focus on a convincing Mimi and Rodolfo was required.

At the end of the first decade Merrill could look back to an extraordinary opening of *Otello* and *La Bohème* with stars of magnitude in imposing productions and beyond that to the splendors of the second season with *Turandot* and *The Tales of Hoffman*, which gave emphasis to the power of the chorus Louise Sherman had developed. In the ten years there had been a sumptuous *Aida*, a svelte *Don Giovanni*, a finely crafted *Traviata*, an enthralling *Don Carlo*, and perhaps the grandest of all, Wagner's *Die Meistersinger von Nurnburg*. Audiences relished these and other productions. For Denver it was cause for just pride. The determination to give Denver exciting, authentic opera had been paramount to Merrill's planning. His unquenched sense of purpose brought a broad range of opera to Denver both on an artistic and professional level.

Exotic and Irrational   163

'Ballo' grips audience in its tension

River of Faith

Opera Colorado will tackle Britten's enigmatic play that turns into religious lesson

Opera Colorado's 'Don Carlo' a not-to-be-missed production

Toni Businger's sets for "Die Meistersinger von Nürnberg"

Hans Sachs workshop.

The Church

Opera Colorado Begins a Second Decade

For a corps of Denver opera-lovers, proscenium opera at the Buell Theatre was a godsend. For musical as well as visual reasons their strong preference was for opera with a scenic focus and a vibrant sound. Merrill believed Opera Colorado in-the-round had been unique but he needed to attend to supporters of traditional operatic presentation. The Buell, with its 2,800 seats, was to become more and more an essential of the seasons, despite its uneasy acoustics and unpopularity with audiences because of seating arrangements.

In late July 1992, Merrill announced a change for the upcoming eleventh season. *Die Meistersinger* had left a debt of $180,000, and the threat of losing more with an unfamiliar *Macbeth* was enough to remove it from the schedule. There had even been talk of canceling the scheduled *Rigoletto* but Merrill was adamant about doing this popular Verdi tragedy, which he would direct. It promised to be a draw. "The board felt we have to pay...our debts as soon as possible. We've been in the black for some years now and we will only have one year out, I assure you." In the spring, at Boettcher, Julius Rudel would conduct Merrill's production of *The Marriage of Figaro*.

Anton Guadagno would conduct Thomas Halliday's production of *The Barber of Seville*.

When *Rigoletto* was done at the Buell in November 1993, Merrill took a leap of faith in assigning the challenging lead role to Yalun Zhang, the Chinese baritone who had been a well-received Renato in *A Masked Ball* as well as Rodrigo in Don Carlo. Zhang coached with Cornell MacNeil for this great role, shortly after winning the coveted Pavarotti International Voice Competition. In the Denver Post, Jeff Bradley wrote that "Unless I'm mistaken, we saw the start of a major operatic career; Denver baritone Yalun Zhang was simply sensational in the title role of Rigoletto." Zhang, strong both in voice and in character, was surrounded with a solid cast. Cheryl Parrish brought a sweet, accurate soprano but not many flights of imagination to the role of Gilda. Swetan Michailov from Bulgaria was back as the Duke with some good work yet lacking consistency. Alfredo Silipigni led a conventional performance without much orchestral dash. The placement of microphones at the stage front was also good news in resolving acoustical problems at Buell.

With two operas from plays by Beaumarchais, a celebratory mood stirred the air. An airy, spirited *Marriage* was a plus, a delight led by maestro Rudel to scintillating results, and Merrill directed for lightness and subtlety. Stephen West was a solid Figaro, not yet at home with Mozart as he had been with Wagner. Erich Parce was a convincingly suave Count. Sheryl Woods was an endearing Susanna. Pamela South made the most of "Dove Sono" but her voice at times had an unaccustomed edge. Marcia Ragonetti was smart and funny as Cherubino, giving radiance to her arias. All subsidiary roles were well done. Merrill had indeed discovered how to resolve what he had earlier considered unsolvable problems at Boettcher for this opera.

The *Barber* came as close to disaster as any Opera Colorado production in all its years. Lackluster performances by Pablo Elvira as Figaro and by Mimi Lerner as Rosina dulled the edges. Curt Peterson was a pleasing exception to the rule as Almaviva and

Donald Sherrill was an amusing Bartolo. Ara Barberian as Don Basilio clowned excessively in Thomas Holliday's overwrought attempts to direct comedy. There was zestless playing by the Colorado Symphony let by Anton Guadagno. It was a grim experience.

At the end of February 1994, *Madama Butterfly* arrived at the Buell with Elizabeth Holleque as Cio-Cio-San, directed by Merrill and conducted by Janos Acs. Holleque ranged from quite accomplished to tentative. She did not yet have the Cio-Cio-San character down. Rick Moon was adequate as Pinkerton, but the real pleasure was hearing the authority of Richard Stillwell's Sharpless. Katherine Hegierski was a surprisingly effective Suzuki. Another triumph was that of Douglas Perry as Goro. There was fine orchestral playing by the orchestra under Acs.

The bold undertaking of the great Strauss comedy, *Der Rosenkavalier*, with all its numerous roles and considerable length, was successfully carried out at the end of April 1994. Merrill assembled a strong cast with Ashley Putnam, an Opera Colorado favorite, as the Marschallin, another favorite, Stephen West, in his first Baron Ochs, newcomer Gwendolyn Jones as Octavian, and Cheryl Parrish as Sophie. Alexander Sander who had led *Die Meistersinger* with such authority, returned for this demanding work. Everything seemed posted for the successful production it turned out to be. In the Rocky Mountain News, Marc Shulgold wrote that "one could hardly imagine a more perfect Marschallin than Ashley Putnam who sang and acted on Saturday evening with impeccable purity and understanding" while Jeff Bradley in the Denver Post praised her for having "deepened her interpretation and gained in vocal assurance" since hearing her in the role at the Santa Fe Opera.

Gwendolyn Jones was quite believable as Octavian, singing with luster and acting with energy and poise. Stephen West was more suited to Baron Ochs than to Mozart, and he gave every indication of becoming a masterful Ochs; a great-humored buffoon and still an aristocrat. Cheryl Parrish brought youthful authority to Sophie with gleaming top notes. In the huge cast, Peter Strummer sang and acted with his usual zest while Marcia Ragonetti was strongly in character as Annina. Thomas Poole was the Italian Tenor, musical although slightly strained. Sander led the Colorado Symphony in sumptuous playing.

Flawed by the same kind of overwrought action that destroyed the *Barber*, Thomas Holliday's production of *Lucia di Lammermoor* could not mesh the intense drama of the work. Jean Robertson's rocky landscape was a further irritation. Sally Wolf's Lucia had ardent moments but in sum was ineffectual. Yalun Zhang was a venomous and powerful Enrico and reliable Kevin Langan was a fine Raimondo. Patrick Denniston's Edgardo was not badly sung but failed to energize the role. Janos Acs led the orchestra in what for him was a perfunctory reading.

Lucia was Holliday's final directing for Opera Colorado. He submitted his resignation as Assistant to the General Director in April, immediately prior to the opening of *Lucia*, to be effective June 1. His resignation was announced immediately preceding the opening of *Der Rosenkavalier*. Jeff Bradley reported in the Denver Post that a letter circulated to friends disclosed matters coming to a head in a dispute with Merrill over English surtitles for *Der Rosenkavalier*. Merrill told Bradley that "I don't think that's [the surtitles] what it really was about—it was perhaps a contributing factor. I think Tom felt he wanted to do more than he was able to do here. He's done a wonderful job in our puppet operas and education programs, and he's had a chance to direct three operas which is good. Tom has decided to pursue some other interests. There wasn't enough directing for him here, I think." However, Holliday would continue later with Opera Colorado, directing the Joseph and Loretta Law Center for young artists.

At the end of May Merrill disclosed to Marc Shulgold some dismaying financial figures. Although *Butterfly* had been a sell-out at the Buell, *Der Rosenkavalier* had not done well and sold 7,790 tickets at 76% of capacity. *Lucia* was nearly as much of a disappointment with 80% of capacity sold. Risk was telling Opera Colorado to stick with the familiar. "Another risky season could put us on the brink," Merrill told Shulgold, but that's always been true. Two bad years and we're on the ropes." Art versus economics was, as always, lurking on the fringes of opera production. That was why *Macbeth* was replaced by tried and true *Aida*. By now Merrill had learned to be guarded in his public announcements of future plans. "There's no point in announcing the specifics because singers drop out, occasionally forcing repertory changes."

By 1995, thanks to Joseph and Loretta Law of Hong Kong, parents of long-time supporter Dennis Law, Merrill had the young artists program he had always thought to be a key element of the opera company. This endowment funded schooling for eleven young artists.

In February 1995, *Albert Herring* was staged by Merrill at the Shwayder Theater with musical direction by Thomas Cockrell, then assistant conductor of the Colorado Symphony, which provided thorough musical preparation to match the stylish performance directed by Merrill. A number of highly promising young singers participated. Daniel Marcy was a standout as Albert, while Elizabeth Bryan was a proud Lady Billows, and Julianne Best a very pleasing Miss Wordsworth. Marcia Ragonetti used her practiced stage experience to present a fine Nancy, while Bret Howsden, Douglas Biggs, and Richard Pearson filled other roles.

In early March, *Tosca* was on stage at the Buell, with Elizabeth Holleque as Floria Tosca, Cesar Hernandez as Cavaradossi, Justino Diaz as Scarpia, Yalun Zhang as Angelotti, and Steven Taylor as the Sacristan. Jeff Bradley thought it was "something to cheer about." He praised Holleque for turning the central role into "a fascinating, multilayered personality." Diaz's robust baritone and suave acting drew praise, and the smooth vocal production of tenor Hernandez promised a strong future for him. Janos Acs was as always authoritative. This production came close to selling out, showing that indeed there was an audience for proscenium opera.

A lavish re-staging of *Aida* by Bodo Igesz at Boettcher in late April lacked the dramatic impact of Merrill's earlier outing. The old problem of chemistry among principals prevailed. Gwendolyn Jones was a sumptuous Amneris and Yalun Zhang a powerful Amonasro.

With a pallid Jeanne-Michèle Charbonnet as Aida and a weak Miguel Sanchez Moreno as Rhadames the focus was never sure. Herbert Eckhoff was a strong King, and there was a gaudy triumphal entry scene, choreographed by Cleo Parker Robinson. Janos Acs made the most of Verdi's great score.

In May, what turned out to be the surprise was Rossini's *La Cenerentola*, staged by Merrill on a magic box designed by Jean Robertson. From this box emerged drawers for each of the sisters' rooms, tables, mirrors, a fireplace, setting a disarming tone for an opera which tries to bring fairy-tale lightness to reality. Merrill had technical support to realize his imagination. Best of all was the presence of Richard Boynynge to shape and pace the work in full Rossinian glory. Mika Shigematsu sang her roulades with ease and style, lacking only in a bit of sparkle. Glenn Seibert's lyric tenor was nicely used, never forced, and his acting had appeal. Jozsef Gregor carried on amusingly as Don Magnifico and Marcia Ragonetti and Julianne Best were absurdly comic as the sisters. Earle Patriarco was a polished Dandini, and George Hogan did a neat turn as Alidoro. This was an ingenious and spirited production.

The fourteenth season in 1996 started out ambitiously with *The Marriage of Figaro* presented at the Teikyo Loretto Heights Theater by the Joseph and Loretta Law Artist Center. Casting was promising with Jamie Offenbach as Figaro, Robert Best as Count Almaviva, Julianne Best as Susanna, Elizabeth Wiley as the Countess, Emily Herrera as Barbarina, and Rosemary Ricci as Marcellina. Two performances were well attended, and a well balanced cast made the trek out to Teikyo Loretto Heights worth the effort. Thomas Cockrell was the able conductor.

There was anticipation of Wagner's *The Flying Dutchman* which would be given at the Buell for four performances. There were no big names, none of the singers who had been so closely identified with Opera Colorado. With the superb musical leadership of Klaus Donath and an inspired Merrill, the production was a major triumph. Merrilll borrowed sets from the New Orleans Opera which worked quite well, but it was a directorial accomplishment with the handling of groups and lighting which provided the final excitement. Victor Von Halem, a giant of a bass-baritone, scaled the heights of the Dutchman with elemental power and musicality, and Jeanne-Michèle Charbonnet far surpassed in vocal rapture the previous year's *Aida*. Other roles were well done, with Herbert Eckhoff an impressive Daland. Douglas Biggs, from the Young Artists Center, shone as the Steersman, Timothy Mussard was a capable Eric, and Rosemary Ricci very able as Mary. Of course there was triumphantly powerful choral work prepared by Louise Sherman.

Die Fledermaus played in late April with the popular Robert Orth, a comic Eisenstein, Pamela South as Rosalinda, and Cheryl Parrish as Adele. Micha Hendel directed and Alexander Sander conducted a frothy but forgettable production.

Cosi fan tutte followed with the fine Richard Boynynge back to give elegant shaping to Mozart's ingratiating melodies. There was a fine ensemble quality to the performance, with an admirable new voice in mezzo Leah Creek. Ms. Creek was another promising singer from the Young Artists Center, who in February had won the Met auditions in Denver, and was a sparkling Dorabella. Christine Akre, a winner of the Fourth Annual Pavarotti Competition, effervescent as Fiordiligi. Sheryl Woods returned for a comic Despina and Stephen West was in fine voice for Don Alfonso. Erich Parce was a suave Gugliemo and Glenn Siebert was a pleasing Ferrando. In Merrill's direction there was polish and not too much horseplay. It was a joy to hear the Mozart music dealt with so authoritatively by the Colorado Symphony under Boynynge. In the Rocky Mountain News Shulgold wrote that "Opera Colorado's production... succeeds wonderfully. Visually, this may be the best Opera Colorado show in a decade."

Don Giovanni had been done with such elegance and popular acceptance early in Opera Colorado's history that it seemed natural to try it again in 1997. But with finances looming ominously over its shoulder, it contended with young singers lacking the experience to qualify them as truly Mozartean singers. Kelly Anderson was a promising baritone, Pamela South was an experienced but not ideal

Donna Elvira. Kay Paschal was quite satisfactory as Donna Anna. Stephen Morsheck had the voice but not the manner of Leporello. Conductor Bruno Aprea lacked authority. It was not the special production required of the work.

Faust, on the other hand, was a superb production, splendidly cast and staged in a grand manner. Richard Boynynge was back to lead the Colorado Symphony in the kind of polished, idiomatic playing in which he excels. With Donald Kaasch as an ideally voiced Faust, this Colorado native in his first Opera Colorado performance, displayed the sensitivity and musicality that have marked his career. Victor Von Halem returned for Mephistopheles, a strong, dramatically conceived devil. Maureen O'Flynn was a captivatingly beautiful Marguerite with a lovely lyric soprano. Erich Parce again was the Valentin, making the most of the great aria with his smooth baritone. The Opera Colorado chorus was heard to grand effect. Merrill was in fine form in his directorial duties.

At Boettcher and at Buell, Merrill had conquered challenges in halls basically unsuited for opera. But they were the only venues at hand.

Exotic and Irrational   173

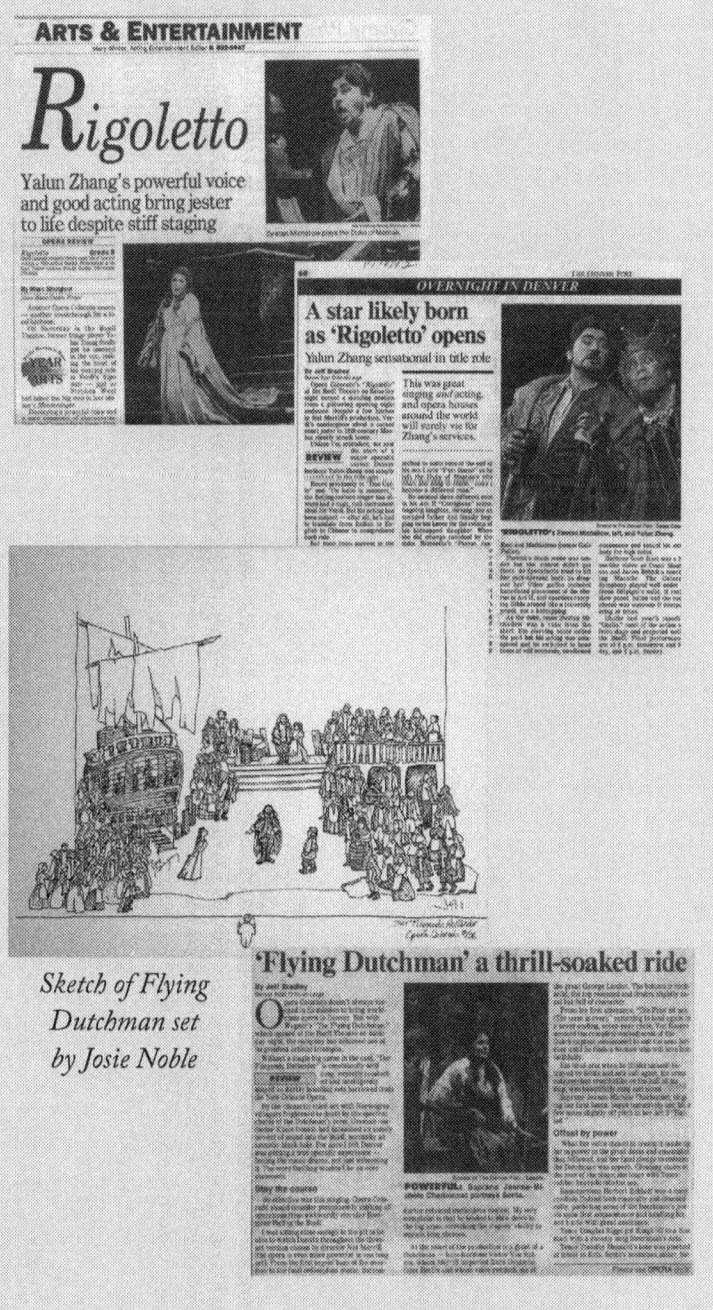

Sketch of Flying Dutchman set by Josie Noble

Seifert Takes the Helm

For more than fourteen years, Louise Sherman had developed a stirring, splendid chorus that was a hallmark of quality. She had been known to be ill with cancer, and her death on February 11, 1998, ten days prior to the opening of *Carmen*, came like the withered flowers in *Faust*. The hopes for the sixteenth season were devastated.

Carmen opened for four performances under Merrill's stage direction at the Buell on February 21. It appeared that Opera Colorado was indeed being tested, for Robynne Redmon, the Carmen of the production, broke her left arm in a rehearsal fall, while Patrick Dennison, the Don Jose, was nearly downed by a viral infection. Somehow Redmon was able to establish Carmen's volatile spirit, finding vocal colors to do this, and Denniston survived his pre-opening problems to deliver an impassioned Don Jose. In Opera News Glenn Giffin praised conductor Christian Badea for "snapping his tempo along. With everyone's attention riveted to the job at hand, a creditable, if restrained, performance resulted."

Ahead were *Salome* and the double bill of *I Pagliacci* and *Gianni Schicchi*. But until March 4, no one knew the extent of drama that would circle about Opera Colorado this season when Nathaniel Merrill's resignation was announced by Stephen Seifert, Opera Colorado Executive Director. Seifert told the press "He has for personal reasons withdrawn from stage-directing *Salome* and resigned his post as artistic director of the company. Everybody can understand given the circumstances of the past several weeks what that entails. This shouldn't be viewed as some kind of huge disruption." Asked why Merrill was leaving in the midseason, Seifert responded, "I don't find it odd in view of all the circumstances. It's stressful enough to do an opera and he's been burdened by an additional blow and did a terrific job under the circumstances. This transition is an inevitable feature of the life of any company. Leadership has to pass at some point to others. The company is prepared to move on with its future in the city of Denver and all of us view that future as very bright."

Seifert had come on the board prior to the 1989 season, and was known as an astute young lawyer. An opera buff, he had become chairman of the board. He was listed in the *I Pagliacci/ Gianni Schicchi/ Salome* program as Executive Director, and he and board chairman Eleanor Caulkins co-signed a statement in that program stating that "Everyone at Opera Colorado who makes the stage come alive on stage each year is very grateful to you our audience and donors for your loyalty and generous support. We're excited and energized by all the new opportunities available to us. Opera Colorado has a brilliant future thanks to the splendid foundation which Nat Merrill and Louise Sherman built. We're confident that you will want as passionately as we do to be a part of Opera Colorado's future."

What indeed was the reason for Merrill's departure? It is easy to imagine that there were problems in managing the company. Financial problems could be suspect and there might be disagreement about repertory—what works would trouble a generally stable financial condition. Was there disagreement about the usage of Boettcher? As the founder of in-the-round opera, Merrill might have been indignant about rumored plans to turn Boettcher into a thrust stage venue, and close out the rear seating. Were determined forces clashing behind the scenes? Was Merrill becoming arbitrary, difficult to deal with? Whatever triggered Merrill's departure is a matter that very likely will not ever be disclosed.

The future loomed uncertain. For a time it seemed a search would be carried out on the national level for a successor but it rapidly became clear there was no time, so Seifert was named to head Opera Colorado.

In the Rocky Mountain News Marc Shulgold wrote an editorial on Nat and Louise. "This amazing couple served tirelessly as the mom and pop of one of Colorado's most important cultural attractions." Shulgold wrote without detail of Merrill's departure raising "questions about unrest within the company. The official silence from the board of directors doesn't instill confidence, either." Shulgold subsequently reported on a talk with Seifert in which Seifert declined to break the board's agreement that it speak with one voice—that of its new executive director.

At the end of March, a month preceding the *Salome* opening, Jeff Bradley wrote in the Denver Post of an extended conversation with Seifert in which he anticipated excitement over a repertory not previously employed, with *The Magic Flute, Macbeth*, and *Romeo and Juliet* forthcoming. There were to be "creative and imaginative approaches" which would "show people a different look and tone and imagination." Gordon Robertson, technical director; Jean Robertson, scenic director; acting music director Ruth "Cissy" Baker, and acting chorus master Micha Hendel were to be involved, along with artistic administrator George Twombly. There would be continuity, Seifert promised. Bradley went on to note that "Merrill was criticized for repertoire, a sometimes abrasive personal style, and his insistence on circular opera in Boettcher Concert Hall, allowing singers to turn their backs to a majority of the audience. But whatever his shortcomings, he was experienced, decisive and often put on a spectacular show."

For all his accomplishments at The Met, at Central City, and elsewhere, Merrill conveyed a proprietary sense that made arguments with him problematic. There had not been public evidence of this, but he was justifiably set in his ways and not easy to convince of a need for changes in repertory or approaches to staging. He and Louise established Opera Colorado as a viable company which raised the level of artistic achievement for opera in Denver to highly professional standards. Their regard for young talent was important. The need to expand repertory, as in the stagings of the Britten church operas, was crucial. Merrill's successes stood as a challenge to the new management, and it was clear from subsequent remarks that his admirable record had been accepted without dispute. There was thus considerable speculation about the forthcoming spring season.

To read over the Post review the words "'Salome' a Sweeping Triumph," and in the Rocky Mountain News, "Cast mesmerizes in 'Salome'" was evidence of the excitement Seifert had anticipated. Seifert had been blessed in obtaining the services of Hans Niewenhuis as director and Klauspieter Seibel as conductor, who joined together to key movement and music into a sizzling presentation which somehow avoided stress on the erotic and concentrated on character. Seibel drew tempestuous color and pacing from the full-throated Colorado Symphony. Niewenhuis concentrated his powers on the fury of the on-stage struggle.

It was the Salome who made the ultimate impact. Ljuba Kazarnovskaya had sung Desdemona to Placido Domingo's Otello at the Met and was supposedly the first Russian to undertake the role of Salome. She had a singular triumph in the role in a fiery blend of singing and acting. She moved like a dancer, so she went easily into her dance. Her voice cut through the large Straussian instrumentation with untiring power. Her Jokanaan was Victor Von Halem, one of Opera Colorado's great discoveries, in another demanding role. His powerful bass-baritone and personal dignity served him splendidly. There were others who made strong contributions, like William Lewis as a corrupt Herod and Mignon Dunn, no less vividly decadent as Herodias. Stephen West was a strong

First Nazarene and Richard Crawley a bold young Narraboth. Everything about this production deserved praise.

The double bill of *I Pagliacci* and *Gianni Schicchi* went well enough. Stephen West was back for the wily Florentine schemer of the Puccini with enlarged vocal and acting talents. Emily Herrera charmed with her Lauretta and there were a number of singers from the Young Artists Center.

I Pagliacci derived most of its drama from Yalun Zhang's potent Tonio. No other performances measured up to his relentless fury. Antonio Nagore gave a dark dimension to Canio in a good realistic performance but Elizabeth Holleque never seemed to get a clue as to her character. Peter Furlong was a bright and dapper Beppe. Alfredo Silipigni conducted with minimal flair. Opera Colorado had begun its transition.

Early in 1999, Marc Shulgold wrote a column reporting on a conversation with Stephen Seifert, now Executive Director of Opera Colorado. Asked about relations with Nathaniel Merrill, his predecessor, Seifert responded "He's my guest opening night" at *The Magic Flute*. Shulgold called this "A nice, symbolic gesture." Seifert, called by Shulgold "a soft-spoken, no-nonsense man," wanted to deal with nuts and bolts. "Our audit at the end of 1998 showed we had a $26,800 surplus—our largest in history" and noted, "I think that says people are supporting us." He further noted that Opera Colorado had matched a $250,000 challenge grant and that ticket sales for 1999 were $50,000 ahead of figures for the same period of the previous year. Seifert raised the question, "The test is, do people support the mission? With this organization, they have and they will."

A major policy step was taken to convert Boettcher into a thrust-stage theater, eliminating those seats considered to be "behind" the stage which would permit use of more conventional scenery. "Over the years, we've averaged 85% of the seats sold in the Buell but only 80% in Boettcher... I think people stayed away because they didn't like opera-in-the-round. So we decided to take a firm, obvious, inventive approach. We are delivering a message that says this will be the same intimate theater as before, that the experience will be as dramatic. Acoustically, it should be better as well."

Plans for 2000 were to be announced in March. "We want to propose a season with a reason—we're working toward a millennium theme (with repertory) choosing works that celebrate the human spirit. "We need to justify repertory to the community—it's our burden to help people approach the art. But we don't want to be seen as pandering. I don't believe Denver is that different from any other city," Seifert indicated, without specifics of expansion of activities.

The pressing business at hand was the forthcoming production of *The Magic Flute*. The opera had been done on the desk-top sized stage at the Barnes School of Business by Robert Lansing in the early 50's and by Norman Johnson's Denver Lyric Theater in a production devoid of animation or color. Not until 1989 had it been done at Central City, and then it was underpopulated.

In a bold step, Julius Rudel was signed both to conduct and direct the production, which would utilize settings by Maurice Sendak, the famed artist of books for children. Donald Kaasch, who had given a memorable *Faust* in the 1997 season, was signed for Tamino and the fine Gwendolyn Bradley was signed for Pamina. Judith Christin, whose husband, Larry Glenn, is a voice instructor at the Lamont School of Music, was brought in from The Met for the Third Lady. Everything seemed adjoined—casting, production, and musical values all contributed to a totally successful event. Rudel saw to it that there were no excesses, musical or dramatic, but more importantly established the "magical, goofy, compassionate" mood, as Bradley called it in the Post.

Jake Gardner returned from being seasoned in Europe to do an affable Papageno, making the most of his common man and his humors. Donald Kaasch in the less showy role of Tamino had his finest moments in the extended solo scene in Act II in which his beautifully placed tenor rang clear and expressive. Gwendolyn Bradley as Pamina sang exquisitely and Cyndia Sieden as the Queen of the Night ripped the rafters with her second aria. Arthur Woodley showed a stirring resonance as Sarastro. Judith Christin was joined by Marcia Ragonetti and Diane Bolden-Taylor as three splendid ladies. Young Artist Center singers Lisa Walecki as Papagena and Peter Furlong as both a Priest and First Armed Man showed confidence and ability. There was a strong energy at work on the stage that used imagination and fun to charm the audience.

You could tell from the kind of headings over the reviews in the dailies that the new regime was working. Over Jeff Bradley's review of *The Magic Flute* ran the words "'*Flute*' pure magic at Buell Theatre" while in the Rocky Mountain News over Shulgold's review it was "'*Flute*' delivers its magic."

In spring 1999, lots of hard work lay ahead for preparing *Macbeth* and *Romeo and Juliet*. A season of opera based on Shakespeare plays had been planned long before the release of *Shakespeare in Love* which had received an Academy Award as the best film of 1998, thereby stimulating popular interest in these plays. *Macbeth* and *Romeo and Juliet* would bring strongly contrasting operas to Opera Colorado. There was boldness in Seifert's casting of Boulder native Cynthia Lawrence as Lady Macbeth, a role she had never sung. Seifert assigned conductor Matthias Kunsch to conduct the opera and Lynn Binstock to direct, both new to Opera Colorado.

Macbeth had been scheduled for the 1989 season but shaky finances had necessitated its replacement by *La Traviata*. An infrequently performed opera, it required daunting vocalism from its Lady Macbeth. It had been seen in an unsuccessful production at Central City. This Opera Colorado production would be the opera's first major presentation in Colorado.

Cynthia Lawrence had been building up a strong career—most recently in October 1998 at Chicago Lyric Opera in Marvin David Levy's operatic version of Eugene O'Neill's *Mourning Becomes Electra*. She partnered Luciano Pavarotti in concerts throughout the world, and sang Elettra to Placido Domingo's Idomeneo at Chicago Lyric Opera. She made a New York City Opera debut as Cio-Cio-San in November 1991 and her Metropolitan Opera debut as Rosalinda in *Die Fledermaus* was in December 1997.

Soprano Lawrence approached the role of Lady Macbeth as bel canto, using a lyric voice with colors to establish the character. She was serious about the acting of the role. As a student at the University of Colorado she had been an usher for 25 performances of the play in the University's Shakespeare Festival, so had a complete familiarity with its demands. She told the Post's Jeff Bradley "I was trying to find what makes her tick, I must be honest, there's not much in my life I can draw on for this part."

In an interview with the Rocky Mountain News's Shulgold, Lawrence told of pestering Merrill and Louise Sherman for a role with Opera Colorado, and of having no invitation from the company until a change in management offered her Lady Macbeth. She drew on her vast experience with Pavarotti. "Standing next to him, I just take it all in. I've learned so much, particularly the Italian style of singing. It's not tangible, but it's something you can learn." In March during rehearsals she was given leave to fly to Las Vegas to perform with Pavarotti.

With her powerful technique she created a coruscating Lady Macbeth who indeed would stop at nothing to achieve her desires. She brought an icy intensity to the role and sang her ferocious arias with beauty of tone, never fearing to use a harsh sound for expression. Justino Diaz was a strong Macbeth, virile enough to realize his ambitions yet sorrowful amidst the resultant carnage. It was a superb job. Herbert Eckhoff had walked off his role as Banquo several weeks before opening but Gabor Andrasy was a good substitute. Peter Furlong was a stalwart Malcolm and Douglas Biggs made his Macduff effective. Julie Simson was a confident Lady in Waiting.

Matthias Kuntsch was a demanding conductor who made the opera move and controlled its dramatic pitch. Lynn Binstock as stage director seemed ill at ease in the overly elaborate set with too many steps and other pitfalls for the singers' comfort. A bolder, simpler set would have improved the production.

It might have been a good idea to pair the two contrasting Shakespeare tragedies but unfortunately, *Romeo and Juliet*, the romance of the "star-crossed lovers," failed to jell because of casting problems. Faith Esham had been a delightful Susanna at Santa Fe in the early 80s but she no longer had the vocal sheen that had been so pleasing. She was not enough of an actress to take Juliet as her own. Adam Klein had done creditable work at Central City but seemed vocally uncertain at Boettcher and the kind of lyrical singing required of Romeo was not in his voice. Peter Furlong was a vividly dramatic Tybalt and Marcia Ragonetti made a comic Gertrude with her fuming and fussing. The leads did not match in vocal style or in acting. Director Patrice Saint-Pierre could do little to create an immortal romance. There were moments of choral grandeur and of incisive drama but they were not sustained. Conductor Michel Singher knew the score and there was fine playing by the CSO but to little avail.

The young artists in the Joseph and Loretta Law Artist Center of Opera Colorado showed increasingly effective talents, and in June 1999 they were presented in an excellent production of Puccini's *Il Tabarro*. This grand *guignol* tale is not in the same league as its cohort *Gianni Schicchi* but in a carefully staged production, with Thomas Holliday doing effective work, it was a worthy effort. Thomas Cockrell conducted the Lamont School of Music student orchestra ably.

Dean Thoma was the jealous barge owner and Li Hui Zhang his vain, flirtatious wife. Her lover was the appealing Tibetan tenor Dor Ji Ci Ren, and they provided a believable dramatic center. Peter Furlong and Derrick Ballard were animated stevedores and Hilary Burtt was outstanding as the ragpicker. Peter Furlong and Lisa Walecki had a nice turn as two lovers. Merrill's determination to have this program was justified by the efforts of these young singers who also were involved in main stage productions.

As the search for an artistic director continued, Executive Director Seifert was saying that Opera Colorado was seeking a set of operas to celebrate the millennium with justifiably major works. Just before the 1999 spring season he announced the 2000 season of *Madama Butterfly, Porgy and Bess,* and *Fidelio*. The Puccini would provide income, the Gershwin would bring a strong community outreach, and the Beethoven would be a powerful expression of the kind of human compassion required for a new century.

Diana Soviero was to have the title role in *Butterfly*. She had not been in Denver for Opera Colorado since 1989 and the memorable *La Traviata*. Since then she had been mentioned for several productions which never materialized. Her husband, Bernard Uzan, director of opera at L'Opera de Montreal, came to direct and the sets also were from Montreal. Christian Badea, conductor of the most recent *Carmen*, would lead the Colorado Symphony.

There was good news prior to the opening in that the production was all but sold out. There was always an audience for *Madama Butterfly*, and by purchasing all the tickets, supporters confirmed their reliance on Opera Colorado to bring them the best. The name of Diana Soviero may not have been familiar to most of these ticket buyers but Puccini's name had a resonance that played powerfully. As a beautifully sung, deeply felt and gracefully enacted Cio-Cio-San, Soviero, despite being beset with a cold, made a lasting impression.

In the Rocky Mountain News Marc Shulgold wrote of Soviero's "triumphant performance" and her "impeccable pitch and dynamic range" though he found the voice less attractive than it had been. Glenn Giffin in the Denver Post thought she had made a slow start but by Act II believed "this was artistry to savor" and "A Butterfly of utter conviction." A division of opinion on Craig Siriani's Pinkerton was reflected by Shulgold who wrote of his "thin, light tenor" and that he "rarely connected with Cio-Cio-San." Giffin wrote of his "clear and affecting tenor" and "a supple lyricism tied to a suavely masculine timbre." I thought his voice lacked the needed richness.

There were fine supporting elements with Judith Christin's classic Suzuki and William Stone's Sharpless, caring and sung with a warm baritone. Jonathan Green was an adroit, vocally nimble Goro and Dean Thoma a sympathetic Yamadori. Where Giffin likened the set to "old packing crates... without human scale," Shulgold wrote of the "elegant unit set" borrowed from the L'Opera de Montreal. It was generally appreciated as an uncluttered set which avoided excessive Orientalism. Christian Badea led a vital, energetic performance by the CSO.

In early April there was announcement by Executive Director Stephen Seifert that James Robinson had been signed to a three-year contract as Artistic Director of Opera Colorado. Seifert recommended him as "a bright, energetic young stage director who has made a big impression in the opera community... I believe Jim is one of the next generation of leaders in the opera world. We are proud that he has chosen Opera Colorado for such an important commitment and we eagerly anticipate the bright future we can create together." Seifert further said that "Robinson is... noted for his creative interpretations of classic works" and that "he appreciates the need and opportunity for opera productions to make strong visual statements... We expect exciting new approaches to both repertory selection and dramaturgical and design choices under Jim's leadership." Among contractual elements was Rohinson's commitment to reside in Denver for six months of each year.

Along with this announcement came word of the works to be done in Robinson's first season, beginning in February 2001. In February at the Buell there would be *Turandot*, which Robinson had produced for the Minnesota Opera in 1995, in a version he believed returned the opera to the character of the original Gozzi fable. At the end of April two operas new to the repertory, *Ariadne auf Naxos* and *Orpheus and Eurydice* would be performed at Boettcher. Robinson would direct *Orpheus and Eurydice*. The Strauss *Ariadne auf Naxos* would be done by a director to be announced.

Robinson was born in Wheeling, West Virginia, attended the University of Tulsa and the University of Minnesota. His degree was in music composition. He was at the Santa Fe Opera as a Production Assistant in 1988 and 1989, and as Assistant Stage Manager in 1990 and 1991. He returned to Santa Fe in 1993 as Stage Director for the Strauss *Capriccio*, a much admired production, and in 1996 he directed Stravinsky's *The Rake's Progress*. He staged the American premiere of George Antheil's *Transatlantic* for the Minnesota Opera, and had been active with the New York City

Opera, the Los Angeles Opera, and at Wolf Trap Opera in Vienna, Virginia. His produced repertory ranges from *Norma* to *Eugene Onegin* to Ned Rorem's *Miss Julie* and Weisgall's *Six Characters in Search of an Author*, and countless productions of Mozart, Puccini, and Verdi. There was no question of his considerable experience.

In 2000 for Glimmerglass Opera, Robinson staged *La Bohème*, and set it in 1914 Paris. Peter G. Davies in New York Magazine credited Robinson and his designer, Allen Moyer, with filling the stage with "one fanciful invention after another." One invention was Act Three set in the railroad yards amidst stacks of coffins of war dead. Davies hailed Robinson for his treatment of "character rather than surroundings." Late in March 2001 a video of the *Bohème* production was presented on PBS. It showed considerable success in transferring the action to the 20th century and particularly in making convincing the opera's bohemians. Musetta arrived in a grand motor car, a light bulb hung over the garrett of Act I , and a a clown in a death's head brought up the second act's procession. It was hard to locate the inn of Act III—it was somewhere off stage. With a huge locomotive and the coffins there was no room. The production demonstrated what Robinson could do with an able cast.

To assure financial continuity of the educational programs, the 17th Annual Opera Grand Ball was held at the Hyatt Regency Hotel shortly before the *Porgy and Bess* opening, with 250 guests who heard vocal selections by Priscilla Baskerville, Bess in the forthcoming Porgy.

Gershwin's *Porgy and Bess* had not previously been produced by Opera Colorado but in June of 1987, with Center Attractions, it had co-sponsored a production from the Houston Grand Opera. A Denver mounting of this opera with its requirement of a large, all African-American cast was a challenge. The Gershwin Family, which licenses productions of *Porgy* insists on this casting. The four performances originally announced had sold out, and a fifth performance was set, and it too came close to selling out.

As Sarastro in the 1999 *Magic Flute*, Arthur Woodley had displayed his imposing bass-baritone to elevating effect. His Porgy was eagerly anticipated. His strength of voice and character touched just about every aspect of the production with quality. Willie Anthony Waters from Connecticut Opera was music director, giving excitement to the work. The large chorus, drawn from Denver churches and prepared by Ruth Baker, gave a potent lift to the many demands for exultant and radiant moods. Cleo Parker Robinson directed *Porgy* as her first operatic venture. There was admirable work with characterizations yet there was haphazard encircling of the stage with daisy chains that broke the affecting reality created by principals. Jean Robertson's set was not abstract enough to serve the multiple scenes of the opera and there were too many steps for the singers.

Priscilla Baskerville was an eloquent Bess but honors went to Angela Simpson whose memorable "My Man's Gone Now" halted the production for rousing applause. Lawrence Craig spun the 'Sportin' Life' songs jauntily and moved like a dancer. There were a lovely "Summertime" from Siphiwe McKenzie and fine vignettes by Charmaine Anderson as the Strawberry Woman and Robert Mack as the Crabman. Jeffrey LaVar was a menacing Crown.

In the Denver Post, Glenn Giffin wrote that it was "superbly cast... voices of real distinction." News critic Shulgold found the production "awkward" at Boettcher, in the round, with "too many distractions" but "the production succeeds where it must—in the singing."

Not since 1947 when Beethoven's single opera, *Fidelio*, was done at Central City had there been a staged Colorado performance. With Julius Rudel as conductor and stage director repeating the dual assignment which had been so markedly successful with *The Magic Flute* in 1999, this was another challenge to Opera Colorado's resources. It was therefore a credit to the opera community that ticket sales for the four performances sold an impressive 92% of capacity.

Jeanne-Michèle Charbonnet came for Leonore and Gary Lakes was Florestan. Dale Travis from Chicago Lyric Opera and the Santa Fe Opera sang Rocco, and Robert McFarland dealt with Don Pizzaro. Arthur Woodley stepped over from Porgy to perform

Don Fernando. Peter Gage Furlong and Lisa Walecki from the Joseph and Loretta Law Young Artist Center showed their superior merits as Jaquino and Marcellina. This was not a spectacular cast but its strength was in its ensemble and its sensitive response to Rudel's musical mastery.

A decision to update the opera to 30s fascistic times made sense. A nearly abstract set by Jorg Madlener and Midori Kurihana, who design for the Aspen Opera Theater Center, was striking in its huge door but dangerous in the cross-boards that threatened to trip performers. The set proved that boldly abstract sets do work at Boettcher.

Charbonnet impressed with the admirable power of the great first-act aria, but there were times when a more incisive register would have brought greater strength to the performance. Her drab uniform was in keeping with the style of the production. Gary Lakes started out strongly in his big aria at the start of Act II but he ran out of power at the climactic moment. He was hardly the physically diminished prisoner of the drama.

The strongest performance was that of Dale Travis as Rocco, warm and richly voiced and always in character. McFarland was a vehement Pizzaro, furious but in fine vocal control. Lisa Walecki's Marcellina was a lovely performance from a promising young soprano. Furlong's Jaquino had a forthright charm and vocal aptitude that made it a role that counted. It was a pleasure to hear the brief measures of Arthur Woodley singing as Don Fernando. Rudel saw to it that Beethoven was honored by this production, and the Colorado Symphony was essential to this vision. Together, *Fidelio* and *Porgy* sold 15,637 tickets, setting something of a recent record.

Bringing in *Turandot* for the 2001 season, when memories of the 1984 production were still green, was the kind of challenge Robinson was geared to take on. His production was originally created for Minnesota Opera in 1985 and has had 22 stagings in eight different houses. Robinson believed in putting a contemporary face on the opera, done with oriental splendor in 1984. His thinking was that Gozzi's fable needed to play at a remove from realism. He and his designers wanted propulsion, so rolling steel scaffolds, one of them nearly thirty feet high, were devised. Chinese calligraphy, fabrics, and elements of Oriental scenic painting were projected on the rear wall, furthering efforts to avoid realism. In performance, the production seemed to be cluttered with heavy stage traffic, although the projections were effective. The three ministers, Ping, Pang, and Pong, were set atop elaborate rolling skirts with drivers to push them around, which added to the movement but not especially to coherence.

Casting was uneven with Jeanne-Michèle Charbonnet, a Princess Turandot who could not locate a focus for her voice until midway in her big aria. When she found her voice, the singing was warm and true but her acting did not compensate. As Calaf, Antonio Nagore's acting was no more than adequate, but the audience had come to hear "Nessun dorma," and they were not disappointed in his shining delivery. Vocal and acting honors went to the Liu of Theresa Santiago, a superb young talent with a voice of major quality. Her two arias, done with admirable sensitivity and color, were high points in the performance. Ping, Pang, and Pong were vigorously done by Dean Thoma, Jason Baldwin, and Peter Gage Furlong. Kenneth Cox was a strong Timur and Thomas Poole sang the Emperor effectively.

Special praise is due conductor Marcello Mottadelli in his American debut. He led the Colorado Symphony in a performance of fine musicality. Ruth Baker's chorus in the delicate "Moon" episode and in more clangorous phases caught the contrasts expertly. In all, it was a lively performance, stronger in its powerful musical realization by conductor Mottadelli than in Robinson's ambitious but spotty staging.

In 1954 when Strauss's *Ariadne auf Naxos* received its Colorado premiere at Central City, which was very possibly an American premiere as well, almost no one in Colorado knew the work. At Central City it had preceded the San Francisco 1957 premiere as well as the 1962 Metropolitan debut. Over the years it had won many to believe it the finest Strauss work. Others ranked it at the top of their short lists of favored operas. *Ariadne* is for the connoisseurs, not immediately accessible.

Robinson wished to distinguish his first season with uncommon works and *Ariadne* certainly qualified in that category. In casting he went to the top for his Ariadne, signing Christine Brewer who had enjoyed a triumph as Ariadne in Santa Fe in 1999, and who was scheduled to sing Strauss' *The Egyptian Helen* in the Santa Fe Opera summer program in 2001. Ashley Putnam, who had given her stamp to the role of the Marschallin of the 1994 Opera Colorado *Rosenkavalier*, was signed to do the Composer.

Robinson was determined to have a new look, so he engaged Allen Moyer, designer of the Glimmerglass-PBS *Bohème*, who studied the new configuration adopted by Opera Colorado. Over the rear seating Moyer threw an imposing hillside, variously used in the production. An opera with severe changes in dramatic tone throughout was a challenge to Italian stage director Lorenzo Mariani. In the Prologue he worked for a graceful flow of movement rather than the more essential establishment of the conflict between the imperious Major Domo and the artists hired to perform.

Strauss and librettist Hofmannstahl did not make things easy for *Ariadne* productions. Though the Prologue was done in English, Boettcher acoustics prevented newcomers from understanding what was going on. Also, the SuperTitles malfunctioned, fading in and out, another confusing element.

There was a major imbalance of orchestra and singers. During the prologue singers were left without adequate orchestral support, and the audience left to seek the continuity so essential to comprehension. The stage action failed to clarify. To some degree, the performance was still in rehearsal mode. Ashley Putnam as the Composer acted with great conviction but no longer had the vocal sheen for which she was remembered. There was an abundance of temper in her portrayal but her singing was over the top emotionally and vocally. There was a stylish Major Domo from Greg Thornton of the Denver Center Theatre Company, a workmanlike Music Master from Jake Gardner, as well as Thomas Poole's Dancing Master, and an imposing Footman by greatly promising Charles Edwin Taylor. All these efforts were lost in Mariani's uneven stage direction.

The opera was a different matter. Allen Moyer's graceful, green brocade hillside was a lovely backdrop to the rococo bedstead on which Ariadne grieved. The nymphs, moved on paths along the hillside. With elegant chandeliers, the scene was an idyll ready to be shattered by the comedians. Christine Brewer sang with a vocal elegance fashioned from a pure and rich sound and admirable control. An ample woman, she characterized Ariadne with insightful, evocative singing rather than with obvious emotion. The Bacchus, Ian DeNolfo, was an uncouth tenor, with no clear talent. The three stylishly graceful nymphs, elegantly gowned in rococo fashion, were enchantingly sung by Marcia Ragonetti, Delorosa Munoz, and Lisa Wilson.

Lynette Tapia delivered Zerbinetta's staggering aria with lilt and a soprano that was silvery in the high register, sometimes inaudible in the lower register. Vitali Rozynko as Harlequin was someone to watch out for, a fine young baritone. Jason Baldwin, Peter Gage Furlong, and Matthew Lau were animated and vocally sure as the other comedians. Conductor Klauspeter Seibel and director Mariani seemed in the Prologue to be on different wavelengths. In the opera, music and movement seemed to blend to create the kind of rapture opera should bring. More rapture lay ahead.

What a pleasure to welcome a wholly fresh and relevant operatic production like that of Gluck's *Orpheus and Eurydice*. It was not a trendy or deconstructive affair so much as a bold, invigorating look at one of the oldest operas in the repertory. Its seamless magic was a triumph for director/choreographer Doug Varone and James Robinson his co-director.

There had been intimations of a novel approach to the classic opera, one not offered in Colorado since the 1941 Herbert Graf/Robert Edmund Jones/Frank St. Leger production at Central City. That had been in the classic, Grecian mode. At the time, St. Leger was quoted in Time as saying "we got the god-damned twaddle out of it." There were fears that Robinson, in removing traditional approaches, would replace them with elements foreign to the noble beauty of the work.

Varone and Robinson conspired successfully to set the opera in American 30s Depression times. Varone began the work with his eight dancers in white on a bare stage. Suddenly jeans and house dresses dropped from the rafters and the dancers become actors in a community of clapboard houses where a chorus is likewise dressed in jeans and house dresses. The marvel of the production was the manner in which principals, dancers, and chorus were all on the same plane of energetic movement. This flow held to the graceful tempo of the music, establishing a poetic, generous world in which the chorus commiserates delicately with Orpheus in his loss.

Theodora Hanslowe took Orpheus as her own, offering a performance as strong in singing as in acting. She gave a natural male dignity to the role, an open yet guarded emotional state. The singing was eloquent, the movement generous and free. In Act II in a series of charming lifts, the dancers clothed her in a tuxedo. Franzita Whelan was a lovely Eurydice, a soprano of delectable timbre and strength whose singing with Hanslowe in Act II was a vocal highlight of the performance. Lynette Tapia replaced Julie Cox at a late hour to deliver a charming Amor.

Not enough can be said of the sweep of movement provided by the eight dancers of the Doug Varone company, dancers whose fine style brought grace to the performance. The chorus was dramatically effective and individually characterized. The musical direction of conductor David Agler was discreet and acute at the same time. Allen Moyer's simple setting with miniature clapboard houses and a weathered signboard on the hillside were essential to setting the understated style of the production.

In the 2001 program were listed the operas for the 2002 season, with *Tosca* to arrive in February at the Buell, and *Eugene Onegin* and *Hansel and Gretel* to come as the spring season. The gamut from *Tosca* to *Hansel and Gretel* was wide, evidence that Robinson intended to reach all tastes and ages, with Tchaikovsky's *Eugene Onegin*,

Opera Colorado's first Russian opera, included for musical sophisticates.

Two weeks after the season concluded, the resignation of Stephen Seifert as Executive Director was announced. Seifert had joined the board in 1989 and soon became chairman of the board. In 1998 he became executive director after Nathaniel Merrill resigned. Seifert told Shulgold at the Rocky Mountain News "I'll take pride in the fact that I'm stepping aside for someone who can take this company to the next level."

Opera's Merrill resigns post

'Salome' a sweeping triumph

'Flute' pure magic at Buell Theatre

'Fidelio' symbolism nailed down

Captivating 'Orpheus' soars

Russell Arrives Cautiously Adventurous

Stephen Seifert was succeeded as president and general director by Peter Russell, who came from the Lindemann Young Artist Development Program at the Metropolitan Opera where he had been since 1997. He was chief administrator of the Wolf Trap Opera Company at Vienna, Virginia, from 1984 to 1997. To Marc Shulgold of the Rocky Mountain News, Russell spoke of Opera Colorado Artistic Director James Robinson, with whom he had worked at Wolf Trap beginning in 1994. "Jim does push the envelope in order to get to the essence of the story... I knew that if I were to accept a position with a company, I had to admire the artistic director—and I do." Russell described himself as "cautiously adventurous... 100% [in] support" of what Shulgold referred to as "Robinson's sometimes daring approach." For 2002, Opera Colorado's twentieth season, Peter Russell would be in command.

Little daring was to be found in the production of *Tosca*, which opened the season at the Buell. There were lavish scenic designs by Jean-Pierre Ponnelle, a rich playing of the Puccini score by the Colorado Symphony under Richard Buckley, but no generally recognizable names. Elizabeth Whitehouse was an attractive presence as Tosca who rose to the occasion in the most demanding moments to create a vulnerable yet proud woman. Greer Grimsley was not the most frightening of Scarpias but his imposing baritone made the Act I finale outstanding. In Act II he menaced Tosca with arrogance and vocal force. Julian Gavin was a believable Cavaradossi, doing his big arias with power and pleasing tone. Stage director Garnett Bruce kept the drama going but failed to provide a memorable experience. The melodrama was either missing or overly familiar.

Hansel and Gretel, a surprising entry into the Opera Colorado repertory, served to remind one of the beautiful Humperdinck score. The production by Peter Rothstein aimed at updating the classic tale but the work resisted modernizing. Its simplicity requires a traditional approach. The modern touch was seen as overly literal. The production was enlivened by the witch of tenor William Saetre, both fey and menacing, who cycled around the stage like the wicked witch of the *The Wizard of Oz*. He required a large stage to maneuver on but otherwise the stage was too spacious for an intimate opera. Kelly Kaduce was convincingly youthful and innocent as Gretel, and Mary Ann McCormick brought luster and boldness to Hansel. Judith Shay Burns sang the Sandman and the Dew Fairy prettily. Scott Terrell led the Colorado Symphony to expressive heights.

The first Russian opera ever to be done by Opera Colorado was Tchaikovsky's *Eugene Onegin*, his opulently scored, dramatic telling of the Pushkin poem. James Robinson directed the performance with settings by Bruno Schwengl which were starker than required. The production was highlighted by some fine singing from a strong cast and chorus. Emily Pulley gave a full-throated and winning performance as Tatyana. Robinson chose not to have her compose her letter as she sang, but to start the letter upon completion of the aria. Mel Ulrich performed at a high level as Onegin, an aristocrat unable to forget his social position, but ultimately a beggar for Tatyana's love. As the central character, he gave focus to the production. There was a stirring Lensky from tenor Andrew Richards who sang the character's drama with ardent feeling. The most tradition-breaking element in the production was the funereal procession that occurred during the brisk polonaise. Previously, in the ball scene, the chorus huddled inexplicably at stage rear right. Robinson did get the principal's characterizations down.

Financially opera is not an easy win. A weak economy hurt attendance figures, as was shown in a review of local arts organizations by Marc Shulgold in June, 2003. The budget had been balanced even though ticket sales were down. The difference was made up by insurance payments for the fire in Opera Colorado offices which destroyed records and forced a move. The figure of 22,176 attendees for twelve performances averaged out at 1,848 per performance. Balancing a budget meant passing on the superstars and lavish scenic values. The lesson, tough as it was, had to be learned by compromise.

Two sure-fire productions and one novelty were set for 2003, a season that promised to attract those with a taste for the familiar as well as those in search of a popular Broadway musical. Robinson would direct both *Lucia di Lammermoor* and *Sweeney Todd*, and Sharon Ott from the Seattle Repertory Theater came for *Don Giovanni*.

The last time Opera Colorado took on *Lucia* was a disaster. Aside from the furious Enrico offered by Yalun Zhang nothing worked. It was time for a fresh attack on one of opera's most popular works. Things suggested an unravelling when the Lucia, Dina Kuznetova cancelled because of "vocal exhaustion." Miraculously, James Robinson's first choice, Jennifer Welch-Babidge, originally sought but then apparently not available, found an opening, and came. Kyle MacMillan at the Denver Post exclaimed "Quite simply, the budding star turns in the most electrifying performance in an Opera Colorado production in recent memory." (But he had not seen Cynthia Lawrence as Lady Macbeth.) MacMillan went on to praise the ease of her ornamental bel canto and her stamina. Shulgold found her technique secure from to top to bottom—her control of dynamics remarkable.

Jorge Antonio Pita as Egardo showed a smooth lyricism, while Scott Hendricks as Enrico commanded a suave villainy with potent singing. The untraditional setting by Christine Jones was a reminder of the rocky field of the 1994 production, and seemed not to make sense. Stephen Lord's conducting was sensitive to the delicate fabric of the score as well as to the pacing.

Stephen Sondheim's 1979 musical, *Sweeney Todd*, is only now entering opera houses, with a Chicago Lyric production preceding Denver's by but a few months. Sondheim's musical gifts, as well as his sense of drama and frequently hilarious prosody, have placed him at the peak of composers now writing for musical theater.

James Robinson directed a top-notch cast in an engrossing performance. Fortune led him to a baritone born to do Sweeney Todd, the Demon Barber of Fleet Street. Alan Ewing, large and prepossessing, with a voice to match, took command of Todd's fury. The rich role of Mrs. Lovett was appealingly done by Phyllis Pancella. Her eagerness to serve Todd was matched by the infectious and ripe lilt she gave her singing. There was an enthralling performance by Marcia Ragonetti of the Beggar Woman, who turns out to have been Todd's wife. On stage throughout the production, she filled the performance with awe, darkening the mood with her ghastly, ghostly presence. John Packard was a stalwart Anthony, and Tonna Miller captivated as Johanna. There was an outstanding bit by Jason Baldwin as Pirelli, animated and effusive. Doug Jones took his part well, with a particularly sweet participation with Pancella in the "Nothin's gonna harm you" duet. Michael Devlin was a strong figure of hypocrisy as the Judge. David Agler led an incisive, mercurial performance.

An effort to re-imagine *Don Giovanni*, perhaps the greatest of all operas, is a dangerous undertaking but Robinson, guest director Sharon Ott, and designer Allen Moyer put forward a production that succeeded in turning the opera on its head. Moyer's set, with the names of women scribbled on the stage floor and plastic hurdles with women's eyes, was a matter of contention. Some thought it was great and others considered it one of the least appealing sets ever at Opera Colorado. It did make people sit up and react.

Casting was excellent with David Pittsinger vocally strong but dramatically weak in presence. Eduardo Chama was as good a Leoporello as one could wish, with a fine, robust baritone and a stage presence lively without going over the top. Chad Shelton sang Don Ottavio's "Il mio tesoro" with a sweet sound and technical prowess. As Donna Anna, Franzita Whelan was a lovely presence. She handled her challenging arias capably without force, but was somewhat lacking in stylistic finesse. Maria Kanyova, who had been enrolled in the Joseph and Loretta Law Center for Young Artists of Opera Colorado, a lamentably vanished program, brought a fiery elegance to Donna Elvira, handling the vocal acrobatics without blemish. Margaret Lattimore was an engaging Zerlina with an attractive voice that may have been a bit heavy for the role. Dale Travis seemed miscast as the Commendatore. His voice was not sufficiently deep or powerful and he was not directed to be an avenging figure. Vitali Rozynko displayed a pleasing baritone as a suitably morose Masetto.

Sharon Ott's direction gave the singers ample opportunity to develop their characterizations. She was another stage director who could not get the lighting right in the mistaken identity scene at the start of Act Two. It appeared the action took place at dusk rather than at night. It was demeaning to Elvira to be in such a predicament. She has enough baggage as it is. There was ravishing playing by the Colorado Symphony under Dean Williamson, whose pacing of the lengthy score never lost the elegance of the music.

There had been something of a contretemps at a rehearsal for home-schooled children when David Pittsinger, as Don Giovanni, was making out with a scantily dressed supernumerary. The children's chaperone sent e-mails to parents criticizing the action. General director Peter Russell asked director Shaon Ott to tone down the scene. Pittsinger told Shulgold the "desired effect was to make it sexual. It was Sharon's way of showing what goes on in the privacy of the Don's house." He went on to tell Shulgold that he had four-year old twins, and "I would have no trouble with them seeing this show."

This production played to a 93% capacity. 13,833 tickets were sold for *Don Giovanni* and *Sweeney Todd*, compared to 11,746 for the previous year's *Eugene Onegin* and *Hansel and Gretel*. But then, *Porgy and Bess* and *Fidelio* sold 15,637 tickets, and *Porgy* had been a sell-out for five performances.

Casting for the twenty-second season was announced in the program for the previous season. For *La Bohème*, Pamela Armstrong was selected for Mimi and Emily Pulley as Musetta. James Robinson's production from Glimmerglas Opera and New York City Opera, seen nationally on PBS, was set. The choreographer Doug Varone, on the basis of his favorably received *Orpheus and Eurydice*, was picked to direct the *Barber*, with Ian Greenlaw as Figaro, Patricia Risley in an Opera Colorado debut as Rosina, John Tessier as Almaviva, and the versatile Dale Travis as Dr. Bartolo. Elizabeth Futral, known for numerous glowing performances at Santa Fe, would come for Violetta in *Traviata*, with the well-regarded young tenor Eric Cutler as Alfredo, and the popular Scott Hendricks as Germont. These operas were a bow towards financial security but the likelihood of their being staged traditionally was very slim. Robinson would always be concerned with re-imagining opera in fresh terms. And it turned out his casting was the stuff of operatic dreams.

Not only was Puccini's beloved opera one of the most familiar in the repertory, but James Robinson's *La Bohème* production was familiar to many. Casting was a harbinger of increased concern about getting the best voices and actors available. There was a determination to refresh these old friends. The move to early World War I times seemed pertinent. It evoked an extra dimension of pathos. The opera kindled new responses. As described earlier, Act III took place in the railroad yards on the outskirts of Paris, and Musetta made a grand entrance in a motor car. A death's head led the parade at the conclusion of Act II. In all details it was an affecting performance.

Pamela Armstrong was vocally supreme as Mimi, sensitively endowing her character with the bloom of her voice. Emily

Pulley gave extravagant sweep to Musetta. The men were strong with Emmanuel di Villarosa's fine lyric tenor matching Pamela Armstrong's in emotional strength. Mel Ulrich's Marcello was vigorous and virile. Oren Gradus delivered a fervent coat aria, and Vitali Rozynko completed a strong quartet. Ashraf Sewailam doubled effectively as Benoit and Alcindoro. The rich textures of Puccini's lustrous score were drawn out by conductor Stephen Lord in beautifully balanced playing by the Colorado Symphony. Allen Moyer's sets were right on target. This was a great artistic and financial success.

None of the *The Barber of Seville*'s tired mold or hoary humor was present in Doug Varone's expansive take on this classic. It was a swirling, whirling madcap of physical ingenuity. Varone brought his dance company with him to spark the production. He imagined taking the familiar opera for a romp to the realms of buffoonery. The overture was danced as a way to introduce the characters, and the buoyant movement was altogether engaging. Updated to the 50s, this was a knockout of a production; audacious, thriving on its talented cast, providing the audience with the rare spectacle of singers who could and did dance, climb ladders, and stay out of the way of rolling doors, mattresses, and a couch. It was a zany show and Rossini would have loved it.

Ian Greenlaw was a Figaro, lately a Las Vegas entertainer, with a rowdy head of red hair, wearing an aqua jacket and light blue trousers, and carrying a microphone. His baritone was resonant. In this production his infectious charm set the key for light-hearted comedy. Patrica Risley was ideally cast as Rosina, a woman spicy and adorable, with a rich mezzo-soprano and vocal agility to spare. Graceful in movement, she danced her way into the comedy. John Tessier's Almaviva was perhaps not so noble an aristocrat as he might have been but he made up for this in the sweetness and deftness of his tenor. Dale Travis almost walked away with the opera with his deft Dr. Bartolo, played out with his adroit sense of character. Up-and-coming Christopher Feigum took on Don Basilio in a genuinely comic spirit, raising laughter with his "Calumnia" aria.

Elizabeth Brooks as Bertha entered fully into the comic spirit of the production. The chorus danced along with the principals.

There was abundant drama in James Robinson's fresh realization of *La Traviata*, Verdi's early classic. There were no tricks of updating. By articulating the weathered opera in terms incisive and revelatory, the Dumas tragedy received a production that was spectacular without surrendering to cliche or orthodoxy. Robinson mastered the drama with powerful demonstrations of understanding. Opera Colorado had executed a coup in obtaining Elizabeth Futral for Violetta. A brilliant production brought more life to *La Traviata* than anyone could have imagined. Further enlightenment came from the fine casting of Scott Hendricks as Giorgio Germont and Eric Cutler as Alfredo. It was a passionate performance, anchored in the truth of character.

Futral's superb vocal attributes, personal beauty, and grace were served by her strong sense of character. With Robinson, she developed a strong persona, a woman of fine passion-stirring temper. There were many moments to savor. Among these, her wandering ghostlike through the opulent red splendors of her salon, drinking champagne in solitude. In Scene I, Act II, her restless state was shown in sudden swift turns. As Germont starts to depart before she has finished with him, she demonstrates her strength of character by suddenly seizing his coat from him.

Robinson built a convincing relationship between Violetta and Germont. Here Germont appeared more concerned with a possible detriment to his investments than with his family being involved with a woman from another world. In movement, gesture, and attitude Futral and Hendricks ranged the course of the conflict with power, making the most of this masterful scene.

Much was expected of tenor Eric Cutler. As Alfredo in the busy Act I he was dry of voice but from the start of Act II the voice was refreshed into a golden lyric tenor. As a son kicking off his traces to find love with a woman of notoriety, he was a shy yet an ardent lover. True love too late comes to him. In a strong cast Marcia Ragonetti's gracious Annina was a fine presence, while John Fulton, Kellie J.

Van Horn, Sha Appenzeller, and Daniel Fosha made themselves noticed in small roles.

An elegantly gowned and suited chorus, prepared by John Baril, was as fine as the Opera Colorado chorus of early days, moving gracefully in Robinson's blocking. Stephen White led the Colorado Symphony through the delicacy of the preludes to Acts I and III. The musicianship of the Colorado Symphony was on exemplary display throughout the opera. Bruno Schwengl's opulent scarlet salon for Act I was dazzling, while his costuming completed an elaborate scene. The white-on-white wintry trees of Act II were strongly in contrast. Scene 2 in Flora's salon was all purple. Violetta's tragic fall was underscored by a background of industrial buildings.

This artistically gratifying season brought remarkable financial figures. 27,683 seats were sold for the twelve performances. This was a jump from the 21,610 seats sold for the 2003 season. It would be a challenge to maintain such sales in coming seasons.

For the 2005 season Russell and Robinson took a leap, naming it in publicity as "A Season To Remember." In its repertory of Handel's *Julius Caesar*, *Rigoletto*, and *The Marriage of Figaro*, they seemed to have touched all bases. For the Handel it was again a time for a coup—making it in its casting the increasingly admired Stephanie Blythe as Caesar and the superb Elizabeth Futral as Cleopatra.

Robinson directed his offbeat concept for the opera, which he set in Hollywood of the 30's, turning Roman forums into period spectacle. The updating did not establish a coherent story line; there were moments of spellbinding spectacle along with moments of utter confusion. It was a half-baked notion which emerged as Robinson's whim.

The singing was notably good, with Stephanie Blythe's dark-hued powerful mezzo played against Elizabeth Futral's radiance for dramatic effect. Nancy Maultsby as Cornelia gave a touching performance that anchored the opera in more reality than any other character. Patricia Risley, who had adorned the Barber, continued to impress with her incisive mezzo. There was fine work by the Colorado Symphony under Graem Jenkins's authoritative direction. Overall it was a mixture of the astute and the stumbling.

Rigoletto was even more of a visual problem, again lifted to musical heights by a fine cast. The production by Thaddeus Strassberger was literally set in the dark, updating the scene to the present. Strassberger aimed at creating "a setting we can connect to here in Denver." The problem was that the eloquent music and the drab setting failed to match, or to illuminate the tragedy.

Again the singing raised the performance to something to recall with pleasure. Christopher Robertson sang a profoundly touching Rigolettto and Jennifer Welch-Babidge was a winning, pathetic Gilda. Julian Gavin looked like a depraved Count and sang like a young singer of promise. Mark Morash conducted ably but little good can be said of James Schuette's sets or of Mimi Jordan Sherin's lighting.

With *The Marriage of Figaro* Russell and Robinson struck gold. It was a perfect realization of Mozart's comedy. Like *La Traviata* in the previous season, it took a contemporary look at a distant period. Casting could hardly be improved upon. Christopher Feigman was a light-hearted, richly voiced Figaro, Mariusz Kwiecien dashing in character and beautifully voiced as the Count, Maria Kanyova an enchanting Susanna, and Norah Ansellem quite breathtaking in her delectable arias. The ensemble was outstanding, with funny character work by Ashraf Sewailam and also by Leslie Remmert Soich as Marcellina. David Agler led the Colorado Symphony in admirably sensitive playing, while Robinson's staging was strikingly well-paced against James Schuette's active sets. This was indeed a production to remember.

The following season would be in a house specifically designed for opera and dance. It would open with Denyce Graves, Julian Gavin, Pamela Armstrong, and David Pittsinger in *Carmen* with Stephen Lord conducting, all in the newly opened Ellie Caulkins Opera House ingeniously built within the Quigg Newton Denver Municipal Auditorium, the name applied to the Auditorium in

2002. The opening in November 2005 would be the first of eight performances, which previous to the opening was close to a sell-out in the 2,280 seat house. Following in February 2006 would be Bellini's *Norma* and in April, Mozart's *The Abduction from the Seraglio*. "A new era begins... in a new house with a bold new style" is the way President and General Director Peter Russell and Artistic Director James Robinson heralded the future of Opera Colorado. There would be much more for future audiences to remember.

Always a New Beginning

The early death of touring opera as it had become was a good thing, for touring opera had given itself a bad name. The companies had become ragged, and audiences in their newly acquired sophistication declined to support mediocrity. It was certainly no artistic loss. Deprivation provoked support for superior local talents. It was unfortunate that local efforts to provide opera of merit took so long. Hard-earned Denver money came to the cause of independent opera. That so many of these efforts sputtered out was regrettable. There had been signs of possibilities. Eventually the long-awaited buds flowered.

There were extravagant theaters, the Tabor Grand Opera House and the Broadway Theater. Denver support for touring companies was originally a novelty, then a frequent cultural visitation. Glamorous artists—Emma Abbott, Adelina Patti, Nellie Melba, Mary Garden, and Geraldine Farrar—and the Metropolitan Opera came. Audiences had reason to attend, and their tastes were cultivated by these enticing performers.

A continuing belief that opera could amount to something, even if produced locally, gave impetus to Father Bosetti's Denver Grand Opera. Though it often mirrored the impoverishment of the old touring companies, it managed to take a foothold in Denver. Father Bosetti understood popular tastes, which he merged with his own affection for opera. As a means of funding the Catholic Charities, this organization lasted for over thirty years. The company gave Denver memorable appearances by Bidu Sayao and Dorothy Kirsten and introduced opera audiences to such home-grown talents as Francesco Valentino, Richard Dworak, Fred Nesbit, and Marvin Worden.

It was not enough that individual voices and performers were heard. Opera should be arousing, theatrical. John Newfield understood that if opera were to build a twentieth century audience it must endow the stage with feeling, dramatic or comic. Under his driving and sometimes coruscating demands, Denver was being provided with opera that had vitality. John Newfield had a vision of what opera in Denver could be. Regrettably, without a financial base he could not sustain the dream. When Newfield's endeavors collapsed in financial distress, it became clear that despite offering such major talents as Licia Albanese and Norman Treigle, Denver audiences wanted even more glamor than these superior singers offered. The movers and shakers of the Denver cultural scene withheld approval of the Newfield era, content to await each summer's offerings at Central City.

Arthur Schoep had experience in conducting, staging, and performing but despite his expertise, he never solved the mystery of how to mount an opera. Nicholas Laurienti had ample music in his head but no professional experience.

With the exception of Father Bosetti and his Catholic Charities support, none of these efforts would connect with a reliable funding source. There was no security in opera. Doing opera on a shoestring meant setting priorities and getting the right balance. Balancing acts were always a trick. Unless there were a recognizable name from the operatic world, audiences would not come out and give. But if there were such a name there would not be enough money to carry the increased costs. These were rough times for those who put themselves forward to develop opera in Denver. They were always too busy to notice until it was too late that they lacked depth in support.

Oddly enough, it was as a result of the Central City Opera House Association's dallying with the prospects of doing opera in Denver that Opera Colorado did arrive. In 1975 the Board of the Central City Opera House Association announced an impending fund drive to support opera in Denver. That year it sponsored the ill-fated *Aida* but the following year there was luster in an outstanding *Bohème*. The Denver Center for the Performing Arts was just then coming into being, and the Central City board believed it might become a wing of that organization. (see: Young, Allen. *Opera in Central City*. Denver: Spectrographics, 1993.)

When Robert Darling came to Central City as Executive Director, he viewed the newly built Boettcher Concert Hall at the Denver Center for the Performing Arts with interest, and soon scheduled *Salome* for 1978, the first opera done in-the-round in that space. Because losses for *Salome* were considered minimal, the Central City Opera House Association announced that in the following year *La Traviata* and *The Flying Dutchman* would be produced at Boettcher. Shortly, these productions were canceled; fiscal responsibility and long-term fund-raising forced this decision.

While Merrill was at Central City in the early 60s, he became aware of the strong base of Denver support for the Central City Opera. At Central City Merrill had raised its strong standards to new heights with fine casting. Striking sets by his excellent teammate Robert O'Hearn made the small stage seem large. These productions glittered in their concepts. Although he had staged 27 operas at the Metropolitan Opera, a change in managerial controls had left him out. He had been the only American stage director at The Met which meant he chose cast, conductor, and designer. Looking about in the 70s, Merrill was provoked by the void of operatic activity in Denver. In 1981 he and his wife Louise Sherman, a coach at the Metropolitan, moved to Denver, and shortly announced that beginning in 1983 Opera Colorado would produce opera at Boettcher Concert Hall.

Almost single-handedly Merrill brought major opera to Denver. His indispensable right-hand was Louise Sherman, who created the superb Opera Colorado Chorus, which ranked among the finest ensembles in American houses. She coached all the principal singers.

The rest is history, it might be said. Like history, there were free-falling finances and all the headaches and heartaches that go with artistic activity in America. The financial problems encountered as Denver bounced from boom to distress reflected the costly venture that was opera. There is never a perfect time for investment in the arts. For Opera Colorado and Merrill, the very early eighties had seemed the right time to arrive but an oil crisis affected major donors in the mid-eighties and big plans had to be withheld. Merrill had always said that in order to succeed, Opera Colorado must bring the great international stars.

Opera Colorado's principal claim to fame was that it performed in-the-round. It also, as promised, featured artists of international renown, bringing in Placido Domingo, Jon Vickers, Eva Marton, and Aprile Millo. He also nurtured Denver area singers such as Stephen West, Hao-Jiang Tian, Marcia Ragonetti and Yalun Zhang. The look was new and the sound of Boettcher, with a "voice lift," satisfied most audiences.

When the Buell Theatre opened in 1991, Opera Colorado began utilizing this proscenium hall for a single production each year. The box-office numbers increased substantially over Boettcher, which led to the decision in 1998 to cease doing opera-in-the-round and turn Boettcher into a thrust-stage venue. This decision coincided poignantly with Louise Sherman's death and Nathaniel Merrill's resignation.

The occasions on which artistry had been breathtaking were many. The opening scene of *Otello* riveted patrons like nothing in Denver's opera-going experience had ever done. Domingo in *La*

Bohème swept the audience with his elegant emotional projection. Eva Marton at her enthralling vocal peak in *Turandot* was memorable. The romantic conflict of *The Tales of Hoffman* was a unique fulfillment.

The ability to mount spectacle was grandly shown in *Aida*. A *Don Giovanni* of compelling suavity met its great challenge. Jon Vickers came for his mighty *Samson* and O'Hearn proved his ability to mount the terrifying destruction of the temple. There was a rare composure to a *Traviata* in which Diana Soviero in an understated production gave a memorable performance. Verdi's *Masked Ball* and *Don Carlo* whipped up further interest in Verdi grandeur.

There were wonderful adventures with Wagner—*Die Meistersinger von Nurnberg* and *The Flying Dutchman*—both noble productions. There was artistic success with *Der Rosenkavalier*, a robust *Faust*, an endearing *Magic Flute*, and an inspiring *Fidelio*.

Nothing is easy in the world of opera. Bringing compatible singers together to fuse the spirit of a production requires taste and strength of purpose. These productions represented the fruition of the great tradition. They gloried in a conservative way of doing things. That was the way the 20th century opera audience liked its 19th century operas.

It was the new management of James Robinson that stood Denver opera on its ear. With co-director and choreographer Doug Varone he staged a charming, updated *Orpheus and Eurydice*—a foretaste of things to come as opera moved into the 21st century. It could hardly have been bettered. The tone was caught in imaginative details, in the zest of the dancers and the relish of the chorus, led by the singularly motivated performances of the principals. In April 2004 Varone returned to direct and choreograph, with his company of dancers, a dashing production of *The Barber of Seville*. Along with Robinson's *La Bohème* and *La Traviata*, Opera Colorado enjoyed boasting of a sold out season—reason for exclamation.

Reviews in Opera News reflect a continuing assault on the conservative tradition both in Europe and in the United States. Some feared that Robinson in his zeal to refresh opera might cross the border into the bizarre. Conflicts between an audience confirmed in its liking for the stability of the Merrill years and a younger audience wanting an ever newer look and sound were bound to occur.

Not all opera goers approved of Robinson's stagings. There were letters to the editors in the Rocky Mountain News complaining about the *Barber* but there were as many hailing it. Robinson told Marc Shulgold of the News that "There are good traditions and bad traditions. A lot of tradition is the last bad idea. Whatever you think of a production of ours, there will always be visual, dramatic, and musical integrity. Our goal is to sell tickets and exciting casting is as important as staging. You've got to educate your audience. People want to see how far you can push things."

He further added that the 2005 season would open with a *Julius Caesar*, "staged like a movie musical of the 30s," and justifying this by noting that Handel "viewed opera as a contemporary entertainment." *Rigoletto* and *The Marriage of Figaro* would be "different if not outrageous." But Robinson did have a strong base to build on with the great success of his 2004 season.

Denver voters in November 2002 approved a bond issue to refurbish the 1908 City Auditorium to create a new performance hall, specifically designed for opera and dance. Architects Peter Lucking and Rick Brown of Semple Brown Design, P.C. were chosen to design, and the first major decision was to build within the shell of the old hall. The auditorium was gutted, down to the ground, and a 2,280 seat opera house was in the planning stage.

A generous donation of $7 million was made by the family of Mrs. Eleanor N. Caulkins, popularly known in the opera world as Ellie. She is a tireless worker for opera in Denver and nationally on the Board of the Metropolitan Opera, and the new opera house would be the Ellie Caulkins Opera House. A brilliant opening of historic grandeur inaugurated the Ellie, as it came to be known, on September 10, 2005. The smartly-gowned and tuxedo-dressed audience filled the sold-out occasion to discover a truly eye-stunning hall.

The architects worked with acousticians Robert Mahoney and Associates to provide the *sine qua non* of an opera house, acoustical properties that would never require amplification. Indeed at the opening, General Director Peter Russell remarked that in all his years of addressing audiences this was the first time he had done so without amplification.

There was a formidable gathering of singers, led by Renée Fleming, Ben Heppner, James Morris, Hao Jiang Tian, Yalun Zhang, Emily Pulley, Theodora Hanslowe, Julian Gavin, Robert Orth, Garrett Sorenson, and Colorado-based singers Cynthia Lawrence, Stephen West, Judith Christin, Charles Taylor, and Marcia Ragonetti, with Stephen Lord conducting the Colorado Symphony and the Opera Colorado Chorus. A world premiere of a composition by Jake Heggie was sung by Kristin Clayton with the composer accompanying. It was a genuine gala. True to promises, the acoustics were striking in the clarity and warmth of the sound.

Opulent visually, the hall's red seating and generously curved side balconies all lead to ideal sight lines. The hall itself achieves a remarkable sense of past and present, with elements of the original structure utilized throughout the lobby areas. Artists are well cared for with large dressing rooms. Audiences have the benefit of the Figaro captioning system, placed at the back of the seats. Everything seems to have been delivered as ordered.

The powerful stimulus of the Ellie will resound for many years, challenging directors designers and artists to surpass themselves. Not since the construction of the Tabor Grand Opera House in 1881 (demolished in 1964) and the Broadway Theater in 1890 (demolished in 1955) has there been a fit house for opera. Too many all-purpose theaters mostly demonstrated their lack of fitness for any single artistic medium.

A fine house is crucial to the success of opera. It means that patrons will experience opera in an ideal situation. They will see and hear great works, old and new, at their best. The adventure that is opera never ends. The human voice and the actor come together to inform and delight. Opera is always exotic and irrational, funny and tear-jerking. That's why we keep going.

Denver moves ahead into what should be a golden age of artistic life. There is always a new beginning and at the present we are on that threshold.

Exotic and Irrational 215

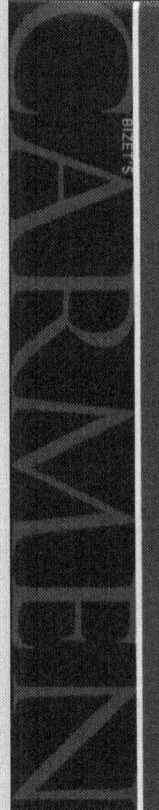

OPENING OPERA COLORADO'S FIRST SEASON AT THE ELLIE CAULKINS OPERA HOUSE NOVEMBER 2005

36A Rocky Mountain News

PEOPLE &

A fresh 'Carmen' opens at the Ellie

By Marc Shulgold
ROCKY MOUNTAIN NEWS

We're all familiar with the fury of a woman scorned — but what about a man who's been unceremoniously dumped? If Opera Colorado's production of *Carmen* is the measuring stick, the furies of hell can't compare.

As staged in the Ellie Caulkins Opera House — the first such production in the new facility — this is a deep journey into the darkness of a deteriorating mind.

Sanity slowly crumbles as obsession grows. Not a pretty sight.

Yet, director James Robinson's view of the beloved Bizet opera never turned oppressive or unwatchable — or imitative. As we've come to expect, Opera Colorado's artistic director is uninterested in following well-worn paths.

In the opening performance on Thursday, Robinson revealed a novel approach to *Carmen*, an opera that has been twisted and turned any number of ways.

The curtain rose on a deliberately amateurish-looking set — a painted backdrop meant to capture the opening scene's opera-comique feel (at least, in Robinson's view). Once we've been taken into the dark world of Lillas Pastia's café, the darker world of a smuggler's paradise and the fatally black world of the Seville bullring, the painted drop gives way to a backstage view of a burned-out theater.

Why? Beats me. But it works wonderfully.

Credit designer Allen Moyer for creating an evocative setting

Carmen
■ **Grades:** A-
■ **When and where:** repeated with two casts at 7:30 p.m. today, Tuesday, Friday and Nov. 12, with 2 p.m. matinees on Sunday and Nov. 13 in the Ellie Caulkins Opera House, 14th and Curtis streets.
■ **Information:** 303-357-2787

that expands in its disheveled look as the story unfolds. In the finale, the full destruction is unveiled, dwarfing the ill-fated Carmen and Don Jose as they play out their final scene.

But then, does any of this matter, when Denyce Graves is singing the tempestuous gypsy? She is, of course, the reigning diva of the role. This is truly a star vehicle — a rarity in recent seasons for Opera Colorado.

It's easy to understand how Graves has come to own this intriguing character. She is a commanding presence, a stunning creature and a brilliant actor. Her spoken dialogue exchanges with Jose (not always audible, alas) revealed her complete understanding of Carmen's complexities. And, despite a perceived cardboard view at the gypsy, Graves shows us how Carmen changes, how she comes to understand herself as clearly as she understands men.

Trouble was, Graves was not in terrific voice on Thursday. Her burnished mezzo never fully opened up. In her early pair of hits, the *Habañera* and *Seguidilla*, there was an unwelcome restraint and monochromatic delivery. But her unconcealed sultriness and in her subtly shaded self-awareness, Graves easily drew us into Carmen's world.

Her Jose on Thursday was Julian Gavin, who resisted the temptation to go over the top in his portrayal of a spurned lover-gone-mad. The voice was a bit forced early, but blossomed in the *Flower Song*.

The two major supporting roles were sung marvelously by Pamela Armstrong (a sweet Micaela) and David Pittsinger (a commanding Escamillo). Nice work from Timothy Mix (Morales), Christopher Job (Zuniga), Rebecca Koenigberg (Frasquita) and Marcia Ragonetti (Mercedes). The ensembles such as the rapid-fire quintet and the *Card Scene* were particularly effective.

Best of all, however, was the toreador parade — in particular, the brilliant work of the Opera Colorado Chorus and Colorado Children's Chorale. Portrayed in dramatic slow motion, it proved a tour de force, as the chorus of onlookers moved slowly but sang rapidly.

In the pit, Stephen Lord and the Colorado Symphony provided a robust accompaniment, although the thrilling opening prelude lacked muscle. Generally, the Ellie served as a fine place for unamplified opera — as long as the singers or speakers projected out into the house and not into the wings.

In a novelty for the company, an almost-complete second cast will offer three performances. Will Beth Clayton out-Carmen Denyce Graves? Stay tuned.

Curtain lifts on Ellie Caulkins Opera House

Matthew Staver | Special to The Denver Post
A crowd builds in the lobby before the sold-out gala opening Saturday night at the new Ellie Caulkins Opera House in downtown Denver. More than a dozen opera singers performed in the three-hour concert.

Debut hits the high note

By Kyle MacMillan
Denver Post Fine Arts Critic

After two years of construction, painstaking preparations and steadily building anticipation, the $92 million Ellie Caulkins Opera House opened Saturday evening with a spectacular gala concert presented by Opera Colorado.

The theater in the Denver Performing Arts Complex has been touted by the architects and others involved in the project as one of the best in the world. So, the immediate question, of course, was: How good is the sound?

And, to everyone's relief, the answer is: excellent. The opera house passed its first major test with flying colors.

Any immediate doubts were erased when tingles ran up and down the spine as celebrated soprano Renée Fleming glided effortlessly into a soaring version of the aria, "Ebben? No andro lontana," toward the end of the first half.

Black-tie crowd: More than 2,000 people from old and new Denver join in the festivities. > Bill Husted, 8C

Rather than serving as an impediment like previous theaters where Opera Colorado has performed, this building embraces and supports the sound, from the booming basement notes of bass-baritone Hao Jiang Tian to Fleming's floating high notes.

> See **ELLIE** on 8C

Acknowledgements

To those whose wisdom and the kinds of advice that smooth out the barnacles on a book's hull I owe special thanks..

Charles L. Ralph's enthusiasm for its substance confirmed me in my belief that the book would be valuable and also entertaining. This provided strong propulsion to the project. His many editorial suggestions and especially his contributions to the early historical chapters have enriched the text.

The meticulous reading by Dr. John Graves and Dr.Mary Kime and their comments helped enormously . Nathaniel Merrill , a principal in this history, gave generously of his time. I thank Stephen Seifert and Marcia Ragonetti for their acute suggestions which came out of totally dedicated involvement in the operatic world.

The many departed , whose dreams and endeavors gave them the courage to pursue what was always difficult, deserve the gratitude of the people of Denver. As they confronted the challenges of an artistic world they believed to be just beyond the horizon they gave life to the cultural life of Denver. I give my thanks to them as I hold them in memory. They are Monsignor Richard Hiester, Marvin Worden, John Newfield, Kurt Felsenburg, Edwin Levy, Ross Reimuller, Russell Porter, Cecil Effinger, and Normand Lockwood. Their irreplaceable and inspirational contributions to this city make this work possible.

I thank Stuart Steffen wherever she may be for sharing her experiences in the early days of the Denver Lyric Opera and which continued into the beginnings of Opera Colorado

I need to thank my publisher Dr, Gary White for his enthusiastic and unfailing support of this project.

Allen Young

Photo credits

Newspaper clippings, posters, and programs taken from the collections of Allen Young and Charles Ralph.

Page xxiii Photos of the Broadway Theater: Copyright © 1995-2005 Denver Public Library, Colorado Historical Society, and the Denver Art Museum. Used by permission.

Page 20, Governor's Guard Hall: Copyright © 1995-2005 Denver Public Library, Colorado Historical Society, and the Denver Art Museum. Used by permission.

Page 21, Frances Rose Rosenzweig: Uchill, I., 1957, Pioneers, peddlers, and tsadikim, Quality Line Printing, Boulder, CO. Used by permission.

Pages 143, 164, 173, Sketches of stage sets from the Nathaniel Merrill Collection. Used by permission.

Index

A

Academy of Music, 6
Acs, Janos, 137, 146, 148, 150, 155, 157-158, 167-170
Addison, Adele, 43
Adelaide Randall Comic Opera, 3, 6
Adriana Lecouvreur, 112
Agler, David, 192, 198, 204
Aida, xiii, xx, 8-10, 12, 15-18, 26, 79, 111, 115, 121, 134, 136-137, 143, 161, 169-171, 209, 211
Albanese, Licia, xx-xxi, 12-13, 41, 123, 208
Alexander, Anita, 113
Alexander, Harold, 34
Amahl and the Night Visitors, 94
Amato, Pasquale, 34, 92
Amelia Goes to the Ball, 26, 149, 153
American Institute of Musical Studies, 115
Amter, Dulcy, 92
Anderson, Charmaine, 187
Anderson, David, 115
Anderson, Kelly, 171
Anderson, Kevin, 145, 147
Andrasy, Gabor, 182
Andrea Chenier, xviii
Anne O'Neill, 26
Ansellem, Norah, 204
Antheil, George, 34, 62, 94, 96, 185
Antoine, Arthur H., xix
Antoine, Josephine Louise, xix, xxiv
Apollo Club, xii
Aprea, Bruno, 172
Argento, Dominic, 73
Armstrong, John, 146-147
Armstrong, Karan, 86, 88
Armstrong, Pamela, 200-201, 204
Arroya, Martina, 133
Artists Corporation of New York, 27
Ashton, John, 116
Aspen Music Festival, 39, 124
Aspen Opera Theater Center, 188
Atwater Kent Audition Contest, xix

B

Badea, Christian, 175, 184-185
Bagnios, Elaine, 86
Baldwin, Jason, 189, 191, 198
The Ballad of Baby Doe, 4, 97
Ballard, Derrick, 183
Ballinari, Stefan, 15
Barab, Seymour, 43, 51
The Barber of Seville, xx, 26, 30, 43-44, 52, 54, 56, 66, 151, 166, 201, 211
Barberian, Ara, 17, 167
Barnes School of Business, 111, 180
Barstow, Josephine, 149, 151, 153
The Bartered Bride, xx, 36
Bartoletti, Bruno, 124, 126
Basilio, Don, 39, 44, 52, 167, 201
Baskerville, Priscilla, 186-187
Bass Clubs, xvi
Baum, Kurt, 12
Bayreuth, 83-84, 159
Beattie, Herbert, 103, 106
Beaumarchais, 166
Beecham Opera Company, xiii
Beethoven, 184, 187-188
Bell, Campton, 44, 91, 101
Benjamin, Arthur, 50
Berg, Alban, 148
Berlin Royal Opera, xv
Bernard, Pierre, 2

Best, Julianne, 169-170
Best, Robert, 170
Biggs, Douglas,
  169, 171, 182
Bijou Opera Bouffe
  Company, 3
Bimetallic Investment
  Company, 8
Bing, Rudolf, 38, 124
Binstock, Lynn, 181-182
Bird, Isabella, 107
Bizet, 145
Bjoerling, Jussi, xix, 12, 18
Black, William, 35,
  39, 41, 43, 94
Blackwell, Harolyn,
  149, 151-153
Blythe, Stephanie, 203
Bobick, James, 152, 154
Boettcher Concert Hall,
  88, 121, 128, 149-
  150, 177, 209-210
The Bohemian Girl, 2
Bolden-Taylor, Diane, 181
Bonini, Peggy, 39
Booth, Philip, 133
Borge, Victor, 45
Boris Godunov, 31
Bosetti, Joseph J., 11, 23
Boston Grand Opera
  Company, 13
Boston Ideal Opera
  Company, 3
Boston Lyric Opera
  Company, 8
Boulanger, Nadia, 100
Bowles, Paul, 98
Boynynge, Richard,
  170-172
Bradley, Gwendolyn, 180
Bradley, Jeff, 156, 166-
  169, 177, 181-182
Breisach, Paul, 15
Brewer, Christine, 190-191
Briarcliff Manor, 28
Brico, Antonia, xx, 33, 35
Britten, Benjamin, 93, 149
Brittle Silver, xii
Broadway Theater, xii-xiii,
  xxiii, 7, 25, 70, 207, 213
Brola-Harrison Voice
  Studios, xiv
Brola, Jeanne, xiii

Brooks, Edward J., xiii
Brooks, Elizabeth, 202
Brooks, Lane, xiii, xxiii
Brown, Pat, 50
Brunner, Richard, 131, 159
Bryan, Elizabeth, 169
Buckley, Richard, 155, 195
Buell Theatre, 150,
  155, 165, 181, 210
Burchinal, Frederick,
  69, 88, 104, 136
*The Burning Fiery
  Furnace*, 152, 154
Burns, Helen, 77
Burns, Judith Shay, 196
Burtt, Hilary, 183
Busch, Fritz, xviii, 13
Busch, Hans, 81
Busch, Robert, 79
Bush, W. H., 7
Bush, William, 5
Businger, Toni, 124, 127,
  146, 155, 160, 164
Byers, William, x, 3

C

Cadore, Ernesto, xviii
California Opera
  Company, 3, 6
Calvé, Emma, 9
Calvin, John, 100
Camp St. Malo, 25
Campora, Giuseppe, 87
Capitol Opera
  Company, 111
Carleton Opera
  Company, 3
Carmen, xiii, xv, xviii,
  6-8, 11-12, 14-16, 35-36,
  69-70, 80, 87, 104, 113,
  145-146, 175, 184, 204
Carnegie Hall, xvii
Carroli, Silvano,
  124, 127, 133
Caruso, Enrico, xv, 10, 22
Casteler, Rene, 14
Caston, Saul, xvii, 43, 56,
  69, 79, 82, 84-85, 106
Cathedral of the
  Immaculate
  Conception, 24, 26
Cathedral Opera
  Company, xvi, 25

Catholic Charities,
  xvi, 25, 208
Cavalleria Rusticana, xiii,
  xv, 9, 15, 25, 81, 116, 151
Central City Opera,
  xvi, xx, 16-17, 65,
  77, 121, 123, 209
Central City Opera House
  Association, 17, 123, 209
Cervi's Journal, v, 51, 85
Chama, Eduardo, 199
Champagne Night of
  the Stars, 132
Chapin, Schuyler, 124
Charbonnet, Jeanne-
  Michèle, 170-
  171, 187, 189
Charles A. Ellis Opera
  Company, 8
Chautauqua Opera, xx
Chavez, Abraham, 106
Cheesman Park, xx, 11, 53
Cheyenne Opera House, 5
Chicago Church Choir
  Opera Company, 3
Chicago Grand Opera
  Company, xv, 9
Chicago Lyric Opera,
  105, 123, 181, 187
Chicago Opera Company, 3
Chotzinoff, Blair, 127, 129
Christin, Judith, 180-
  181, 184, 213
Cillario, Carlo Felice,
  124, 126
Cincinnati Opera, xix
Civil War Centennial
  Year, 101
Civilian Conservation
  Corps, 80
Classic Chorale, 51
Clayton, Kristin, 213
Cockrell, Thomas,
  169-170, 183
Cohron, Leonora, 14
Cole, Deborah, 147
Colonel Jonathan, 73-74
Colorado Ballet, 28
Colorado Children's
  Chorale, 103
Colorado Federation of
  Music Clubs, 48

Exotic and Irrational   221

Colorado Mountain
  Club, 81
Colorado National Guard, x
Colorado Opera Club
  of Denver, xii
Colorado Springs, xii,
  xvii, 5, 25, 106, 113
Colorado State Teachers
  College, xvii
Colorado State
  University, 58, 86
Colorado Symphony
  Orchestra, 148
Colorado Women's
  College, 56, 104
Columbia Concerts, xvii
Comley-Barton
  Company, 3
Connecticut Opera, 187
Conried Opera Company, 9
Consul, The, 94, 104
Conti, Alberto, xviii
Cooper, Lawrence, 88
Coppola, Anton, 147
Corkin Theater, 104
Corona, Leonora, 14, 16
Cortez, Viorica,
  133-134, 136
Cossa, Dominic, 85
Costa, Mary, 87
Cotrubas, Ileana, 124
Covent Garden, xiii,
  xv, xviii, 145
The Coventry Narrative, 96
Covillo, Lillian, 28
Cox, Julie, 192
Cox, Kenneth, 189
Craig, Lawrence, 187
Crickard, Lewis, 105
Crucible, The, 71, 76,
  103, 119, 123, 160
Csonka, Paul, 38
Culver, Anne M., 112
Cunningham,
  Robert, 66, 68
Curlew River, 149, 152, 154
Curtin, Phyllis, 85-86
Curtis Institute, xvii
Cutler, Eric, 200, 202

D

Dahlby, Steve, 93
Damrosch, Frank, x
Damrosch, Walter, xvii

Damrosch Opera
  Company, 7
Damrosch-Ellis Grand
  Opera Company, 8
Darling, Robert, 73, 209
Das Rheingold, 160
*The Daughter of the
  Regiment*, 1, 69-70
Davies, Peter G., 186
Davis, Agnes, xvii
Davis, Eric, 17, 48-
  50, 52, 54, 56
Day, Larry, 58
Dedrick, Helen, 36,
  39, 48, 50-51
Defrere, Desiree, 15
Delacote, Jacques, 146
Delacote, Joseph, 130
DeLuca, Giuseppi, 10
*Demon Barber of Fleet
  Street*, 198
Denniston, Patrick, 168
DeNolfo, Ian, 191
Denver, Junior
  League of, 77
Denver Archdiocese,
  21, 134
Denver Art Museum, 117
Denver Auditorium,
  xx, 9, 21, 27, 204
Denver Botanic
  Gardens, 118
Denver Centennial
  Program, 102
Denver Choral Union, xi, 3
Denver Civic
  Symphony, 28, 105
Denver Concert
  Chorale, 112, 117
Denver Conservatory
  of Music, xvii
Denver Grand Opera
  Company, xvi,
  11, 25-27, 33
Denver Lyric Opera, 63,
  65, 69, 72-73, 76-77,
  85, 111, 113, 117, 160
Denver Lyric Theater,
  47-49, 51, 55, 61, 63,
  73, 77, 82, 180
Denver Music Hall, 6

Denver Opera Association,
  33, 36, 39, 41, 43,
  45, 47, 85-86
Denver Opera Club, xi-xii
Denver Opera Company,
  114-117, 123
Denver Opera House, 4
Denver Post, v, xvi, xviii,
  xx, 11-12, 14, 25, 27,
  45, 72, 75-76, 83, 104,
  106, 112, 123, 131,
  134, 156, 166-168,
  177, 184, 187, 197
Denver Symphony
  Orchestra, xvi-xvii,
  12, 18, 28, 36-37, 41,
  43, 56-57, 59, 61, 69-
  71, 77, 79, 85-86, 96,
  105-106, 112, 117-118,
  124, 127, 130-131, 133,
  135, 137, 147-148
Denver Theater, x, 16,
  47-49, 51, 55, 61, 63,
  68, 73, 77, 82, 91,
  93-94, 180, 207
Denver Times, 4, 9, 34
Denver Vocal Society, xii
Der Rosenkavalier,
  151, 167-168, 211
DeSett, Louise, 17
Deutsche Oper, 104
Devlin, Michael, 198
Diaz, Justino, 128, 130,
  150, 155-156, 169, 182
Dickenson, Jean,
  xvii, 11, 26-27
Dickinson, Emily, 57
Die Fledermaus, 36, 43-
  44, 86, 105, 114-115,
  123, 135, 171, 181
Die Meistersinger, xiii,
  7, 150, 158, 161,
  164-165, 167, 211
Die Walküre, 7, 80-81, 88
Dinhaupt, Frank,
  xvii, xxiv, 24, 26
A Doll's House, 94
Domingo, Placido, 122,
  124, 128-129, 149-151,
  155, 178, 181, 210
Don Carlo, 104, 150,
  154-155, 161, 166, 211

Don Giovanni, xviii,
  14, 17, 31, 105, 121,
  134-137, 150, 161,
  171, 197-200, 211
Don Pasquale, 30, 49,
  51, 54, 75-76, 160
Doscher, Barbara, 149
Dransfeldt, Fred, 114
Duke of Mecklenburg's
  Royal Theater, xiv
Duman, Nellie Mae, 124
Dunning, Angela, 149, 153
Dworak, Richard, 30,
  34-35, 41, 48-49, 54,
  82, 93, 95, 208

E

Eagleson, Leonard, 131
East, Thomas, 44
East Denver High
  School, xiv
Eastman School of
  Music, xx, 55
Eckhoff, Herbert, 88,
  170-171, 182
Edbrooke, W. J., 4
Eddy, Nelson, 12
Effinger, Cecil, 12, 105
The Egyptian Helen, 190
Elias, Rosalind,
  87, 130, 132
Elitch's Garden Theater, 28
The Elixir of Love,
  150, 154-155
Ellie Caulkins Opera
  House, 204, 212
Ellis, Brent, 86-88, 147
Elvira, Pablo, 133,
  135, 151, 166
Emma Abbott Opera
  Company, 5
Emma Juch Opera
  Company, 7
Engel, Lehman, 48
Esham, Faith, 183
Estatieva, Stefka,
  150-151, 155
Eugene Onegin, 186,
  192, 196, 200

F

Falstaff, xvii, 39, 103,
  115, 146-147
Farberman, Harold, 85

Favre, Jean, 70-72, 76, 119
Fazah, Adib, 128-129
Fee, Roger Dexter, 30,
  94, 100, 102-103
Feigman, Christopher, 204
Fernald, Beverly
  Christiansen,
  112-113, 116
Fernando, Don, 188
Ferrera, Maria, 18
Fetsch, Rudolf, 34,
  40, 44, 46, 50, 94
Fiamma Izzo D'Amico,
  157-158, 161
Fidelio, 31, 80, 82, 123,
  183, 187-188, 200, 211
Flagstad, Kirsten, xv, 12
Floyd, Carlisle, 71,
  103, 118, 160
The Flying Dutchman,
  11, 170, 209, 211
Forrester's Opera House, xi
Foss, Lukas, 93
Frank, Joseph, 130-131, 137
Fredericks, Richard, 62, 98
Fredman, Martin, 155
Fremstad, Olive, 9
Fried, Howard, 70
Furlong, Peter Gage,
  188-189, 191
Futral, Elizabeth,
  200, 202-203

G

Gadpaille, Warren,
  49, 57, 60
Garden, Mary, 9, 22, 207
Gardner, Dorothy, 57
Gardner, Jake, 180, 190
Garner, Bob, 134
Gavin, Julian, 196, 204, 213
Gedda, Nicolai,
  130-131, 149
*The Gentleman
  Desperado*, 107
German Grand Opera
  Company, 11
Gershwin, 183, 186
Schicchi, Gianni, xx, 30,
  33-34, 104-105, 145-146,
  150-151, 176, 179, 183
Giffin, Glenn, 72, 75-76,
  104, 107, 112, 118, 129,
  131, 134, 175, 184, 187

Gilman, Lawrence, 14
Gilson, Franklin, 92
Golden Age of Opera, 28
Goldowsky, Boris, 17, 55
Goldowsky Grand
  Opera Theater, 16
Golschmann, Vladimir, 85
Gordon, David, 105
Gotterdammerung, 160
Governor's Guard
  Hall, 4, 20
Gower, John H., xii
Gradus, Oren, 201
Graese, Judy, 71
Graf, Herbert, 13,
  80-81, 83, 191
Grand Army Magazine, 2
Grand Opera of Nice, xiii
Grant, Alexander, xix
Grau English Opera
  Company, 3, 6
Grauer, Laura, 36
Greater Denver Opera
  Association, 33, 36,
  39, 41, 43, 45, 47
Green, Jonathan, 184
Greenawald, Sharon
  Evans, 66
Greenlaw, Ian, 200-201
Gregor, Jozsef, 170
Grimsley, Greer, 196
Guadagno, Anton,
  133, 153, 166-167
Guido, Josephine, 16
Gustafson, Nancy,
  135, 149, 151

H

H.M.S. Pinafore, xi-xii, 3
Hadley, Jerry, 124, 129
Haenisch, Natalie, xiv
Hale, Robert, 61
Halfvarson, Eric, 129,
  131, 150-151, 160
Hall, Janice, 88
Hamburg State Theater, 158
Hanna, L. G., 6
Hanslowe, Theodora,
  192, 213
Hao, Tian Jiang, 146,
  151, 160, 213
Harrold, Jack, 128
Harshaw, Margaret, 81

Haverly's Church Choir
 Opera Company, 3
Heggie, Jake, 213
Hegierski, Katherine, 167
Hello Out There, 69-70
Hendel, Micha, 171, 177
Hendricks, Scott,
 197, 200, 202
Herbert, Ralph, 67
Herbert, Walter, xx, 36,
 38, 40, 43-44, 46
Hernandez, Cesar, 169
Herrera, Emily, 170, 179
Hilker, W. C., 6
Hillock, Russell, 52
Hilty, Richard, 51
Hindemith, Paul, 34
Hines, Jerome, 13, 80
Hinman, Leroy R., 10
Hogan, George, 170
Hogue, DeRos,
 112-114, 116
Holleque, Elizabeth,
 167, 169, 179
Holliday, Thomas,
 158, 167-168, 183
Holm, Hanya, 97
Holman, Libby, 98-99
Holt, Charles L., 51
Holt, Henry, 18
Hong, Hei Kyung,
 131-132, 150
Hotter, Hans, 114
Houston Grand
 Opera, 36, 186
Howard, Frank, 2, 51
Hugenots, Les, 8
Hughes, P. T., 6
Hunt, Alexandra, 98
Hunt, W. F., xii

I

I Pagliacci, xx, 9, 29, 33,
 81, 116, 145, 176, 179
Igesz, Bodo, 169
Il Tabarro, 104, 183
Il Trovatore, 2, 15, 26, 66,
 111, 113, 116, 121, 133
An Incomplete Education, 57
Indiana University
 School of Music, xvii
International Council of
 Opera Colorado, 130

International House, xx,
 48-49, 51-52, 56, 69, 82

J

Jackson, Bruce, 69-70, 72
Jacobs, Lore, 48
Jagel, Frederick, 41, 79
Janzen, Donna Bricker,
 35, 58, 70, 72
Johnson, Broadway, 70
Johnson, Dick, 82
Johnson, Norman,
 65, 77, 85, 180
Jones, Betty, 18
Jones, Christine, 198
Jones, Doug, 198
Jones, Gwendolyn, 167, 169
Jones, Isola, 149, 153
Jones, Spike, xix
Jorn, Karl, 26
Joslin, J. Jay, 6
Joyce, James, 95
Julius Caesar, 39, 203, 212
Jumping Frog, The, 93

K

Kaasch, Donald,
 xxi, 172, 180
Kaduce, Kelly, 196
Kaiser's Royal Opera, xv
Kansas State Teachers
 College, 92
Kauffman, A., xi
Kavrakos, Dimitri, 150, 155
Kayser, Kathryn,
 35, 92, 94, 101
Kazarnovskaya, Ljuba, 178
Keeley, Walter, 28
Kennedy, Kevin, 126
Kent, David, 85
Kim, Shinja, 88
King Theodore, 56
Kirsten, Dorothy,
 xxi, 12, 31, 208
Klein, Adam, 183
Klemperer, Otto, xvii
Knoll, Richard, 72
Kostelic, Jeanne, 50-51, 59
Kovalevsky, Cecilia,
 48, 50-51, 82
Koyke, Hizi, 11, 15
Krall, Heidi, 81
Kuntsch, Matthias, 182
Kuznetova, Dina, 197

L

La Bohème, xiii, xx, 8,
 12, 16, 30, 37, 43, 59,
 90, 124, 126, 128,
 150, 158-159, 161,
 186, 200, 210-211
La Cenerentola, 88,
 104, 146, 170
La Gioconda, 8
La Rondine, 57-58
La Scala, xiii, xviii, 26, 112
La Serva Padrona, 48
La Traviata, xvi, xx,
 14-16, 26-27, 29, 41,
 46, 67, 80, 85-87, 112,
 146-148, 151, 181, 184,
 202, 204, 209, 211
Laciura, Anthony, 147-148
Lacy, Robin, 37, 40,
 97, 100-101
LaGuardia, Vince Jr., 104
Lakes, Gary, 187-188
Lakmé, 60, 112
Lambardi Opera
 Company, 8
Lamberti, Giorgio, 133
Lamont, Florence, xvi-
 xviii, 20, 26-27, 30
Lamont School of Music,
 xvi-xvii, 10, 27, 30-31,
 50, 62, 69, 82, 88, 91,
 93-94, 114, 180, 183
Lamont Singers, xvi
Land of Promise, 100
Langan, Kevin, 135-136,
 149-154, 158, 161, 168
Lansing, Gladys, 79, 111
Lansing, Robert, 79, 180
Latouche, John, 4
Lattimore, Margaret, 199
Lau, Matthew, 191
Laurienti, Nicholas,
 112, 208
LaVar, Jeffrey, 187
Lawrence, Cynthia,
 xxi, 181, 197, 213
Le Pauvre Matelot, 38, 51
Lee, Ming Cho, 149, 153
Leigh, Jennifer, 112-116
Lescaut, Manon, 136, 157
Levine, James, 37
Levy, Edwin, xx, 34, 37,
 40, 92-93, 96, 102

Ligi, Josella, 137
Lindemann Young
  Artist Development
  Program, 195
Little Johnny Mine, 8
The Lively Arts, v,
  81, 83-84, 99
Livingston, Mike, 82
Lockwood, Normand, 99
Lohengrin, xiii, xvii,
  7-8, 26, 31
London Conservatory
  of Music, xvi
London Promenade
  Concerts, xviii
Lord, Stephen, 198,
  201, 204, 213
Loretta Law Young
  Artist Center, 188
Loretto Heights
  Performing Arts
  Center, 74
Louisiana State
  University, 92
Lucking, Peter, 212
Lulu, 115, 123, 148

M

MacAllister, Scott, 88
Macbeth, 26, 103, 115,
  151, 165, 169, 177,
  181-182, 197
MacDonald, Jeanette, 12
MacMillan, Kyle, 197
MacNeil, Cornell,
  125, 145-147, 166
MacNeil, Walter, 127,
  135, 147, 149, 151, 153
Madama Butterfly, xx,
  15, 26, 37, 67-68, 87,
  104, 115, 149, 151,
  158, 167, 183-184
*The Madwoman of
  Chaillot*, 93
The Magic Flute, 31, 67, 73,
  111, 177, 179-181, 187
Maguire's Opera House, 1
Makris, Cynthia, 115, 120
Malady of Love, 48
Malas, Spiro, 76, 88
Malfitano, Catherine, 128
Mancorti, Susanna, 95
The Man in the Moon,
  40, 73, 189

Marchant, Arthur, xii
The Marriage Merchant,
  38, 43, 51
The Marriage of Figaro,
  xx, 26, 39, 57, 151, 165,
  170, 203-204, 212
Marsh, Calvin, 67
Marton, Eva, 131-
  132, 149, 210-211
Marvosh, June Johnson, 114
A Masked Ball, 153, 166
Mastromei, Giampiero, 147
Matisse, Janice,
  112-113, 116
Maultsby, Nancy, 203
Maureen O'Flynn, 172
Maurice Grau Grand
  Opera Company, 8
Maynor, Dorothy, 80
McCarthy, Violette, 35, 41
McCormack, John, 11
McCormick, Mary
  Ann, 196
McCourt, Peter, 5, 7-8
McCourt, Philip, 7
McCracken, James,
  124, 127
McFarland, Robert, 187
McGiffert, Genevieve,
  103-104
McGrew, Rose, xiv, xxiii
McKenzie, Siphiwe, 187
The Medium, 56, 70, 97, 105
Meinke, Ruth, 29-30
Melba, Nellie, 8, 207
Melchior, Lauritz, 80
Melville Opera Company, 3
Menotti, 34, 51, 56,
  70, 93-94, 103
Merrill, Nathaniel,
  xxi, 118, 121, 128,
  176, 179, 193, 210
The Merry Widow, 87, 113
Metropolitan
  Theater, xiii, 6
Meyerowitz, Jan, 57
Michailov, Swetan, 166
Mignon, xvi, xix, 11,
  13, 25-27, 178
Milhaud, Darius, 51
Millo, Aprile, 134, 151, 210
Milnes, Sherrill, 17, 22,
  72, 122, 124, 147, 151

Moe, Daniel, 96
Moldoveanu, Vasile,
  131-132, 137, 149,
  151-153, 158, 161
Monk, Allan, 124,
  128, 150, 155, 157
Montana Theatre, 1
Monteverdi, 118
Moon, James, 57
Moon, Rick, 167
Moore, Grace, 12
Morash, Mark, 204
Moresca, Carlo, 15
Morris, James, 130,
  132, 135, 213
Morsheck, Stephen, 172
Mosely, Robert, 18
Mowatt, Anna Cora, 93
Moyer, Allen, 186,
  190-192, 198, 201
Mozart, xviii-xix, 24, 31,
  39, 41, 51, 58, 67, 87,
  97, 104, 151, 166-167,
  171, 186, 204-205
Mukaida, Mariko, 35
Munoz, Delorosa, 191
Munsel, Patrice, 13
Murgu, Corneliu, 157
Musical America, vi
Musical Arts, 56
Mussard, Timothy, 171

N

Nagore, Antonio, 179, 189
National Opera
  Association, 102
Naughty Marietta, 116
Nava, Carolyn, 105
Neri, Josephine, 26
Nesbit, Fred, 31, 34,
  44, 79, 208
New City Opera
  Company, 117-118
New England Conservatory
  of Music, 55, 58
New Orleans Opera
  Company, 49
New York City Opera, 15,
  38-40, 44, 60-62, 98,
  103, 114, 181, 185, 200
New York Times, xiv
Newfield, John, xx, 33, 38,
  45-47, 52, 73, 77, 208

Nickel, Matilda, 66, 68-70, 72, 74, 76
Nordica, Lillian, 6
Norma, 8, 50, 82, 186, 205

O

Oates Comic Opera Company, 2
Offenbach, 1, 50, 131, 170
Offenbach, Jamie, 170
The Old Maid and the Thief, 51, 93, 103
Olon-Scrymegeour, John, 68, 73
Olson, Jack, 43-44, 69
Opera, Glimmerglass, 200
Opera Colorado, v, vii, xii, xxi, 77, 105, 118, 121, 124, 126, 130-132, 134-137, 145-155, 157-160, 165-168, 170-172, 175-179, 181-187, 190, 193, 195-200, 202-203, 205, 209-211, 213
Opera Colorado Guild, 154
Opera News, vi, 95, 175, 211
Opera Theatre of the Rockies, 77
Order of the Silver Laurel, xiv
Orpheus and Eurydice, 80, 185, 191-192, 200, 211
Otello, 6, 13, 122, 124, 126-127, 130, 147, 150, 155-158, 161, 178, 210
Ott, Sharon, 197-199

P

Packard, John, 198
Pancella, Phyllis, 198
Parce, Erich, 129, 131, 137, 149, 153, 158, 161, 166, 171-172
Parrish, Cheryl, 166-167, 171
Parsifal, xii, xvii, 53
Paschal, Kay, 172
Passmore, E. J., xi
Patriarco, Earle, 170
Patrick, Julian, 71, 76, 160
Patti, Adelina, 6, 207
Pavarotti, Luciano, 124, 181

Peabody Institute, 65-66
Pearson, Richard, 169
Pease, James, 81
Pelargidis, Apostol, 35, 43-44
People's Theatre, 7
Pergolesi, 48
Perry, Douglas, 152, 154, 158, 167
Peterson, Curt, 154, 159, 166
Peterson, Glade, 88
Phipps Auditorium, 15, 57
The Pirates of Penzance, xi
Pita, Jorge Antonio, 197
Pittsinger, David, 199, 204
Poleri, David, 15
Pollard's Lilliputian Opera Company, 8
Polozov, Vyacheslav, 155
Ponnelle, Jean-Pierre, 195
Pons, Lily, xv, 12, 26-27, 80
Poole, Thomas, 146, 160, 168, 189-190
Poretta, Frank, 85
Porter, Russell, 92, 94, 100
Price, Max, 117, 123
Priestman, Brian, 77, 85, 112
Proctor, Elizabeth, 72
Puccini, xiii, 34, 37-38, 41, 57-58, 68, 82-83, 104, 115, 124, 129, 131, 136, 145, 161, 179, 183-184, 186, 195, 200-201
Pulley, Emily, 196, 200, 213
Pulliam Hall, 67, 69
Purcell, 118
Putnam, Ashley, xx, 125, 130, 132, 135, 150-151, 159, 167, 190

Q

Quadri, Argeo, 126-127, 131, 135
Quigg Newton Denver Municipal Auditorium, 204
Quittmeyer, Susan, 130, 132, 135, 151

R

Raether, Keith, 122, 126
Ragonetti, Marcia, xxi, 146-147, 151, 153, 166-167, 169-170, 181, 183, 191, 198, 202, 210, 213
Rains, Ina, xvii
The Rake's Progress, 105, 185
Ramey, Samuel, 154
Rauschnabel, June, 104
Ravel, 100
Rayson, Benjamin, 70, 72
The Red Mill, xx
Red Rocks Amphitheater, 80
Reimueller, Ross, 58
Reinhardt, Max, 38
Renner, Don, 154, 158, 160
Respighi, 99
Ricci, Rosemary, 170-171
Richards, Stiles, 25
Richings-Bernard Grand English Opera Company, xi, 2
Riegel, Kenneth, 86
Rigoletto, xiii, xx, 14, 16-17, 26-27, 30, 34, 49, 72, 76, 104, 113-114, 149-150, 158, 165-166, 203-204, 212
Risley, Patricia, 200, 203
Ritchard, Cyril, 44
Ritchie, Harry, 104
Robert O'Hearn, 135-136, 143, 157, 209
Robertson, Christopher, 204
Robertson, Jean, 146-147, 150, 153, 168, 170, 177, 187
Robinson, Cleo Parker, 135, 170, 187
Robinson, James, 185, 191, 195-198, 200, 202, 205, 211
Rocky Mountain Arsenal, 35
Roggero, Margaret, 15
Roman, Stella, 12
Root, Scott, 152, 154, 158, 160
Rorem, Ned, 186

Rosenzweig, Frances
Rose, xiv, 21
Rossini, 1, 31, 38, 43, 51, 88, 104, 146, 151, 170, 201
Roth, Anne Stein, 29
Rothstein, Peter, 196
Rousse Opera, 153
Rowland, Martile, 151, 154
Rozynko, Vitali, 191, 199, 201
Rudel, Julius, 135, 165, 180, 187
Russell, Peter, 195, 199, 205, 213
Ruy Blas, 94

S

Saint-Pierre, Patrice, 183
Salome, xv, xx, 37, 40-41, 69-70, 176-178, 209
Salzburg Marionette Opera Theater, 131
Salzburg Opera Guild, 38, 47, 51
Samarzia, Anthony, 95
Samson and Dalilah, 10, 79, 136, 148-149, 211
San Carlo Opera Company, 11, 15, 27
Sander, Alexander, 158, 167, 171
Sander, Rolf, 106
Santiago, Theresa, 189
Sargeant, Sir Malcolm, xviii
Sass, Sylvia, 133
Sayao, Bidu, 12, 30-31, 208
Scaggs, Sally, 50-51
Schneider, Charles, 148
Schneider-Siemssen, Gunther, 123, 130
Schoep, Arthur, 55, 61, 65, 85, 208
Schuette, James, 204
Schuler, Duane, 127, 130-131
Schwengl, Bruno, 196, 203
Scott, Elizabeth, 51
Seattle Opera Company, 17, 75
The Secrets of Suzanne, 51
Seibel, Klauspeter, 191
Seifert, Stephen, 176, 179, 185, 193, 195

Sembrich, Marcella, xix, 9
Sendak, Maurice, 180
Sewailam, Ashraf, 201, 204
Shelton, Chad, 199
Sherman, Louise, xxi, 126, 135-136, 147-149, 157, 161, 171, 175-176, 182, 209-210
Sherrill, Donald, 167
Shigematsu, Mika, 170
Shulgold, Marc, 147, 156, 167-168, 177, 179, 184, 195, 197, 212
Shwayder Theater, 169
Siebert, Glenn, 171
Siegfried, 7, 160
Silipigni, Alfredo, 166, 179
Sills, Beverly, 16, 39
Simpson, Angela, 187
Simson, Julie, 157, 160, 182
Singher, Michel, 183
Siriani, Craig, 184
Skari, Vernon, 66, 112-115
Snyder, Delores, 50-52
Soich, Leslie Remmert, 204
Souez, Ina, xvii-xix, xxiv
South, Pamela, 126, 128, 145, 147, 150-151, 158, 161, 166, 171
Soviero, Diana, 131, 147, 150-151, 184, 211
Spence, Patricia, 147, 153
St. John's Cathedral, x
St. Paul Opera, 71, 98
St. Paul's Lutheran Church, 118, 152
Steber, Eleanor, 80, 82
Steffen, Stuart, 59, 61, 66-67, 69, 71, 74-75
Stevens, Risë, 12-13, 27
Stewart, Janet, 66, 68
Stivan, Edgar, 131
Strassberger, Thaddeus, 204
Strauss, Richard, xv, xvii, 37, 39-41, 56, 70, 84, 114, 167, 185, 189-190
Strauss, Johann, 114
Stravinsky, 95, 105, 185
Street Scene, 82
Strummer, Peter, 167
Sullivan, Brian, 82
Suor Angelica, 104
Surinach, 98-99

Surinach, Carlos, 98
Susannah, 103, 118
Sutherland, Donald, 102, 106-107
Sweeney Todd, 197-198, 200

T

Tabor, Baby Doe, 7
Tabor, Horace, xxii, 4-5, 7
Tabor Grand Opera House, xi-xii, xxii, 4-5, 7, 34, 96, 207, 213
The Tales of Hoffman, 9, 80, 104, 123, 130-131, 161, 211
Tamagno, Francesco, 6
Tannhäuser, xiii, xv, 7
Tapia, Lynette, 191-192
Taylor, Charles Edwin, 191
Taylor, Steven, xxi, 105, 146, 148, 154, 158, 160, 169
Tebaldi, Renata, 87
Teikyo Loretto Heights, 170
The Telephone, 70
Terrell, Scott, 196
Tessier, John, 200-201
Tetrazzini, Luisa, 9
Thais, 9
Thoma, Dean, 183-184, 189
Thompson, Hugh, 44
Thomson, Virgil, 94-95
Three's A Crowd, 98
Time Magazine, vi, 83
Toczyska, Stefania, 146
Tokady, Ilona, 150
Torrigi, Richard, 15
Tosca, xiii, 9, 62-63, 88, 115, 132-134, 150, 169, 192, 195-196
Toscanini, 13, 27, 41, 99
Toth, Andor, 106
Tourel, Jennie, 12, 114
Townsend, Betty Jane, 44, 50-51, 54
Traubel, Helen, 80-81
Travis, Dale, 187-188, 199-201
Treigle, Norman, xx, 39, 43-44, 208
Trout, Mary Beth, 69-70
Tucker, Ernest, 132
Tucker, Marji, 68, 72, 76

Exotic and Irrational 227

Turandot, xviii, 112, 115, 123, 130-131, 147, 150, 161, 185, 188-189, 211
Turner Hall, 2, 4

U

Udell, Belle, 15
Ulrich, Mel, 196, 201
University of Denver, xvi, xx, 20, 25, 30-31, 34-35, 44, 50, 62, 69, 91, 93-94, 98-99, 102-103, 111, 113-114

V

Valente, Benita, xx-xxi
Valentino, Francesco, xvii, xxiv, 26, 29, 208
Van Gorden, George, 30, 35, 93
Van Ham, Irene, 104, 115
Varone, Doug, 191-192, 200-201, 211
Verdi, xiii, xvii, xix, 13, 23, 26, 41-42, 66, 103-104, 113, 116, 124, 135, 147, 149-150, 153, 155, 157, 165, 170, 186, 202, 211
Verrett, Shirley, 122
Vickers, Jon, 136, 145, 210-211
Vinay, Ramon, 13
Von Halem, Victor, 171-172, 178
Von Suppe, 50

W

Wagner, xii, xvii, 7, 11, 15-16, 26, 80, 83-84, 89, 103, 150, 158-161, 166, 170, 211
Walhalla Hall, 4
Walker, John, 86-87
Walker, Mallory, 74-75
Ward, Robert, 71, 149
Warner, Beverly, 50-51, 82
Warren, Leonard, 12
Waters, Willie Anthony, 187
Weckbaugh, Eleanore, 29, 34
Weill, Kurt, 82, 94

Welch-Babidge, Jennifer, 197, 204
Wells, Patricia, 87
Welting, Ruth, 130, 132
Werther, 114
West, Stephen, xxi, 18, 127-128, 130-131, 133, 135-137, 146, 149-151, 155, 159, 166-167, 171, 178-179, 210, 213
Western Michigan University, 49
Whelan, Franzita, 192, 199
White, Roi, 93
White, Shirley, 106, 115
White, Stephen, 203
Whitehouse, Elizabeth, 196
Wilcox, Carol, 86-87
Wilcox, Charles McAllister, 24
Wilcox, Martha, 25, 92
Williamson, Dean, 199
Williamson, Waldo, 93-94, 99
Wolf-Ferrari, 51
Woodley, Arthur, 180, 186-188
Woods, Porter, 87
Woods, Sheryl, 151, 155, 166, 171
Worden, Marvin, 30, 57, 59-61, 68, 79, 208
Worstell, Ron, 104
Wozzeck, xix, 148
Wright, Patricia Baxter, 104

Y

Yauger, Marguerite, 18
Young, Elizabeth, 25
Young, Rebecca, 118
Young Artists Center, 171, 179
Young Artists of Opera Colorado, 199

Z

Zhang, Yalun, 149-151, 153-155, 166, 168-169, 179, 197, 210, 213

www.ingramcontent.com/pod-product-compliance
Lightning Source LLC
Chambersburg PA
CBHW022056160426
43198CB00008B/252